Advance praises for *Taking Bullets*

"For more than forty years Haki Madhubuti has deployed his considerable intellect and skill as a poet and essayist to inform, enlighten and arm us to wage the necessary battles for self-determination and human rights. In *Taking Bullets* he hits the target again. This book is a refresher course and a primer to prepare us for what we need to do in an era of epidemic state sponsored or sanctioned violence against black people, especially African American men. But make no mistake, this is not just lamentation. It is Haki deciphering a complex system of enemies and their minions. It is a demand that we stand up and be responsible for our own liberation. In *Taking Bullets* we have been given a tool to fight and build and also evidence that Haki Madhubuti remains an important thinker and doer in our struggle."

—Michael Simanga
author of *Amiri Baraka and The Congress of African People*

"Haki Madhubuti's *Taking Bullets* is an outstanding and brilliant critique of the stark realities of contemporary Black people in the United States. Professor Madhubuti, a lifelong activist, essayist, educator, poet, social historian, commentator, editor/publisher and institution builder, dismayed by the fatal shooting of 12-year old Tamir Rice, uses his pen as a weapon to confront and challenge inequality, injustice and racism in American society. He offers a very insightful and thorough analysis of the urgency of reckoning with the dilemmas of being Black. He persuasively agrees and summons his readers to take a unified and concerted stand to eradicate inequality, injustice and racism moving towards social justice."

—Diane D. Turner
author of *Feeding The Soul: Black Music, Black Thought*

* * *URGENT* * *URGENT* * *URGENT* * *

The pervasive and common lie that police officers give after killing unarmed Black men and boys is that the officers feared for their lives. A white police officer, Michael T. Slager of North Charleston, South Carolina, used lethal force against an unarmed Black man, Walter L. Scott, as he ran away from him on Saturday, April 4, 2015. According to the New York Times *(4-8-2015), officer Slager shot eight bullets striking Mr. Scott "five times—three times in the back, once in the upper buttocks and once in the ear—with at least one bullet entering his heart." After a livestream video emerged detailing the entire murder, officer Slager's original story of the incident was disproved and he was dismissed from the force, arrested, and charged with the death of Mr. Scott. This is a rare occurrence in the U.S.; most police officers are immediately believed and return to work. The video from a caring young Black man made the difference in this case. This book is an on-the-ground analysis of these types of deaths that are never-ending in the Black community in the United States. The horror and acts of pure terrorism are the Emmanuel 9, the forced death of Sandra Bland in Texas, and the 16 shots in fifteen seconds into the body of a 17 year-old, Laquan McDonald by a Chicago police officer as other CPD officers looked on, did nothing and lied about what really happened, until after thirteen months when the official video showing the actual murder of Laquan was released. These deaths will not be the last.*

Taking Bullets

Taking Bullets

TERRORISM AND BLACK LIFE
IN TWENTY-FIRST CENTURY AMERICA
CONFRONTING WHITE NATIONALISM, SUPREMACY,
PRIVILEGE, PLUTOCRACY AND OLIGARCHY

A Poet's Representation and Challenge

Haki R. Madhubuti

With an Appendix
The Constitution of the United States and the Bill of Rights
The United Nations—Universal Declaration of Human Rights

Third World Press Foundation
Chicago

First Edition
Printed in the United States of America

ISBN 13: 978-0-88378-361-0
20 19 18 17 16   8 7 6 5 4 3 2 1

Library of Congress Cataloging-in-Publication
Names: Madhubuti, Haki R., 1942-
Title: Taking bullets : terrorism and Black life in twenty-first century
America : confronting white nationalism, supremacy, privilege, plutocracy
and oligarchy / Haki R. Madhubuti.
Description: First edition. | Chicago : Third World Press Foundation Books,
2016. | "With an appendix: The Constitution of the United States and the
Bill of Rights." | Includes bibliographical references and index.
Identifiers: LCCN 2015035690| ISBN 9780883783610 (paperback : alkaline paper)
| ISBN 9780883783627 (cloth : alkaline paper)
Subjects: LCSH: African American young men--Social conditions. | African
American boys--Social conditions. | Terrorism--Social aspects--United
States. | Violence--Social aspects--United States. | Healing--Social
aspects--United States. | Community life--United States. | Man-woman
relationships--United States. | United States--Race relations. | United
States--Social conditions--1980-
Classification: LCC E185.86 .M337 2015 | DDC 305.242/108896073--dc23
LC record available at http://lccn.loc.gov/2015035690

To and for a dear friend and brother
who gave all and more—he is missed
Dr. Walter P. Lomax Jr.

To the poets, artists and keepers of our culture
Amiri Baraka
Jayne Cortez
Ruby Dee
Derrick Bell
Gil Scott-Heron
Jon Onye Lockard
Yosef A.A. ben-Jochannan
Walter Dean Myers
Ronald Walters
Chokwe Lumumba
Abena Joan Brown
Chenjerai Hove
Julian Bond
Frances Cress Welsing
and
Chinua Achebe, Grace Lee Boggs, John Coltrane, Curtis Mayfield,
Studs Terkel, Howard Zinn, Stuart Scott, Nina Simone, John O. Killens,
Henry L. English, Darwin T. Turner and Tony Judt

And for the men and women who gave me early life
Maxine Graves Lee
Richard Wright
Malcolm X (El-Hajj Malik El-Shabazz)
Margaret and Charlie Burroughs
Dudley Randall
Hoyt W. Fuller
Barbara A. Sizemore
Gwendolyn Brooks
Ossie Davis
Martin Luther King, Jr.

and
my family, biological, cultural and extended
including
Wesley Snipes, Danny Glover, Chester Grundy, Khephra Burns,
Herb Boyd, Useni Eugene Perkins, Alexander Gabbin, Haile Gerima,
Ronald Rochon, Keith Gilyard and Errol A. Henderson

A Special Acknowledgement and Thank You to
Charles J. Ogletree Jr.
Matthew D. Brinckerhoff
Jonathan S. Abady
Emery Celli Brinckerhoff & Abady LLP
Attorney Jeff Whitehead

This document is being published by Third World Press Foundation. I must give credit to Bakari Kitwana for the idea of my writing about this very delicate problem that is not foreign to me. Serious credit must be acknowledged around the input of my executive assistant Rose Perkins and Third World Press staff member Antoine Lindsey. I must thank Willalyn Fox, Gwendolyn Mitchell, and Dr. Michael Simanga for reading and providing feedback on this document; and my granddaughter, LaJenne Alcantar, for helping with the bibliography for this book. Thanks to Melissa Moore, Kristina Wheeler, and Jasmine Bundy for copy editing. Thanks to Denise Borel Billups for the book's overall design and for her generous kindness throughout this process. Serious thanks must always be given to my wife and partner in life and struggle, Dr. Carol D. Lee (Mama Safisha Madhubuti), to my children and grandchildren, and to my friends in the struggle throughout the nation who have supported us and continued on the front line of this continuous battle for liberation and cultural, political, economic, and living space in the United States. A Special Brotherly thank you to Paul Coates, Kassahun Checole, William E. Cox, and Anthony Rose. The love they have shown for Black people cannot be quantified. And always, a thank you to my adopted grandfathers W.E.B. DuBois and Paul Robeson, and to a serious liberation fighter, Harry Belafonte.

Contents

Preface
ALSO MUST BE NOTED

The writing *of Taking Bullets: Terrorism and Black Life in Twenty-first Century America* began during the months following the November 2014 killing of Tamir Rice, a twelve-year-old boy shot to death by a white Cleveland police officer. With the murders of Trayvon Martin, Michael Brown, Oscar Grant, Eric Garner, Justus Howell, and Walter Scott, the urgency of this book is more apparent. The deaths of these individuals were, without question, acts of state terrorism against Black boys, men, and the Black community.

As the book unfolded, my thoughts kept returning to President Obama and his six-year fight against the Republican Party and their allies, especially Fox News and right-wing talk radio, which have never acknowledged his presidency. They have done everything within their power, including interfering with the President and the Secretary of State's negotiation with the foreign government of Iran. This has never been done before in the history of the country. I think daily of his wife Michelle and the constant agony that she must endure. I think of their children Malia and Sasha who go to bed each night praying that their dad, a Black man, the President, will return to them each night.

This book is also for all the senseless deaths of Black men and women by state violence and terrorism that we will never hear of—and to all children of all cultures who I hope will grow up without being contaminated and acculturated by the deadly ideology of white supremacy/white nationalism or religious nationalism. We all do what we have been taught to do. Hatred of the other is a learned activity. White supremacy and white nationalism are not only political and economic, but also cultural.

To always do that which is good, just, correct, and right, regardless of culture or race, are taught and learned. All adults, mothers, fathers, grandparents, aunts, and uncles have choices; which will we take? We need another political, cultural, and economic movement of like-minded people who understand the life and death struggles that the great majority of citizens in the U.S. and the world endure each day. This book—as well as all of my work—is a small contribution to that effort. I write as a poet who loves this country and understands suffering and struggle and is acutely aware of the transformative power of language used in the defense of people, especially young people and children.

"The ability to ignore unwanted facts is one of the perogatives of unchallendged power. Closely related is the right to radically revise history."

—From *Because We Say So* (2015)
by Noam Chomsky

"Our justice system can prevent blacks from killing blacks in the same way that it prevents whites from killing whites: by investing time, money, and police resources into proving that blacks are valuable to our society—by extending them material and cultural support while aggressively investigating and prosecuting the perpetrators of their violent deaths. Unfortunately, such a commitment is expensive and arduous, and it requires white Americans to admit that, in some ways, black-on-black crime is an outgrowth of historic white-on-black crime. It's much easier to watch TV's one hundreth Natalee Holloway special and tolerate cops who write off black murder victims as subhuman."

—From "Making Black Lives Better" by Cord Jefferson, a review of Jill Leovy's *Ghettoside: A True Story of Murder in America* (2015) Published in Feb/Mar 2015 issue of *BookForum*

"In a single year, in case after case, across many sectors of the economy, federal agencies caught big companies breaking the law—defrauding taxpayers, covering up deadly safety problems, even precipitating the financial collapse in 2008—and let them off the hook with barely a slap on the wrist. Often, companies paid meager fines, which some will try to write off as a tax deduction.

The failure to adequately punish big corporations or their executives when they break the law undermines the foundations of this great country. Justice cannot mean a prison sentence for a teenager who steals a car, but nothing but a sideways glance at a C.E.O. who quietly engineers the theft of billions of dollars."

—Senator Elizabeth Warren
Op-ED New York Times (1/29/16)

Blackness
is a title,
is a preoccupation,
is a commitment Blacks
are to comprehend—
and in which you are
to perceive your Glory
. . . .
The word Black
has geographic power,
pulls everybody in:
Blacks here—
Blacks there—
Blacks wherever they may be . . .

—Gwendolyn Brooks
Primer for Blacks

Taking Bullets

"The white race is the cancer of human history; it is the white race and it alone—its ideologies and inventions—which eradicates autonomous civilizations wherever it spreads, which has upset the ecological balance of the planet, which now threatens the very existence of life itself."

—Susan Sontag, *Styles of Radical Will*

As I write these words, the changing backdrop of America's political and domestic scene is focused on Missouri where Governor Jay Nixon activated that state's National Guard when he and the state's white leadership anticipated a serious Black rebellion, or as he called it, a "riot," in the city of Ferguson. This action spurred in the wake of the Grand Jury's decision not to indict police officer Darren Wilson for the murder of Michael Brown, an unarmed Black[1] teenager. I emphasize "murder" because upon reviewing and studying the case, any sane, objective, fair-minded person, and any person with knowledge of the United States' history of Black boys and men's relationships to local and national "law" enforcement and the legal establishment, would conclude that there is "legally" and logically only one possible outcome: murder.

Two years earlier in July of 2013, with a similar backdrop in focus, the majority of the national Black community and others thought that the Trayvon Martin case was clearly one of murder. Let me remind you of its conclusion: a jury acquitted George Zimmerman of second-degree murder and manslaughter charges for Martin's 2012 death.[2] These two cases—and countless more—are indicative of the climate of mistrust that confronts Black men and boys in twenty-first century America.

---

[1] Black is capitalized when referring to people of African ancestry and of the African Diaspora. I have been writing capital B on Black people for over fifty years. Also see Professor Lori L. Tharps. *New York Times* op-ed, "The Case for Black with a Capital B" (11/18/14).

[2] The federal government has decided not to bring charges against Mr. Zimmerman in his murder of Trayvon Martin, a teenager who was standing his ground without a weapon, against a grown man approaching him with a weapon. As of 3/4/15 the Justice Department of the federal government decided not to bring civil rights charges against Darren Wilson in the case of Michael Brown, but did issue a scathing and severe analysis of the city's government including the police department of Ferguson, Missouri, in their relationship to its African American citizens. It is clear that the city of Ferguson was involved in criminal conspiracy and represented a citywide criminal enterprise against its Black citizens.

Haki R. Madhubuti

As the nation enters the second decade of this century with its first Black President, Barack Obama, the Black population on his watch is in deep, white-rooted trouble, far worse than most people, Black or white, realize. In fact, the African American community, with the possible exception of Native Americans (the nation's first indigenous peoples), was hit the hardest by the 2008-2009 recession. The national Black population has yet to recover from the prolonged crippling and criminal effects of its damage.[3]

The Cassandra cries of the existence of a post-racial America by right-wing pundits, the Tea Party, and the Republican Party are at best their code words. This is a signal for anti-Obamaism and right-wing fundamentalism, to upgrade their unrelenting attack on progressive politics, the Democratic Party, Black people, the poor, and others not in their club. These groups have been widely successful with the recent 2014 mid-term elections with Republicans gaining or buying more governorships and control of Congress. In a *Newsweek* cover story "The White Vote" (10/3/14), Matthew Cooper focused much of his analysis on "working class" and "middle class" white men. He writes that what "a disproportionate number of non-college white men seem to have in common, according to polls, is a profound sense of aggrievement—at the rich for rigging the system and the poor for getting benefits they don't deserve." The poor are generally defined as Blacks, Latinos, and recently poor women of all cultures and races in the United States.

---

[3] The Nobel Prize winner in Economics and the award winning Op-Ed columnist for the New York Times, Paul Krugman, documents this weekly in his columns and most recently in his book, *End This Depression Now* (2012). The former New York Times columnist Bob Herbert, in his remarkable book *Losing our Way: An intimate Portrait of a Troubled America* (2014), also documents and chronicles the loss of the middle class and the rise of the wealthy, and the loss of political power of everyday citizens to the corporate, financial and political elite.

Change the Conversation

Godfrey Hodgson argues in his 2009 book, *The Myth of American Exceptionalism*, that "the history of the United States ought to be seen as only one part of a broader history, not as the teleological preparation of a present and future perfection; as history, that is, and not as patriotic commemoration." He writes that the "expansion of Europe and the African slave trade, through the reformation and the enlightenment, brought about the global competition between the European powers...and the industrial revolution." This aided the United States' current preeminence in the world, especially its rise as a global economy and its part in international hegemony, also known as Empire.

Europe is attached to the United States in its shared history, culture, values, economics, wars, and philosophies of white supremacy and white nationalism—therefore one must understand and acknowledge that race—which fundamentally is a social construct in the United States—is not the exception to its culture; it drives the culture. Race also dictates that we—as Black poets, writers, scholars, workers at all levels, progressives, and mainly those activists who have given their lives to working and studying the issues of race—much like W.E.B. DuBois of the last century—must retake control of the territory of language, ideas, and creative actions. One of many leading the way in this necessary work is the Afrocentric scholar and educator Molefi Kete Asante, whose book, *Erasing Racism* (2003), is an essential guidepost for activists and scholars. The scholar, activist, and Christian, Cornel West, in his latest book, *Black Prophetic Fire* (2015), as in his groundbreaking, *Race Matters* (1993, 2001), and his co-authored *The Rich and The Rest of Us* (2012), continues to fight in the tradition of W.E.B. DuBois, Harriet Tubman, Martin Luther King, Jr., and Malcolm X. Also in this tradition of struggle and scholarship, we have to include the work of Nell Irvin Painter, Fred Hord, Haile Gerima, bell hooks, Errol A. Henderson, Keith Gilyard, Bakari Kitwana, Walter Mosely, Sonia Sanchez, Michael Eric Dyson, Toni Morrison, Charles J. Ogletree, Jr., Ishmael Reed, Carol D. Lee, Herb Boyd, Nikki Giovanni and others.

Race in the United States drives its culture in all the areas of human activity: family, religion, education, economics, politics, media, law, sports, entertainment, health, and of course, the military. The dominant, unspoken, undebated, and therefore unacknowledged narrative in the nation is *race*. This is especially on display in the demonization of Black boys and men as in the recent killing of the unarmed Black teenager Michael Brown by officer Darren Wilson in Ferguson, Missouri. During his deposition, Wilson provided his depiction of Brown as "the most intense aggressive face. The only way I can describe it, it looks like a demon." (*Huff Post* 11/29/14) This demonization of the other—as in enemy—has a long active history in the United States.

From the genocidal elimination and appropriation of indigenous peoples' lands in the Americas, to the enslavement of tens of millions of African peoples and their parallel sub-human bondage in the twentieth century with Jim/Jane Crow, to the internment (a polite word for *imprisonment*) of tens of thousands of people of Japanese heritage during Europe's and the United States' war on the world number two, commonly known as World War II. The rhetoric and nomenclature of race often diminishes the horrific effects of white world supremacy and international white nationalism, which by any measurement is not only alive and well in the twenty-first century but is, most certainly in the United States, a growth industry.

Seldom in this country do we at any level entertain questions of global colonization, genocide, white settler land-theft, or whole-people enslavement because of race, color, economics, or location. The essential core and fundamental definition of North and South America is in its history of white domination of Native peoples, whether in the Americas, Africa, or Asia. We cannot understand or seriously approach with any ounce of the truth United States' history without confronting how the nation was formed, maintained and developed; and how it grew and prospered in its systematic conquering, colonization, elimination, and enslavement of Native peoples. The seizing of American land is not a pretty story and its development is less appealing to young minds committed to the "land of the free and the home of the brave" narrative. The historian Roxanne Dunbar-Ortiz makes this very clear in her timely book, *An Indigenous Peoples' History of the United States* (2014), where she documents in vivid, un-flowered language the systematic destruction of Indigenous peoples, the first people of this nation. This state-terrorism still lives with us today in the total unfiltered demonization, economic control, enslaved education, and mass-incarceration of Black and Brown men. Paralyzing and failed politics border on outright fascism, anti-intellectualism masquerades as knowledge, and liberating values over power, direct, and determine the daily existence of Black people, poor people, and non-white people in the United States. These facts cannot be minimized or negated. In 1970 when Wendell Berry wrote *The Hidden Wound*, he was thirty-four and on his way to becoming the much honored and respected poet, fiction writer, essayist, and farmer that he has become. *The Hidden Wound* is autobiographical, perceptive, and honest. Both sides of his family were in the slave-owning business and as he recounts this history one feels that there is a place in our culture that has turned its back on this type of truth telling:

> It seems to me that racism could not possibly have made merely a mechanical division between the two races; at least in America it did not. It involves an emotional dynamics that has disordered the heart both of the society as a whole and every person in the society. It has made divisions not only between white people and black people, but between black men and black women, white men and white women; it has come between white people and their work, and between white people and their land. It has fragmented both our society and our minds.

A major stimulus in making the crisis is that white supremacist attitudes and actions are not predicated on doing that which is just or right toward the people (Blacks and others); they have enslaved, killed, raped, imprisoned, forced into "ghettos," marginalized members of society. They have little knowledge of and less respect for Black people, and that is the crisis. Wendell Barry as a poet and as a man who lives close to the land is indeed, a truth teller and in many other areas of life he is in opposition to corporate culture and its many destructive forces.

Remember they who control and create the master narrative also articulate, write, publish, distribute, teach, practice, condone and make official their version of history, which is manifested and celebrated in all their national holidays. The obvious example and clearly the biggest lie is Thanksgiving. This day should be named if we are dealing with the truth, Indigenous Peoples' Genocide Day.

Bold Statements, But True

"The old, old phrase: 'Negroes are the last to be hired and the first to be fired.' This doesn't apply to the Negro maid particularly, though it can. It actually applies, without exception, and with great rigor, to Negro men. One has got to consider, especially when you talk about this whole tension between violence and nonviolence, the dilemma and the rage and the anguish of a Negro man who, in the first place, is forced to accept all kinds of humiliation in his working day, whose power in the world is so slight he cannot really protect his home, his wife, his children, when he finds himself out of work. And then he watches his children growing up, menaced in exactly the same way he has been menaced."

—James Baldwin
interviewed by Studs Terkel

In the West, most certainly in the United States, white people never, and I say *never*, have to think about being white. Being white is an accepted, normal, and privileged existence. However, Black people, African Americans everywhere in the world, especially in the United States, must think about and deal with being Black every day of the year, and this is amplified in the darker one's complexion. Dark-skinned Black men and women have a storm to negotiate each day they step outside their family or comfort zones. All the white systems of organizations, control and definition have been put in place to keep Black men out. To reduce Black peoples' struggles and the definition of their race to "people of color" is to display an ignorance reserved for newborn babies. We must never diminish the critical power that "Black" carries in a white supremacist culture.

If all 42 million-plus Black people in the United States disappeared tomorrow, there is not one job, position, appointment, post, function, manager, executive, professorship, CEO, CFO, general of the military, etc., now held by Black people, including the President of the United States, that could not be filled within a week by white people. In a nation of over 314 million people, the Black population is 42 million according to *Black Stats* by Monique W. Morris. In a nation with a surplus of PhDs, MBAs, lawyers, MFAs, medical doctors, technical non-degree positions and others, too many white young people are jobless. There are millions of white people standing in line and submitting similar resumes from the basements of their parents' homes where they have been forced to move back to after undergraduate school or technical training because of the "recession" of 2008-2009 that is still with us. They are unable to find employment.

> Bottomline, Black people are no longer essential to America's economic labor force.

This is the core fact of our existence in this country and unless we recognize it and plan accordingly, the future will remain a question mark. We must also consider a number of other bold but true statements that will provoke questions and conversations on race and existence in America.

Number 1. Too many Black boys and men know more about football and basketball than their own history, culture, and defining ideas and values. Cultural self-knowledge is not even an afterthought. The major problem in the Black community is one of economic, cultural, political and military ignorance.

Number 2. In hard numbers, there are more poor white people in the United States than poor **Black people.** White nationalist ideology, white skin privilege gives white people opportunities that most Blacks do not have. There is little if any discussion nationally on the acute poverty of Appalachian and Delta Mississippi poor whites. This discussion would introduce the conversation of class inequality among whites and the rich avoid this reality like the plague.

Number 3. If the white rich and wealthy really cared about America's youth, why is student loan debt 1.4 trillion dollars and growing?

Number 4. Black people and Latinos/Hispanics are not in mass numbers leaving the United States. We are here to stay. White people need to seriously adjust their attitudes, actions, and lifestyles, and begin a re-education that leans toward a realistic understanding of people outside of their white world.

Number 5. As long as Barack Obama is President, a great many white voters—middle-class, low income, and highly educated—will vote against their own interests to avoid voting for or agreeing with a Black authority or political figure.

Number 6. Whenever a Black boy or man commits a crime that receives national attention it is generally, fair or not, attached to all Black people. And before we know the race of the offender, most Blacks are saying under their breath, "I hope he is not Black."

Number 7. Black people are not allowed or encouraged to be individuals—from the outside, we are seen as a group, therefore, individually, we are invisible.

Number 8. Black boys and men, unlike some other ethnic groups, do not have effective national lobbying firms, politicians, institutions, or organizations working on their behalf round-the-clock.

Number 9. Drugs are not grown, created, conceived, developed, manufactured, produced, or delivered to the nationwide Black community by Black people. Nor are guns, or any weapons of mass destruction manufactured in the Black community.

Number 10. As an oppressed, dependent, occupied, depressed, vilified, and isolated community, too many young Black men—and some women—see the local selling of drugs as an economic support system, and for a few, a way ahead.

Number 11. Many of the businesses in the Black community do not represent and are not owned by Black people. Black people spend overwhelming percent of their money at white businesses and spend an equal percent of their time criticizing the same people they give their money to.

Number 12. The first level of freedom and liberation is a cultural and political mindset that understands and practices said concepts; the second level is economics. The Black community used to understand this. Integration not only destroyed us economically, but also culturally and politically; this is why an accurate understanding of Black history and culture are essential. White people world over love Black culture, yet have little resistance in dismissing its originators, Black people.

Number 13. The majority of Black people live in fresh-food deserts. It is common knowledge that Black communities are surrounded by and saturated with fast "food" establishments, which base their profits on the sale of quickly fried meats, fish, chicken, and other "foods." Combine this with Black peoples' over-consumption of salt, sugar, and fats and we have a recipe for health crises such as obesity, high blood pressure, and other food-related illnesses. Dr. Carl C. Bell calls these areas "food swaps," he also points out that Black communities nationwide are saturated with liquor stores that contribute to the high rates of alcoholism and to a condition that he and a colleague decibe as "Fetal Alcohol Syndrome" that may contribute to violence exhibited in children born to women with this medical condition. *This is very serious.*

Number 14. If we look at high-end Black communities where the Black upper and middle-class live—this would also include the newly "rich" Blacks—we immediately see one institution that does not function at the highest levels: the public schools, especially the high schools. Also, deep rooted segregation in America still exist, which determines Black wealth creation. (See N.Y. *Times* editorial of 9-15-15, "Segregation Destroys Black Wealth")

Number 15. On the evening of Barack Obama's inauguration (1-20-2009), Frank Luntz, a republican communications specialist called a special meeting of fifteen of the Republican Party's most enterprising thinkers[1] to devise a strategy to put a stop to the progressive agenda of the new President. As reported in Robert Draper's *Do Not Ask What Good We Do* (2012) that, "he and the others in the room were devastated." However, it would take the words of Mitch McConnell's highly Broadcast quote in 2010 that would leave little doubt as to the priorities of their meeting, "The single most important thing we want to achieve is for President Obama to be a one-term President." This is from Mann and Ornstein's, *It's Worse than it Looks* (2012) and to a large degree they have succeeded.

---

[1] Eric Cantor, Kevin McCarthy, Paul Ryan, Pete Sessions, Jeb Hensarling, Pete Hoekstra, Dan Lungren, Jim DeMint, Jon Kyl, Tom Coburn, John Ensign, Bob Corker, Fred Barnes, Newt Gingrich and Frank Luntz.

Number 16. It is an unfortunate fact that President Barack Obama is the most hated, vilified, insulted, lied about, condemned, castrated, cartooned, derided, disliked, loathed, maligned, disapproved of chief executive in the history of the United States. The only other U.S. President that came close was Abraham Lincoln, and he was in the middle of a civil war. The primary reason for this state of white hatred of President Obama is because he is Black, his family is Black, and they live in the nation's White House. If he was white, the Republican would not have dared invited the Prime Minister of Israel to speak before a joint session of Congress.[2] This was indeed a sucker punch to the face of this Black president and a statement to all white people, "we got this."

Number 17. Without a national Black economic strategy and program completely controlled, created, directed, and owned by serious Black people who actually love and care for Black people, especially our children, there is no way there will be complete freedom. As long as there are some urban areas where Black men's unemployment levels approach fifty percent, we cannot seriously talk about liberation. As a result of white inaction on the economic and political front, Black outrage and regional rebellions (white define as riots) will become the *new normal* in keeping with the growth of non-white populations increasingly becoming the nation's new majority.

Number 18. We live in a nation where "power," all ultimate power, resides in the hands, minds, and actions of white men and a few white women. The final decisions, however, in all areas of human activity (including climate change) in the United States, in the great majority of life's situations, reside with white men. All Black men—all Black *people*—in America make choices within the parameters of decisions handed down by white men, with the

---

[2] Please note: Prime Minister Netanyahu, the head of state of Israel, was invited by John Boehner and the Republican leadership to address a joint session of Congress which has never been done before without involvement with the executive branch of government. This was carried off primarily to diminish the statue of the President and embarrass him on the international stage. As we navigate the white supremacist economy, politics, education, media, healthcare, environment, judicial, manufacturing, sports, military and entertainment systems in the United States, the common denominator is that one percent of the super, almost unimagined wealthy—who are white—controls it all. The obscenely rich, like the Koch Brothers, the Walton family, Larry Ellison, Warren Buffet, Sheldon Adelson and others discharge damaging influences over Congress, the Supreme Court, and most state legislators via American Legislative Exchange Council (A.L.E.C.) and other institutions—primarily right wing think-tanks, radio stations and the ever-present Fox News. To add insult to an already divided congress, freshman Senator Tom Cotton organized 47 Republican senators to sign a written letter to Iran's leaders warning them that any deal made with President Obama'a administration will not last after he leaves office. These 47 traitors would not dare undercut the foreign policy of a white president. (See appendix for names)

United States Supreme Court at the top of the pecking order. There are no exceptions, including the President of the United States.

Number 19. If the Black rich lost all of their money tomorrow—which comes to about 41 billion dollars including Oprah Winfrey's fortune at three billion and, according to *Forbes's 2015 Wealth Issue*, Michael Jordan's fortune at one billion—that loss would not negatively or positively affect the national Black community. Why? According to Claud Anderson, the richest among Black people, with the possible exception of Oprah Winfrey, do not in any systematic or measurable way use their wealth to affect real, meaningful, and lasting economic, political, or educational change for the majority of Black people in America. One cannot make this same statement, for example, about Jewish people in the United States, where a sizable portion of their wealth is systematically used to strengthen their people in all areas of human development. Dean Starkman in the July 14, 2014 issue of *The New Republic* documents that the "typical Black family is worth $236,500 less than the typical white family. Equality will be a lie until we close the gap." What else is new?

Number 20. "1.5 Million Black Men, Missing from Daily Life" states the *New York Times* on its front page on April 21, 2015. Walfers, Querly, and Leonhardt, using the work of Becky Pettit of the University of Texas and others, write, "In New York, almost 120,000 Black men between the ages of 25 and 54 are missing from everyday life. In Chicago, 45,000 are missing, and more than 30,000 are missing in Philadelphia. Across the South— from North Charleston, South Carolina, through Georgia, Alabama, and Mississippi and up into Ferguson, Missouri—hundreds of thousands more are missing." These Black men are missing for a number of reasons due to early deaths or because they are behind bars. Those Black men between 25 and 54—"which demographics call the prime age years—[have] higher imprisonment rates [that] account for almost 600,000." The writers also state that "the gap in North Charleston is also considerably larger than the nationwide average" in terms of demographic disparity.

Number 21. Too many Black people are anti-Black. Many Black people would rather be colored, brown or white. We have been taught in so many ways from enslavement to today, from birth to now, to be anti-self, anti-African, and anti-

Africa. Black self-hatred is centuries old and subconscious due largely to white on Black crime and terrorism, see *The Destruction of Black Civilization* (1987) by Chancellor Williams and *Post Traumatic Slave Syndrome* by Joy DeGruy (2005). Black on Black crime exists in America largely because of the deadly history of white on Black crime; any elementary and honest reading of Black history authenticates this fact.[3] Fundamentally, the color question and confusion exist because of this history. White men's rape and sexual abuse of Black women (African women) during the international trade of enslaved Africans produced mixed-race Black people worldwide. White fear and hatred of Black men is at the European heart of their treatment of Black people and other non-whites. This is why, in part, many of the legal systems and sub-systems are created to constrict Black mobility. Also, among many whites—mainly men—there is nightmarish dread of Black retribution or avengement. This speaks loudly to why the lynching of Black men often included public castration. Black people kill Black people in part because we have been taught killing Black people is acceptable and that in the European worldview Black life is not important. Black people do not mass kill white people because they have not been trained to do so and it is not part of their experience, see *Psychopathic Racial Personality* (1985) by Bobby E. Wright. With all of the psychological baggage of which Christianity is central and essential to Black existence in America— it is understandable as to why there exists a love/hate relationship with the United States. Black people know no other land or culture—even with the white supremacist cries of "Go back to Africa." Still among the great majority of Black people, who are culturally "American" they have only recently begun to question that reality and to seek other answers; their love of America knows no boundaries, and they are more willing to fight and die to protect it. This culture of constant and contained oppression has rendered too many Black people in a perpetual state of trauma.

Number 22. A few white men have literally committed the crime of the century that produced the 2008-09 economic meltdown that bankrupted tens of millions of citizens. The criminal activities of the "smartest guys in

---

3 Some of the finest thinkers, scholars and researchers to publish work covering Black life in America and the world confirm this history: Carter G. Woodson, Chancellor Williams, Lerone Bennett Jr., Vincent Harding, Jacob H. Carruthers, Herbert Aptheker, John H. Clarke, W.E.B. DuBois, Eric Williams, Yosef A.A. ben-Jochannan, Edward Wilmot Blyden, Maulana Karenga, Cheikh Anta Diop, John Hope Franklin, John G. Jackson, Tony Martin, Asa G. Hilliard, Amos N. Wilson, Howard Zinn, Studs Terkel, Marimba Ani, Bobby E. Wright, Molefi K. Asante and Errol A. Henderson to name a very few of the finest thinkers, scholars, and researchers to publish work covering Black life in America and the world.

the room" on Wall Street, including the corporate one percent, thousands of global companies, financial firms, and banks, wrecked the national and international economy. The Bank of America, J.P. Morgan Chase, Citigroup, Wells Fargo, Goldman-Sachs, Morgan Stanley, Barclays, Deutsche Bank, Credit Suisse and others yield such an outstanding amount of clout and wealth that they are still too big to fail, even after American citizens, including Black people, bailed most of them out. The six largest banks control over ten trillion dollars, according to Chuck Collins book, *99 to 1: How Wealth Inequality Is Wrecking The World and What We Can Do About It*, which translates into 63 percent of the U.S. gross domestic product. The major point here is that the Obama Administration did not take one CEO, CFO, or any of the governing board members to trial. They, the one percent top bankers and others of the one percent for the most part, walked away with a smile counting their year-end bonuses after committing supreme violence on the nation and the world. They did not burn down a CVS or steal soda; they destroyed Black, Brown, and white people's lives (their pensions, 401(k)s, IRAs, causing foreclosures and bankruptcies) without acknowledgement, guilt or a change of their attitudes or practices that continue to this day. Michael Lewis' book *The Big Short* is a must read to fully understand the recession of 2008/09 and Rena Steinzor's *Why Not Jail?* for an understanding of how the rich "legally" rigged the system and got away with high crimes and *murder* that continues today.

Number 23. According to *USA Today*[4] (8/10/15), "nearly 30 unarmed black men were killed in police shootings in the year since Michael Brown's death on August 9, 2014." Also, according to the *Chicago Tribune*, since the beginning of 2015 – there has been 1,500 shootings in Chicago. One can imagine and do mind mathematics around the number of shootings during the same time nationwide. I will state as emphatically as possible since our forced migration to this land, Black people, people of African ancestry, African Americans have as a people been set up to fail in America's white supremacist culture, politics and economy.

---

4 The listing of unarmed black men shot since Michael Brown's death on August 9, 2014 are: Ezell Ford, Aug. 11, 2014; Akai Gurley, Nov. 20, 2014; Tamir Rice, Nov. 22, 2014; Rumain Brisbon, Dec. 2, 2014; Jerame Reid, Dec. 30, 2014; Artago Damon Howard, Jan. 8, 2015; Jeremy Lett, Feb. 4, 2015; Lavall Hall, Feb. 15, 2015; Thomas Allen, Feb. 28, 2015; Charly Leundeu Keunang, March 1, 2015; Naeschylus Vinzant, March 6, 2015; Tony Robinson, March 6, 2015; Anthony Hill, March 9, 2015; Bobby Gross, March 12, 2015; Brandon Jones, March 19, 2015; Eric Harris, April 2, 2015; Walter Scott, April 4, 2015; Frank Shephard, April 15, 2015; William Chapman, April 22, 2015; David Felix, April 25, 2015; Brendon Glenn, May 5, 2015; Kris Jackson, June 15, 2015; Spencer McCain, June 25, 2015; Victor Emanuel Larosa, July 2, 2015; Salvado Ellswood, July 12, 2015; Albert Joseph Davis, July 17, 2015; Darrius Stewart, July 17, 2015; Samuel DuBose, July 19, 2015 and Christian Taylor, August 7, 2015.

Number 24. Little, if any substantial change politically, socially, culturally, economically, educationally, or spiritually for Black boys, men, people will occur in the world or the United States until there is an unfiltered, honest conversation—with correctives and programs that *work* under the *deadly affects*—locally, nationally and internationally of *white skin privileges* and its *underpinnings white nationalism, white supremacy, i.e., white power.*

Number 25. I have also been asked over my fifty odd years of writing, activism, teaching, and struggle, "Why do you do this kind of work?" My bold statement, in truth, "I love Black people and by extension I love all children of all cultures." I, also, deeply care for poor people where ever they exist. I work daily to challenge and change this world so its works for the great majority rather than for the acute privileged few.

Number 26. Central to any people's tomorrow is memory. Deny a people's past, and you put them at the mercy of those who are in the business of imposing their past, present and future upon others. One's history of oppression, misadventure, and suffering is too often a victim's history and people cannot build a future on the history of the enslaver. The centrality of memory and the gladness and hope of measurable accomplishments must be larger and must encompass the worldview of the majority of any people who seek liberation and a bright future on their own terms. For Black people, the right memory, accurate memory, long memory, history-based memory can be the fuel, the clean protection that jump starts a recalibration of a *liberation narrative.* And, historically, this has always been the case. Remember, the people who control and shape the narratives decide the conversation. History, according to winners, is always quickly and slowly recorded, written, published, taught, and studied. Black boys and men, girls and women need *new love,* Black *unconditional love* and security, need a deep earth rooted love based upon Black cultural knowledge that we (Black families, communities, institutions and people) are our own answer to any bright future.

Number 27. If there is to be a future in America and the world, we must create it. Never give up on young people of all cultures. We must remain *realistic optimists.*

The United States of Empire

Most Black people and others do not realize that the United States is the world's only legitimate "empire" and its rulership is white. The most important institutions of this empire are its economic, legal and political systems and its military. When one adds its court system, especially the Supreme Court, it is not surprising that 1.5 million Black and Brown boys and men are contained and locked-down in the nation's criminal justice system. Most of these boys and men are poor and have had inadequate legal representation. In fact, most of their sentencings have been plea-bargained, and if they become convicted felons, these individuals automatically lose most of their civil rights: voting, most employment opportunities, government-funded housing, quality education, and much more. The empire does not work for all citizens.

Most students of world history are aware of the 1884-85 meeting of major European powers in Berlin. They—Great Britain, Germany, France, and others, as well as the United States, which sent a representative but refused to be a signatory to the final document—were there to discuss empire and "ground rules" that continue European world imperialism. As documented by Thomas Bender in his book, A *Nation Among Nations: America's Place in World History* (2006), the great powers of that time "negotiated a blue print, carving up of Africa among themselves, an agreement that accelerated their imperial expansion and tightened control over their colonies." Also see Errol A. Henderson's book, *Afrocentrism and World Politics Towards a New Paradigm* (1995).

Bender also notes that Americans, in the nature of their own national identity, chose to move on as an Empire on their own terms. He writes, "American republicanism and Protestant Christianity, they thought, were the key notes of their distinctiveness, as were their rejection of imperial ambition." He labels this a "sleight of hand" which thereby obscured "their actual empire by describing it as 'the westward movement' or the 'westward expansion' of their country."

The United States used what is described in much of the historical literature as "the empty land theory" to justify its stealing and conquering of land owned and possessed by Native Americans and Mexicans. Bender writes that, "it has been difficult for Americans to recognize their continental expansion as an empire especially when ethnocentric assumptions obscure the presence of Native

Haki R. Madhubuti

Americans on the supposedly 'empty' land." It is not only the control, settlement, and colonization of land*—which is the only living entity that nobody anywhere is making any more of—it is also the uncontested control of the high seas.

In a recent op-ed article in the *New York Times*, "Our Navy is Big Enough" (3-9-2015), Gregg Easterbrook argues, rather effectively, that the Pentagon's new budget request of $161 billion for the 2016 fiscal year as opposed to the $149 billion already in the budget, is not needed. He claims that no naval expansion is needed and that "the United States Navy dominates. In aircraft carriers, nuclear submarines, naval aviation, surface fire power, assault ships, missiles and logistics, the United States Navy is more powerful than all the other navies of the world." He also mentions the $3.3 billon Zumwalt destroyer, which is the most advanced war ship in the world has advanced cannons that can hit targets 63 miles away. The United States Navy represents just one element of its armed forces that outpaces all other nations. The training of its officer core at West Point, Annapolis, the Air Force Academy, Naval War College, and other U.S. institutions is unmatched in the rest of the world. However, Easterbrook writes that "arguably, naval hegemony is among the greatest American achievements, and one that makes all nations better off. That hegemony is secured by such a dramatic margin that no naval build up is needed...one lesson that officers of other navies learn at the Naval War College is that there is zero chance they will ever defeat the United States in battle—so why even try?" The proposed budget for 2016 does not include that of the Nuclear submarine fleet or the off budget secret space program. Nor does it include Special Forces: the Navy SEALS, the Army Rangers and Green Beret. Nor does this budget include the billions of dollars that are allocated openly and secretly to Homeland Security, the FBI, (especially its joint terrorism task force and its national cyber workplaces across the nation are strictly secret) and the CIA and its international above board and secret bases around the world. This is the U.S. Empire patting itself on the back.

William Appleman Williams' *Empire as a Way of Life* (1980), defines America's strategic and economic rule over a very large portion of today's world as an unlimited quest for resources and military dominance as a necessary psychological and imperial advantage. Williams states, "It is perhaps a bit too extreme, but if so only by a whisker, to say that imperialism has been the

---

*See *Who Owns The World: The Surprising Truth About every piece of land on the planet* (2010) by Kevin Cahill with Rob McMahon. One surprising revelation is that Queen Elizabeth II owns 1/6 of the entire land surface on earth, (nearly 3 times the size of the U.S.

opiate of the American people." This may have indeed been true of America's leadership—political, commercial, and military, but I believe that the average citizen gives it little thought. Williams also writes:

> In thinking about empire as a way of life, we must consider the dynamics of the process as well as a static description of the empire at any particular moment. The empire as a territory and as activities dominated economically, politically, psychologically by a superior power is the result of empire as a way of life. This is particularly important in the case of the United States because from the beginning the persuasiveness of empire as a way of life effectively closed off other ways of dealing with the reality that Americans encounter.... The other meaning of empire concerns the forcible subjugation of formerly independent peoples by a wholly external power, and their subsequent rule by the imperial metropolis. One thinks here of the First Americans and of the northern half of Mexico seized by conquest in the 1840s by the United States and integrated into its imperial system. Or of England's assault on Ireland.

Another example of recent empire would be the British in India and Africa. The United States has replaced British influence in the Philippines and Cuba prior to Cuba's revolution. This nation's adventures in the Middle East, ill-advised as they are, continue despite the uncertainty of a long-term plan, but are still predicated on cheap oil and the false benefits that "democracy" would bring to the region.

It is abundantly clear to political/policy wonks, scholars and informed lay citizens that the Bush/Cheney ill-advised attack on Iraq war/is a horrific act of hubris and war crimes that will never be prosecuted by the World Court or addressed by the United Nations. The ultimate power of the empire is to control the narrative and the courts—national and international. Peter W. Galbraith, the first U.S. Ambassador to Croatia writes in his *The End of Iraq: How American Incompetence Created a War Without End* (2006) about the complete political and cultural ignorance and arrogance of the Bush administration and its total waste of U.S. treasure and influence.

It is common knowledge that the middle-east oil was a prime mover in the decision to invade, in fact it can be argued that it was the major reason. However, Chalmers Johnson in *The Sorrows of Empire* (2004) offers other considerations:

> It would be hard to deny that oil, Israel, and domestic politics all played crucial roles in the Bush administration's war against Iraq, but I believe the more encompassing explanation for our second war with Iraq is no different from that for our wars in the Balkans in 1999 or in Afghanistan in 2001-02; the inexorable pressure of imperialism and militarism.

Haki R. Madhubuti

As the current and only empire in the world the United States' unquestioned backing of Israel has positioned it in the minds of many as the nation's fifty-first state. Most certainly since 9/11 the right-wing of the nation and the state of Israel have been able to use "terrorism" to justify most military acts and request for greater resources in the continued occupation of Palestine and serious oppression of its people, especially children.

Jen Marlowe in an article that was published recently in the *Nation*, "The Children of Gaza" (7/20-27/2015) details the "permanent war" that Israel reigns on occupied Palestine daily. Israel controls most of Palestine, its water, electricity, roads, equipment flow, food flow, education space, and one can go on and on. Marlowe points out that the major conflicts of Operation Hot Winter (2/08), Operation Cast Lead (12/8), Operation Returning Echol (3/1), Operation Pillar of Defense (11/12), and Operation Protective Edge (7/14) produced unimagined material destruction and cost the lives of over 3,826 Palestinian children and adults and 93 Israelis children and adults. Ilan Pappé in his book *On Palestine* (2015) defined "the Israeli policy toward the Gaza Strip as incremental genocide." This is not an over statement. Yet, due to the United States' all out support of Israel, history may not record this sorrowful tale accurately. However, Noam Chomsky in *On Palestine* gives us his educational long view:

> When Israel is on "good behavior," more than two Palestinian children are killed every week, a pattern that goes back over fourteen years. The underlying cause is the criminal occupation and the programs to reduce Palestinian life to bare survival in Gaza, while Palestinians are restricted to unviable cantons in the West Bank and Israel takes over what it wants, all in gross violation of international law and explicit Security Council resolutions, not to speak of minimal decency. And it will—continue as long as it is supported by Washington and tolerated by Europe—to our everlasting shame.

Egypt who signed a "peace" agreement with Israel during the Carter administration also functions as is defined in its best interest even as the recent military controlled government locked up students, journalists, peace activists and others. The rule of military force has become the norm in Egypt, all after the "Egyptian Arab Spring" led by progressives and students who brought down the corrupt government of former President Hosni Mubarak. Egypt, easily is number two after Israel in reception of America's foreign gifts (aid). Between the two of them, America's tax payers (including Black people) contributes in assets of seven billion dollars a year.

With increasing control of East Jerusalem, with relative security from the wall surrounding what is left of the West Bank, and with thousands of remaining settlers east of the wall protected by a strong occupying force, there is a temptation for some Israelis simply to avoid any further efforts to seek a peace agreement based on the Quartet's Roadmap or good-faith negotiations on any other basis.

U.S. support for Israel is hardly the only source of anti-Americanism in the Arabic and Islamic world, and making it less confrontational would not remove all sources of friction between these countries and the United States. Examining the consequences of Israel's treatment of the Palestinians and tacit U.S. support of these policies is not to deny the presence of genuine anti-Semitism in various Arabic countries or the fact that groups and governments in these societies sometimes fan these attitudes and use the Israel-Palestine conflict to divert attention from their own mistakes and crimes. Rather, the point is simply that the United States pays a substantial price for supporting Israel so consistently. This posture fuels hostility toward the United States in the Middle East, motivates anti-American extremists and aids them in recruiting of anti-American fighters. The authoritarian governments in the region also use American influences as an all-too-convenient scapegoat for their own failings, and makes it harder for Washington to convince potential supporters to confront extremists in their own countries. According to John J. Mearsheimer and Stephen M. Walt from *The Israel Lobby and U.S. Foreign Policy* (2007), "When it comes to fighting terrorism, in short, U.S. and Israeli interests are not identical. Backing Israel against the Palestinians make winning the war on terror harder, not easier, and the 'partner against terror' rationale does not provide a compelling justification for unconditional U.S. support."

WHERE EMPIRE IS IN DOUBT?

Indeed, this is a teaching moment. In our centuries of struggle in the United States, from enslavement to the presidency, the whites who have been the closest and most supportive of our struggles have been Jews. Their own history of enslavement, the Holocaust, the founding of the state of Israel, which the Palestinians define as the Nakbeh. Palestinians and the current "insider," and "outsider," problems with the Obama administrations regarding Iran are both painful and instructive. Seldom are Black-Jews relations commented on by Black writers, scholars, leaders, pundits, educators, or lay folks from our communities. These are many reasons for this, however, this is not the place to ponder this important question. All of my comments are made in support of the Iran deal and that of the first and probably only Black President—Barack Obama—whom I will witness in my life time.

There are two key facts that are not debated in the United States, but are well known in Israel. First, that members of Israel's intelligence and military communities have come out openly against Netanyahu's position and are for the Iran deal. J.J. Goldberg, the editor-at-large of the *Forward* and the author of *Jewish Power: Inside the American Jewish Establishment* (1996) states in his 4-24-2015 opinion piece:

> Netanyahu's disagreement with his top brass over Iran strategy has been an open secret at least since January 2011 when he fired legendary Mossad director Meir Dagan. Ever since, Dagan has been accusing Netanyahu of recklessness for his military threats against Iran. Shin Bet director Yuval Diskin picked up the theme after he was cashiered in May 2011. He's been even harsher than Dagan.
>
> Dagan, Diskin and a slew of other security chiefs argue that if Israel attacked Iran's nuclear installations by itself, it would set the Iranian nuclear effort back a year or two at most. Iran could rebuild afterward with greater international sympathy, since it could claim it faced an active threat from the Middle East's only nuclear power, Israel.

And second, the majority of the American Jewish community voted overwhelmingly for Barack Obama twice, and many Jews serve or have served in key positions in his administration.

Seldom are these two facts given serious coverage in the United States. We have been led to accept a world view sanctioned by corporate media, talking heads, and most right-winged pundits that most Israelis in and out of power support the prime minister's position. This is not true.

This Iran deal has affected relationships between Blacks and Jews. Not a forever question mark, but a question. One of the few publications to seriously look at Jewish-Black relations is the *Forward*, a weekly Jewish newspaper with a one hundred year publication record. In a February 27, 2015 edition, the *Forward* ran a front page article by Nathan Gottman, a staff writer, "Will Black Leader's Anger over BiBi's Speech Hurt Long Term Ties?" Mr. Gottman opens his piece by quoting U.S. Representative Charles Rangel, one of the founders of the Congressional Black Causcus (CBC), a long supporter of Israel. Mr. Rangel, the 23-term congressman who represents many Jewish constituents in his district that includes New York City, Harlem, Manhattan's Upper West Side tweeted: "BiBi: if you have a problem with our POTUS's foreign policy, meet me at AIPAC but not on House floor." Mr. Rangel and other African American representatives did not attend Israelis Prime Minister Netanyahu's March 3 speech to a joint session of Congress as an "insider" protest to support Obama's foreign policy, and his administration's negotiated Iran deal. Mr. Gottman's conclusion is that the "speech" will not have long term consequences with the CBC. He is correct for many reasons—CBC fundraising being one—however to fully examine this question that is the CBC's relationship to Israel will require a longer essay.

In the same issue of the *Forward*, Marjorie Golde Kent, the excutive director of Jews For Racial and Economic Justice paints a more examined and nuanced picture of Black-Jews relationship in the United States. She writes that the Jewish community engagement with the #BlackLivesMatter has been mixed:

> Unfortunately, the activist Jewish community has its own race problem. Those of us that have been vocal against police violence and in support of #BlackLivesMatter movement, our activism of the past few months has laid bare this fact: Virtually no progressive Jewish organization has Jews of color in visible leadership.

Majorie Golde Kent as an activist leader in the Jewish community has taken the lead during this very difficult time when the Black-Jewish relationship in the United States is not as close as many think it is. I share her feelings after over fifty years of watching this relationship deteriorate to where it is today. I have been to Israel and I have seen their nuclear facilities in Dimona. I have extended family in Israel and understand their love for the nation. They and I only wish the best for the young nation. But to act, as the most powerful military power in the region less as a victim and more as a responsible force for good and justice. For the lay reader I suggest reading *Jewish Literacy* by Rabbi Joseph Telushkin, *Tikkun Reader*, edited by Michael Lerner, *The Crisis of Zionism* by Peter Brinart, and *Because We Say So* by Noam Chomsky to aquire a deeper understanding of modern Israel.

This fight regarding Iran's Nuclear Accord negotiated between Iran, the United States plus five is about to get ugly. The culture of misinformation, ultra-high hyperbole and lies that the Republican and Tea parties have

Haki R. Madhubuti

unleashed against President Obama and his negotiating team have not only crossed the line of political decorum but have created a new bottom. Mr. Michael Huckabee, a Republican presidential candidate just accused the President of the United States of fashioning a deal with Iran that "march Israelis to the door of the oven." The United States as the last standing empire in the world will receive the brunt of the negative criticism for the Iranian deal, even though it was not possible without six nations plus Iran agreeing to it. To not have received the deal would have placed the United States and the allies in the position of another land war in the Middle East that the great majority of Americans are not onboard with. Have we forgotten 2003 with the Neo-Cons and their right wing chicken-hawks using some of the same language that pushed the nation into Iraq with the "axis of evil" declaration and other fictions?

We went to war without any serious consideration or understanding of the region's culture, language, religion, economics, geography, and governing leadership. The complexity required in making the decision to go to war or not was never debated at the national level among the populous. We rushed into war as a result of listening to the Bush administration leadership led by Vice President Cheney, Secretary of Defense Rumsfeld, Secretary of State Powell, Ms. Rice, Mr. Wolfowitz, editorial boards of major newspapers and magazines, right-wing and middle-of-the-road reporters, columnists, the corporate world who would benefit from the war, the Washington D.C. political spin machine and others, including the state of Israel who would benefit from taking down Saddam Hussein and his government.

Yet this was/is a war crime not experienced by the nations since Vietnam and, therefore, is not common knowledge. However, due to modern communication and social media, a large portion of the western world's population now views this as an international war crime and as a western move against a sovereign nation without any serious evidence that it contained weapons of mass destruction. There was, prior to the Iraq war, loud and legitimate voices and movements against going to war which were ignored. As a result of this criminal act, we have over four thousand U.S. dead fighting men and women, over twenty thousand wounded, seriously maimed and psychologically impaired veterans. We caused the deaths of over one hundred thousand Iraqis, the displacement of millions of others and the destruction of Iraq's infrastructure and historical sites. The damage we inflicted upon the children of Iraq is incomprehensible and as far as I am concerned, unforgiveable. This international crime is part of the reason that ISIL (Islamic State) exist. We must never forget that we sent the best of our youth—white, Black, and brown men and women, mostly teenagers and young people to another peoples' land to kill and occupy it on the white supremacist lips of lies, faulty intelligence and hubris of a very few well-placed white supremacist men and women whose own sons and daughters would never taste the desert sands of the Middle East. We will be dealing with the returning veterans from the Middle East and Afghanistan who have been physically, intellectually and psychologically crippled for decades to come, e.g. Vietnam.

Now, the same group of men who sent us off to war with Iraq is now trying to repeat that dastardly act by advocating a war with Iran. Any person with a working brain who understands the history of Iran and the United States realizes at best that this is complex. Our involvement with Iran has a long and checkered history with major involvement using the CIA to overthrow the democratic elected regime in Iran and install the Shah of Iran. As the current leadership completed its revolution defeating the U.S. and the Shah in taking U.S. hostages, this country declared Iran as a "terrorist" state. Soon after the U.S. supported Saddam Hussein in his war against Iran by supplying him with chemical weapons that he used against the people of Iran. President Obama, Secretary of State Kerry and their negotiating team need to be supported and given credit for their negotiation skills in drafting an agreement that reasonable people from all seven nations can agree upon. Unfortunately, we are now deep into the 2016 of the Presidential campaign and Republican candidates will try to outdo each in demonizing President Obama. It will become clear over the coming weeks that the Israeli lobby, led by American Israel Public Affairs Committee (AIPAC), and others with a reported twenty-five million dollars will not spare any cost in making sure that the President and this deal are torpedoed before the Congress votes on it in September 2015.[1]

The most vocal voice, other than Prime Minster Netanyahu of Israel is former Israeli ambassador to the United States, Michael B. Oren (2009 to 2013). Ambassador Oren is a highly respected historian and an author of many books on Israel and the Middle East. Born in the U.S., Mr. Oren, a citizen of both na-

---

[1] As *Taking Bullets* goes to press, President Obama was able to secure enough votes for the passage of the Iran Accord. However, the right wing of the Republic Party continues to fight for a reversal, as does Prime Minister Netanyahu, as highlighted recently in his address at the United Nations in September, 2015.

tions, brings an insight to the current divide that others do not have. His current book, *ALLY: My Journey Across the American-Israeli Divide* (2015), is in part a complex criticism of President Obama and the current Iran Nuclear Accord. He, as well as others, will over the next month or so bring a hurricane force against Mr. Obama and the proposed deal. Get ready for subtle and not so subtle name calling of anti-semitism gone wild. (See Appendix for excerpts from *Tikkun*)

However, in terms of Black-Jewish relationships, none of this is new, most certainly if one reviews the writing of the great essayist and fiction writer, James Baldwin. Many of Baldwin's essays and interviews on this vital question are reprinted in *James Baldwin, The Cross of Redemption: Uncollected Writings* (2010) edited with an introduction by Randall Kenon. A clear analysis of Baldwin's views on Black and Jews can also be found in Herb Boyd's excellent biography, *Baldwin's Harlem* (2008). One should read Harold Cruise's ground breaking work, *Crisis of the Negro Intellectual* (1967) for a full and nuanced record of a difficult time. Also, just published this year is an excellent analysis and commentary on this most delicate of relationships by Keith P. Feldman's *A Shadow over Palestine: The Imperial Life of Race in America* (2015). His comments on the Student Nonviolent Coordinating Committee, Ambassador Andrew Young, President Jimmy Carter, W.E.B. DuBois, David Graham DuBois, and the Black Panther Party are instructive. One cannot include a discussion on America's empire with a passing comment on modern "legal gang" culture: the FBI, the CIA, and the U.S. court and prison system.

Due to time and space, I can only comment on the baddest "gang" on earth, the Central Intelligence Agency (CIA). My first introduction to the reach and covert actions at the CIA was in the very public fight that Philip Agee had with his former bosses over the publication of this explosive book *Inside The Company: CIA Diary* (1975). Prior to that, it was the super secret assasination of the Congo's first democratically elected Prime Minister Patrice Lumumba. Lumumba, like Kwame Nkrumah of Ghana, was fastly becoming an international hero to pan-africanists worldwide. The CIA had other plans and according to David Talbot's *The Devil's Chessboard: Alan Dulles, The CIA and The Rise of America's Secret Government* (2015), it was President Eisenhower who in August 1960 gave a direct order to the CIA director Dulles to "eliminate" Lumumba. Also see *Dirty Work 2: The CIA in Africa* (1979) edited by Ray, Schaap, Van Meter and Wolf and for a full view of their current action, see *The CIA World Fact Book 2015*.

Terror In The Midst of Prayer and Empire

In our perpetual state of national mourning where our eyes are watered out and our hearts cease to heal at the rate the creator meant them to, we hold hands in profound silence as we remember the Mother Emanuel Nine of Charleston, South Carolina—these nine mothers, fathers, sisters and brothers. Even before burying, before Black earth covered their caskets, too many ministers, media pundits and plain white and Black folks downgraded the terror, that quickened their deaths of our finest in this land, to the "mental" illness and "race hatred" of a single young white man.

He may have acted alone, but he was not alone in his thinking, encouragement, gathering of arms, warped consciousness, confirmation, or ahistorical views and yeses from the millions in the nation who proudly wear and display the confederate flag above their hearts and fly it in all of its *traitorous* glory over a state capital and other institutions. Again, we find ourselves at war with history and culture, entertaining another call for a national conversation on race and a President weary of trying to make sense of and comfort the grief-stricken nation with words from the highest office of the land.

These are the facts, not an opinion or the ignorant ranting of compromised preachers and television pundits. A twenty-one-year-old white man, a citizen of South Carolina, walked into the sacred and spiritual home of the Emanuel African Methodist Episcopal Church of Charleston, the historical home of Black Liberation fighter Denmark Vesey, and fatally killed nine of its members, including the pastor during Bible study. This was a pure act of domestic terrorism, a modern day lynching by a young white nationalist who coolly and calmly assassinated nine Black members of Mother Emanuel.

Domestic violence and acts of terrorism are on the rise in the United States as detailed by Charles Kurzman and David Schanzer in their *New York Times* Op-Ed, "The Other Threat" (6/16/15) where they state that, "The main terrorist threat in the United States is not from violent Muslim extremist, but from right-wing extremists." In their national research, local police agencies across the country identified the "militias, neo-Nazis and Sovereign citizens" as the major threat the nation faces in "regard to extremism." All of this is homegrown, with international connections.

Morris Dees and J. Richard Cohen of the Southern Poverty Law Center also writes in the *New York Times* of (6/22/15), "Racists Without Borders" state that:

> Americans tend to view attacks like the mass murder in Charleston as isolated hate crimes, the work of a deranged racist or group of zealots lashing out in anger, unconnected to a broader movement. This view we can no longer afford to indulge.
>
> When, according to survivors, Mr. Roof told the victims at the prayer meeting that black people were "taking over the country," he was expressing sentiments that unite white nationalists from the United States and Canada to Europe, Australia and New Zealand. Unlike those of the Civil Rights era, who's main goal was to maintain Jim Crow in the American South, today's white supremacists don't see borders; they see a white tribe under attack by people of color across the globe.
>
> The end of white rule in Rhodesia (now Zimbabwe) and South Africa, they believe, foreshadowed an apocalyptic future for all white people: a "white genocide" that must be stopped before it's too late.

The internationalization of terrorism is not a foreign theory in today's social media world. Dees and Cohen will be speaking at a "conference in Budapest about this transnational white supremacism that is emerging as the world grows more connected technologically. The message of white genocide is spreading." Also, David J. Whittaker's *Terrorism: Understanding the Global Threat* gives another view. Clearly our rush to "forgive" this mass murderer within 96 hours of this supreme tragedy is misguided, anti-human and does not allow for proper grieving for the fallen.

As perfectly scripted, displaying the permanent effectiveness of Christian acculturation the Sunday, June 21, 2015 morning services at Mother Emmanuel Church, the Black Christians out Christianed their white brothers and sisters. Before the morning sermon the presiding elder Rev. Norvel Goff Sr. found it necessary to thank the local, state and federal law enforcement agencies for doing their job. He also stated, "A lot of folks expected us to do something strange and break out in a riot. Well, they just don't know us. We are people of faith." I find this statement inappropriate, insensitive and ahistorical, implying whether he meant it or not that the recent uprising and rebellions in Ferguson, New York, Cleveland and other parts of the nation were "riots" and did not include Black people of "faith" and that somehow they were "strange" in their social, political and economic activism.

Informed people do not *riot* against injustice or white terrorism. They study, organize and strategically struggle at all levels—in the streets, on the campus, in front of the White House and in corporate boardrooms. Dylann Strom Roof stated intentions were to start a "race war." An informed Black leadership understands that we cannot pray this away or appeal to any law enforcement agency that all across the country—including Charleston has been seriously compromised.

To label Black reaction to murder, terrorism, deep unemployment, sub-standard housing, poor education, negligible healthcare, etc., as "riot" is to *blame the victim* and give them little credit for analysis of their condition and justified actions and anger. Dr. King states that a "riot" is the language of the unheard. Charles M. Blow, the *New York Times* columnist writes on June 22, 2015 that, "Roof was a young man radicalized to race hatred who reportedly wanted to start a race war and who killed nine innocent people as his opening salvo. If that's not terrorism, we need to redefine the term." There will be no national Black love and forgiveness tour for white terrorists.

I have often stated that racism—white supremacy and white nationalism are a growth industry in the United States and that no new national race tour will solve this nationwide dilemma bordering on a catastrophe. The nationally respected author and talk-show host Thom Hartmann recently asked a simple yet profound question, Why is racism not defined as un-American or viewed as un-patriotic? I wonder how Malcolm X, James Baldwin, Gwendolyn Brooks and Barbara Ann Sizemore would answer such a question. I know my answer!

Blowback

As a student and veteran of Black struggle, it has been an absolute necessity to observe and study the literature of U.S. engagement worldwide. One of the most informed and engaged scholars on U.S. empire is Chalmers Johnson. Johnson, who is no longer with us, was formerly the president of the Japan Policy Research Institute and Professor Emeritus of the University of California, San Diego, and is internationally respected for his series, *The Blowback Trilogy*, including *Nemesis: The Last Days of the American Republic* (2006), *The Sorrows of Empire: Militarism, Secrecy and the End of the Republic* (2004), and *Blowback: The Costs and Consequences of American Empire* (2000), as well as many other books on world affairs. For over fifty years, his voice has been one of deep analysis and honest criticism of his country's adventures around the world.

The term "blowback" was invented by the CIA for its own internal use. According to Johnson's book *Blowback*: "It refers to the unintended consequences of policies that were kept secret from the American people. What the daily press reports as the malign acts of 'terrorists' or 'drug lords' or 'rogue states' or 'illegal arms merchants' often turn out to be blowback from earlier American operations." He argues throughout *Blowback* that the U.S. has over extended itself as empire and presents itself, especially after the fall of the USSR, as the moral and ethical voice of reason and freedom in the world. This message is broadcast almost nonstop on corporate media without serious rebuttal. Johnson documents in his last book, *Dismantling the Empire* (2010), that as a result of our worldwide mis-adventurers, over-spending, dark sites, missions, and total reliance on the military, CIA and American first legislation, we are close to committing "national suicide."

The average citizen—Black or white—has no idea what this cost entails and has no idea of the impact of this economic committment made by the country. According to a Brookings Institution study, "It has cost the United States $5.5 trillion to build and maintain our nuclear arsenal."

This is one of the reasons Johnson gives for the demise of the USSR which with "comparable costs...led to its collapse." Reading *Blowback* puts into context this country's recent wars, however the citizens of this nation are clearly ill served by its mass media—which in the best of circumstances in a working democracy acts as a serious and critical watchdog. John Nichols and Robert

W. McChesney strongly argue that the traditional role of the fourth estate has been effectively compromised by money and politics, and they see a "media crisis" that harms democracy. They write in *Tragedy and Farce: How the American Media Sell Wars, Spin Elections and Destroy Democracy* (2005), that it is "a crisis in which we are seeing the deterioration of political journalism, if not its effective termination. The collapse of journalism spells disaster for any concept we might hold that this is a self-governing society, or even that citizens can fulfill the public role envisioned in our constitution." We can only conclude the correctness of their comments by reading Chalmers Johnson's *The Blowback Trilogy*.

However, there was one more book to come, *Dismantling The Empire: America's Last Best Hope* (2010). This book is a critical and necessary read for those who do not have the time to read the trilogy. This book is a kind of summary with the most up-to-date military information and an analysis that gives the reader a political context within the many secret contexts of the nation's rulers. Johnson, in less than 200 pages, masterfully unravels the secrets of empire. He exposes the cost of empire that extends into the trillions of dollars of tax payers money. The greatest lie told by the U.S. empire is that it operates within budget and that the perceived enemies are larger, growing and more dangerous than they actually are; therefore, our "enemy" fighting agencies, the Defense Department, CIA and Homeland Security, need more, much more money. This unscrupulous, expected, and accepted congressional dance is played out in public with lobbyist and the military-industrial complex directing this annual disgraceful welfare to the armaments industries. Maintaining over 750 bases worldwide with its dark and Black sites including other on-going wars, still cost trillions of dollars to the American taxpayer.

Johnson does his nation a special service by exposing the continued fleecing of the national treasure that for the modern age started with Jimmy Carter and expanded expeditiously under Reagan and Bush, writing:

> Carter, Brzezinski, and their successors in the Reagan and first Bush administrations, including Gates, Dick Cheney, Donald Rumsfeld, Condoleezza Rice, Paul Wolfowitz, Richard Armitage, and Colin Powell, all bear some responsibility for the 1.8 million Afghan casualties, 2.6 million refugees, and 10 million unexploded land mines that followed from their decisions. They must also share the blame for the blowback that struck New York and Washington on September 11, 2001. After all, al-Qaeda was an organization they helped create and arm.

Haki R. Madhubuti

As he continues to expose the "economic death spiral at the Pentagon," the blowback that he writes of also has a destructive effect on the homeland. He describes this allocation of monies as a national disgrace, "Spending hundreds of billions of dollars on present and future wars that have nothing to do with our national security is simply obscene."

His point, as well as the one I am making, is to step back from the "empire" and to begin rebuilding our own nation should be the priority for the twenty-first century. Our other major problem is one of eradicating ignorance, especially the supreme ignorance in the current cultural, political, and economic state of Black people, white people and others in the United States.

A very serious and renewed dilemma crippling the national Black community in the United States is that the great majority of Black people are not exposed to or informed by life-giving, life-affirming, and life-saving information and knowledge. Most of us are not aware of our constitutional rights that are "guaranteed" to us as citizens. And further, we are constantly surrounded by the unhealthy empire excess: "dead food," overcrowded living conditions, poor educational choices, a predatory economy, few *green* spaces, an unjust criminal justice system that overly criminalizes Black and Brown boys and men, and an uncaring, politically-complex healthcare structure that has failed Black, Brown, and poor white people of the nation. We now live in an America where the most cherished democratic values have been compromised by for-sale politicians who are beholden to the one percent of the nation's criminally but "legally" rich and wealthy. They are the movers, shakers, and war mongers of empire, e.g. Iraq, Afghanistan, and others.

The major deed that the empire necessitates is a continued, uninterrupted supply of natural resources to constantly fuel its many national and international enterprises. Oil is the critical, yet highly climate-damaging resource that this modern empire requires and cannot function without. This is not new or revelatory information. If we read and study the nation's most progressive newspapers, magazines, newsletters, and websites[1] and act proactively on the many suggestions

---

[1] Most local libraries—with the possible exception of larger urban libraries—will not subscribe to the majority of my suggested reading list, in no special order: *The Nation, The Progressive, Yes, In These Times, Z Magazine, The New Yorker, The Atlantic, Harpers, The New York Review of Books, Sojourners, The American Prospect, Washington Report, Diverse, Moment, Book Forum, Tikkun, Columbia Journalism Review, Mother Jones, Forward, Extra!, Foreign Policy, The New York Times* (read with a critical eye), *Financial Times, ISR: International Socialist Review, the crisis, The Hightower LowDown, Rolling Stone, Essence, Lapham's Quarterly, Pacific Standard, The Humanist, Ebony, The Africa Report, Women's Review of Books, Ms., Rolling Out, The American Scholar, The Final Call, Irish America, Boston Review, Jewish Review of Books, The Progressive Populist, The Counter Terrorist, Israel Defense, Black Scholar* and from north of the border: *New Internationalist*

Continued to page 33

jumping off their pages or screens, maybe we could see progress and change. This modern empire commands whole scale ignorance from its population—especially its youth, those who will have to fight its illegal and unjust wars.

White on Black crimes are a national and state secret. Study the empire. It is clear that in order for the state to be successful, it must keep its "minority" populations in order; better yet, in check, as in *checkmate*. The three methods of accomplishing this task are (1) subtle and not so subtle force—local, state, and national police forces; (2) determined acculturation that has created an educational system which functions as a patriotic propaganda machine unbeknownst to those it impacts as the first line recruiter for the empire's wars; and (3) enforced living spaces across the nation such as the South and West sides of Chicago, all of Detroit, Black-concentrated areas of Atlanta, Los Angeles, and others. The first level is often substandard housing, urban partitions, or the second level state and federal prison system. Andrew J. Bacevich, in his book *The Limits of Power: The End of American Exceptionalism* (2008), makes the point that all of this talk of globalization by the hard right is:

> In point of fact, however, Globalization served as a euphemism for soft, or informal, empire. The collapse of the Soviet Union appeared to offer an opportunity to expand and perpetuate that empire, creating something akin to a global Pax Americana.

The Bush Administration, under the direct leadership of Vice President Cheney, Defense Secretary Donald Rumsfeld, Secretary of State Condoleezza Rice, Deputy Defense Secretary Paul Wolfowitz, and the entire right wing "Chicken Hawk" sound machine led us into an unjust, offensive war that the less-fortunate of America's Empire—Black, Brown, and poor white people—are still suffering from and paying for. This would include the tens of thousands of veterans of Iraq, Afghanistan, and the dark wars on the planet that we know nothing about.

Attorney and author Vincent Bugliosi's 2008 book, *The Prosecution of George W. Bush for Murder*, was written, researched, and published after the Iraq War

---

Continued from page 32
and *Adbusters*. I also recommend *The Economist*, from England, *The Guardian*, and *London Review of Books*. Any serious list is obviously incomplete, as is this one. The continued call is to support independent publishing at all levels: newspapers, magazines, journals, and progressive online reporting and investigating. Websites and Blogs: crooksandliers.com, thenation.com, motherjones.com, thinkprogress.org, dailykos.com, laternet.org, mediamatters.org, counterpunch.org, inthesetimes.com, truthdig.com, moveon.org, rightwingwatch.com, therawstory.com, thomhartman.com, gregpalast.com, thehuffingtonpost.com, thegrid, BlackAgendaReport.com theRoot, democracynow.com, blackcommentator.com, aclu.org, commondreams.org, wikileaks, znet, worldwatchinstitute, theprogressive, and opensecrets.org. There are many more.

brought death to nearly 4,000 American military personnel, over 100,000 innocent Iraqi men, women, children, and the elderly, and close to two million displaced Iraqis in bordering nations. Bugliosi's issue, as well as that of millions of ordinary American citizens, is that this war is/was not only illegal but has cost the nation its moral foundation, spirit, and soul. The economic cost—according to Joseph E. Stigliz and Linda J. Bilmes—comes in at over three trillion dollars.[2]

The cost of the war continues to escalate because of the recommitment of the United States to Iraq and other parts of the Middle East. As a result of the Islamic State (ISIL) and other Islamic agents in the Middle East, the right wing Republicans continue to call for boots on the ground. Obviously the three trillion dollar cost will rise not only due to the overuse of corporate contractors[3] but also to the failure to adequately provide healthcare, educational opportunities, housing, and employment for returning and retiring veterans. Frances Fox Piven wrote about this "hidden" can of worms early on in her book *The War At Home* (2004) in which she warned the nation of the unseen cost of President George W. Bush, Vice President Dick Cheney, and their cronies' wasteful use of the nation's treasure. It must be emphasized *that the great majority of Americans are totally unaware of the true cost of our foreign engagements* and our undeclared wars against other peoples, for whatever the reasons. I believe that if the citizens knew, there would be a loud outcry for the return of the draft rather than undemocratically sending and redeploying poor white, Black, and Brown men to tour after tour. The empire keeps secrets from its own population well.

My comments on the United States as empire have not seriously looked at the place of Africa—the original homeland of African people—in an international context. As an African man born and living in America, I and my people have had a long, often difficult relationship with that vast continent. Most of us start, in understanding Africa from a state of complete *ignorance*. African people's forced migration to the West has too long been told from the worldview of Europeans and others. Yes, the ideas of W.E.B. Dubois, George Padmore, Chancellor Williams, Ali Mazrui, John H. Clarke, Cheikh Anta Diop, Kwame Nkrumah, and others play a dominate role in my understanding. However, the work of Errol A. Henderson, a political scientist at

---

2 See their *The Three Trillion Dollar War: The True Cost of the Iraq Conflict,* (2008).
3 See *Black Water: The Rise of the World's Most Powerful Mercenary Army* (2007) by Jeremy Scahill and *Licensed To Kill: Hired Guns and the War on Terror* (2007) by Robert Young Pelton. Also, *A Nation Among Nations: America's Place in World History* (2006) by Thomas Bender (pp. 182-245).

Pennsylvania State University must be added to my list of modern Africanist thinkers. He is a major scholar who has dedicated his life's work to enlighten us on Africa and its role in international affairs. *African Realism? International Relations Theory and Africa's Wars in the post-Colonial Era* (2015) is his latest book. It is a must read, especially in the era of "overnight" experts in the land of the internet and Wikipedia. Dr. Henderson's first book, *Afrocentrism and World Politics* (1995) speak loudly to the "current" state of the west's view of Africa and its people:

> There appeared to be, in the European mind, a dichotomization, wherein one set of rules, or one "regime," was applicable to the European, while quite another was appropriate for non-Europeans. Therefore, it was not inconsistent for the European to arduously set about for himself the task of ensuring sovereignty and security for Europeans, while creating conditions for suzerainty and warfare abroad. Although Asian political economies fared little better under European hegemony, Afrocentrists remind us that nowhere was this dichotomy, or hypocrisy, more apparent than in the European's relationship with Africans. Where balance of power was the norm for Europe, divide and conquer was to be for the African, Asian, and Native American. Where "Rights of Man" and "Declarations of Independence" were to be the domain of Europeans, God himself was invoked to sanction servitude and the Holocaust of the Enslavement for the African. As regards the African, this dichotomy, this hypocrisy, was codified near the turn of the century at the Berlin Conference.
>
> At the Berlin Conference of 1884-85, Europeans decided among themselves what parts of Africa they would appropriate for themselves. No Africans were present. It was the action of this pact and that which came out of the later Brussels Conference that initiated the white supremacist regime in Eurocentric world politics. It is this regime that provides the template for the theory and practice of Eurocentric world politics, and it stands as an institutional reinforcement of the white supremacism that is manifest at the worldview level today.

Of the current African scholars writing on international affairs who keeps Africa, African people and, African Americans at the center of his analysis, Dr. Henderson has few peers.

Life's Work and Study

> Every writer's difficult journey is a movement from silence to speech. We must be intensely private and interior in order to find a voice and vision—and we must bring our work to an outside world where the market, or public outrage, or even government censorship can't destroy our voice.
>
> —Sara Paretsky,
> *Writing In an Age of Silence*

I am no stranger to the realities of life's struggles—the slow, sometimes fast, drowning in the richest, most economically, scientifically, technologically, and militarily developed nation in the world. I am no stranger to the love-hate relationship that most Black people have with America. The white majority populations and their politics, economics, education, and overall culture have relegated the great majority of Black people to the back avenues of slow drive without cars. In the 1990s, I completed and published one of the first books to honestly access and detail the condition of Black men, and by extension, the Black family, in the United States: *Black Men: Obsolete, Single, Dangerous? The Afrikan American Family in Transition* (1991). I tried to bring clarity to the Black condition from an insider's point-of-view not contradicted by an "integrated," middle-class upbringing, education, or conscious or unconscious desire to be accepted, liked, or appreciated by whites. I came from and was raised among the poorest of the poor, without a live-in father and with a mother working in the sex trade incapable of weathering this storm of rearing my sister and me. My mother was dead at the age of thirty-four, leaving us on our own to translate the many coming hurricanes.[1]

As a poet, educator, and professor for over forty-four years, a serious reader of literature (poetry, fiction, and nonfiction), businessman, cultural activist, and intellectual, family man and institution builder, I come to my assessment of Black life without the blinders of Negro privilege, rewards or false expectations, or lying promises. I've witnessed the untimely death of too many of our children and people over my seventy-three years. Therefore, I write out

---

[1] I provide greater detail in my book *YellowBlack: The First Twenty-one Years of a Poet's Life, A Memoir*, (2006).

of a passion for life, yet, with a clear understanding of what Black people face in this country. I am clear that if the white rulership really desired quality change, it would start today for us and the ninety-nine percent. Not only do the one percent not care about Black people, they do not care for or love their own people. See Jill Lepore's article "Richer or Poorer" in the *The New Yorker* (March 16, 2015). The real fact of life for most Black people is that we all have horror stories about life in this nation that are never shared outside of one's family. We realize as long as the rulership does not understand or face the root causes of the invention of the Negro people (who were Africans) there will be little justice or peace.

The critical need is for accurate definitions and serious development of a new social justice movement, in America led by young people of all cultures but with serious leadership from Black and brown youth. This movement at its core most immediately addressed, almost all the same issues we fought for in the 60s and 70s: quality education, full employment, adequate housing, single payer healthcare, climate change and clean water rights, police brutality elimination, voting rights, human rights, big banks, corporate welfare, and the constitutional right to life, liberty and the pursuit of happiness.

I write as a poet of African ancestry who is a student of history and politics; and understands the necessary role that culture and economics play in determining any people's tomorrows. In effect, white nationalism, white supremacy, white skin privilege, white history, culture, politics and economics are essentially, at their very core—white power. The history of Black people in the United States from our first landing on these shores and our fighting in the Revolutionary War, Civil War, WWI and II; the resistance to the Black codes, America's civil rights restrictive laws to today's re-segregation, #Black Lives Matter uprisings confirms that resistance to oppression is an active part of our DNA. These battles are a continuation of our history, and if understood accurately we must also acknowledge that there are four ongoing crises that most Black people confront daily:

1. The great majority of Black families have someone close locked down in the criminal justice system—a brother, son, grandson, father, uncle, grandfather including Black women and family attachment also. Their imprisonment consume our time, resources, and thinking and organizing skills. See the *New Jim Crow* by Michele Alexander for more inclusive and nuanced examination.

2. The great majority of Black families in the nation have someone critically ill, suffering from a serious life-threatening medical condition which has a family members institionalized or has caused that ill family member, due to the lack of insurance and money to self medicate, keep quiet or drop out of his/her family all together as not to be a burden.

3. Too many in the Black community are living from paycheck-to-paycheck, or no-check to no-check. The rise of the Black underground economy, as the above ground economy pushes us out, has both negative and positive pathways.

4. We do not have conscious Black wealth creators working 24/7 on our behalf.

I learned very early that most people who are successful experience a loving and intelligent up-bringing that included great schools, serious reading and study skills, some travel (national and international), and an ongoing interaction with people of many cultures. They, early and often experienced the power of ideas—at all levels of human involvement. And, they, quite early in their lives participated in organized music and arts programs as well as organized sports.

Black Men:
Obsolete, Single, Dangerous?
Revisited

In *Black Men*, I tried to provide progressive, practical answers and an analysis for forward movement based at that time upon over twenty-nine years of political activism, writing, publishing, institution building, teaching, family life, world travel, introspection, men's work, formal and informal higher education, internal national political debates, community work, and much, much more. *Black Men* was read, studied and used as reference text across the country in venues as diverse as state prisons and universities, with over a million copies in print.

In 1991, Morehouse College purchased a thousand copies for its freshman class and invited me to the college to provide additional insight into my ongoing work with young brothers and men. Among the many points I emphasized during that seminar, as I did for over a thousand other institutions and gatherings, nationally and internationally, were these core paragraphs that provided a framework for our ongoing conversations:

Oppression is oppression, and to quibble over degrees of oppression, more often than not, is an accurate measure of the effectiveness of white oppression. However, there are some basic male dynamics that need to be understood: men run the world; this is not a sexist statement but one of fact. Also, men fight men (and women) to maintain control of "their" part of the world. There may be women in leadership positions (elected and appointed), but they are there because men see such concessions as politically wise and in their best interest. White men control most of the world—economically, politically, and militarily—and undoubtedly control all of the Western/Northern World.

Other facts are: (1) White men do not fear white women; they are concerned, yes, but fearful, no; white men and women are partners, be it senior and junior partners; (2) White men do not fear Black women. The white man's relationship to Black women traditionally has been one of use, sexually and otherwise; the widespread of color that exists among Black people proves this point—it was white men raping Black women that produced the mixed race Black person. Worldwide (Weisbord, 1975; Day, 1972; Stember,

39

1976; Hernton, 1965); (3) White men do fear Black men. This fear may not be spoken and obvious to many Black people, but if one understands the history of white male/Black male relationships, it is quite evident that it is a history of war, with the horrid and severe physical and psychological enslavement and elimination of Black men by white men (Ginzburg, 1969; Williams, 1974). Sterling Brown's classic words are instructive when he says of white men venturing into the Black community, "they don't come by ones, they don't come by twos, they come by tens."

The Black male/white male confrontation is not only racial and cultural, it is also a serious question of what group of men is going to "rule" the world. The concept of shared power has always been a major question within the white male ethos, especially if it involves the inclusion of men outside their racial or cultural grouping (Tiger, 1969). However, it must be understood that white men actually don't like or trust each other. Their cultural, religious and nationalist wars are legendary. Any serious study of European wars will validate this point. When one analyzes the war-like nature white men exhibit among each other, only the naïve and severely mentally handicapped would expect white male attitudes towards Black males to be any different than they are. These attitudes are historical and cultural and, therefore, psychological (Bradley, 1981; Wright, 1986; Akbar, 1984; Welsing, 1989) and intimate. To change such negative and "natural" attitudes would require a revolution of the most profound kind. Michael Bradley in his book *The Iceman Inheritance* carefully documents the white race's war on the non-western world, and clearly gives reasons for western man's racism, sexism, and killing aggression.

The Black male/white male dynamic can be best described as one of continued and unrelenting war, with Black males being consistently on the losing end of most battles (Williams, 1974; Martinez and Guinther, 1988). One of the major problems is that most Black men in the United States are fighting the wrong war—that is, many are fighting to get a "piece of the pie." Therefore, they do not understand the "bio-social" nature of white males, which is that of conquest, domination and self-development, not one of sharing power or decision-making with the vanquished i.e., former slaves (Storr, 1972; Lorenz, 1962). The best that most Black men can hope and work for within this society is a "job" which, indeed, has been defined by many disillusioned Blacks as a "piece of the pie."

It is true that the future of any people can be measured by its cultural sophistication and the political, economic and military success of its male population in dealing with its natural and unnatural enemies. However, when that male population cannot or does not clearly and definitively identify the enemy, it cannot, on a continuous basis, develop effective means and methods of neutralizing or eliminating said enemy. If this is the case, the future of that people can only be one of doubt and continued subjugation; and subtle, yet effective, elimination and/or subjugation is all but guaranteed in any white-American "multi-racial" situation, especially when the racial minority in that culture is economically obsolete (Willhelm, 1971; Yette,1971) and Black. When a people does not have strong, resourceful, energetic, honest, serious, intelligent, committed, incorruptible, fearless, innovative and fighting men in a world ruled by the force of men, then that people is in serious trouble. When a people does not have men of integrity and vision, long term and lasting development is just about impossible. (*Black Men: Obsolete, Single, Dangerous?* pp. 70-72, 1991)

My position, as of now, is that the Black presence in the United States remains precarious, highly questionable as an essential labor force, and after all is said and done, remains highly misunderstood and largely unwanted or needed at any level of national importance other than cultural enlightenment and innovation, entertainment, sports, military service, and tap dancing.

My doubts are based upon my own life experiences of over fifty years in active Black struggle, nationally and internationally, which included three years of active military service in the United States Army. For over a forty-eight-year span of time that includes building independent Black institutions in Chicago, teaching at Ivy League, Research One, urban, and Black universities, and being a working poet and writer—with over thirty books published as well as poems and essays published in hundreds of newspapers, magazines, journals and anthologies—I have never stopped studying the works of the great minds of my own culture as well as others.

One such mind is that of Professor Charles W. Mills of Northwestern University. In his profound and timely analysis of the Black condition recorded in his book *The Racial Contract* (1997), he writes, "White supremacy is the unnamed political system that has made the modern world what it is today." Mills in his book-length study makes the critical case for the debilitating effects of white supremacy on non-white people and especially on Black people. He also writes:

You will not find this term (white supremacy) in any introductory, or even advanced, text in political theory . . . And this omission is not accidental. Rather, it reflects the fact that standard textbooks and courses have for the most part been written and designed by whites, who take their racial privilege so much for granted that they do not even see it as political, as a

41

form of domination. Ironically, the most important political system of recent global history—the system of domination by which white people have historically ruled over and, in certain important ways, continue to rule over nonwhite people—is not seen as a political system at all. It is just taken for granted, it is the background against which other systems, which we are to see as political, are highlighted . . . Philosophy has remained remarkably untouched by the debates over multiculturalism, canon reform, and ethnic diversity racking the academy; both demographically and conceptually, it is one of the "whitest" of the humanities. Blacks, for example, constitute only about 1 percent of philosophers in North American universities—a hundred or so people out of more than ten thousand—and there are even fewer Latino, Asian American, and Native American philosophers.

One of the major points I make in *Black Men*, which we face hourly in the United States, is the result of local, state, and national white supremacist policies. Law-makers of whom the great majority are white and very protective of their power and sacred-secret spaces will not give any quarter to the former enslaved or recently arriving non-white immigrants. This is one of the reasons that the National Rifle Association is so powerful and effectively constitutes an open yet non-obvious lobbying agency for white people. To many white people, the final solution to any problem is "violence" and, use of their "guns" and "weapons" against any population is their equalizer and final answer.

That is why the armament industry in the United States is enormously profitable, favored, protected, and will not be *out-sourced* like thousands of other businesses and factories in recent years have been out-sourced to China, India, and Mexico. All across the nation the *first line* of white enforcement and protection are local and state police agencies where officers are taught that once you draw your weapon, you shoot to kill. Obviously, this works differently among white folks, Black folks and others. As the nation draws down its military from Iraq and Afghanistan, much of that military equipment will find its way to local and state police agencies. We saw this boldly displayed in Ferguson after the killing of Michael Brown.

Whiteness

"Upheavals of a generation ago. The new white nationalists differ even more from the small band of misfits and psychopaths who formed the heart of the ineffectual neo-Nazi movement of that era. While sharing much in common with the older style of white racist and white supremacy movement, and drawing upon important white supremacist beliefs, the new white nationalism is potentially broader in its appeal and a development sufficiently different from the older racist right to be considered a distinct phenomenon. The new white nationalism, in this sense, might be considered a kind of repackaged, relabeled, and transformed white supremacy that is aiming its appeal at a broader and better-educated audience."

—Carol M. Swain
The New White Nationalism in America (2004)

"Thus the idea that the racial/ethnic majority would dominate the state was an integral part of the context from which European ethnicities emerged to establish control over America. The various White ethnicities coalesced into a "White" majority group that proceeded to establish a privileged social status which has expressed its dominance over non-White groups and over the major institutions of American society. Tom Nairn described this as the practice of civic nationalism."

—Ronald W. Walters
White Nationalism, Black Interests (2003)

This study of terrorism facing Black folks in America and the world is incomplete without an analysis of the growing field of white studies and reflection of the important voices of white activist and thinkers who fight alongside us to end white supremacy and its devastating affect on Black life. The writer Maurice Berger, in his insightful book *White Lies: Race and the Myths of Whiteness* (1999), retells a critical experiment in racial consciousness that was, decades earlier, initiated by the political scientist Andrew Hacker. At that time, Hacker put forth the hypothetical proposition that the government and not genetics determined the race of newborn babies in the United States. One day a visit from a government official responsible for determining race informs you that you were born the wrong color and soon would be "involuntarily returned to your proper race" which is not white. You are told that the government has put aside money to help in one's race transition from white to Black. The question asked by Hacker is how much money would you seek to compensate you for your change from white to Black? The answer from white students and others who earlier had stated that there was little difference and denied that racism was a major problem were "now willing to concede that racism was a problem, and that being Black in America might be more difficult than being white." As far as compensation was concerned, their answers ranged from fifty million to "I would not change." However, the point of the exercise was made: whiteness is indeed a privilege and an advantage that remains widely undocumented in most of the humanities, social science, and political science literature.

Among a small but significant number of scholars, activists, students, and cultural workers, *white studies* has become a serious area of inquiry. Their mission is not misplaced. The global population of people of European ancestry holds stable at around 9 to 10 percent of the world's population. Yet, white people's influence, governance, wealth, systems of economics and politics, control of land, and military reach is international and all far out weigh their numbers.

White studies at its core is about the study of white development, white nationalist thought, and its influence on the majority of white people and others. Moreover white studies is about white people who view themselves, their culture, ideas, production, institutions, and worldview as supreme to all others. This concept of white studies gives the world an unquestioned, yet widely accepted, philosophy of white supremacy. Again, I refer you to Charles C. Mills' book, *The Racial Contract* (1997). Black people are acutely aware of *racism* as defined and practiced by white people. However, many Black and white people have bought into the fiction that anybody could be racist, including Black people. Only white people, fundamentally, can be white supremacists, even though Black people and others who buy into white nationalist philosophy can—even though limited—act and function like white supremacists. Keep in mind that those Black people will be encouraged, paid, and protected by white people. An early scholar in white supremacy is psychiatrist Frances Cress Welsing. Her highly influential book, *The Isis Papers* (1991) raises the question, why does the most informed nation remain seriously ignorant of the negative effects of white supremacy? It is a question whose answer demands that Black people must stop deceiving themselves about their relationship to America and white people.[1]

One of the few historians Black or white to recently and critically look at the development and history of white people is Nell Irvin Painter, Edwards Professor of American History (emerita) at Princeton University. In her book, *The History of White People*, she carefully provides a brilliant, deeply reasoned and passionate study of the "invention of the idea of whiteness." The invention of race theory and the worldwide use of racism (white supremacy) by white people has left serious destruction in its wake. Western civilization is white civilization. Its war-like advances across the world in the last two thousand years have cemented into the minds of millions the effectiveness of western culture. Victor Davis Hanson in *Carnage and Culture: Landmark Battles in the Rise of Western Power*, underscores this point and the United States involvement in it of which he argues has, a "western knack for killing." Most Black people have no idea—and most certainly historically had no idea—what we were up against.

Painter in her heartfelt work confirms that race is indeed a social construct that has largely benefited it's creators: white people. Her book is must-reading for those who seek to go beyond the Fox News Channel's right wing revisionist politics and history. Professor Pointer writes:

> "Those at the very bottom were slaves. Slavery has helped construct concepts of white race in two contradictory ways. First, American tradition equates whiteness with freedom while consigning blackness to slavery."

There are major activists who have actively fought much of their adult lives against white supremacy, as white people immediately come to mind. These persons have been called "white traitors," "self-haters," and other names unprintable. I am referring to Bill Ayers and Bernardine Dohrn. In their revealing semi-autobiography, they cut into the myths, misconceptions and lies of the politically right-wing white supremacists. The life-long partnership of Ayers and Dohrn has been one of on the ground fighters for that which is politically right and just. They have raised their children within this culture and have not wavered as they pursued professional lives to make ends meet. Their lifelong

---

[1] In terms of fairness we must always make critical and studied distinctions between individual whites and the large national groupings. There are good white people in the world; the major problem is that there are not enough of them and those who exist generally do not make public policy, command armies, control vital institutions, or manage enormous amounts of wealth.

fight as anti-racist, counter-white supremacist activist has been a model for all of us but particularly young white serious activists. Their book, *Race Course: Against White Supremacy* (2009), is a one-of-a-kind and a must-read. One other political activist designated as a "race traitor" by the enemies of this country is Tim Wise, who has traveled the nation for over a decade speaking truth to his own people and others. He has been a progressive fixture on many of the college and university campuses of the nation analyzing white supremacy. As a counter-white supremacist worker he has published many books; I strongly suggest these two: *White Like Me: Reflections on Race from a Privileged Son* (2011) and *Color-Blind: The Rise of Post-Racial Politics and the Retreat to Racial Equality* (2010).

Most certainly with the recent passing of Studs Terkel and Howard Zinn, we have lost two men who had devoted their lives to progressive politics, educational enlightenment, anti-racism, and counter-white supremacy work. Their many books are a testimony to what is possible when the impediment of fear of Black people is not an issue. They helped create an enlightened racial environment that they incorporated in their work and shared their findings with their own people as well as Blacks and others. They talked and practiced a way of life of progressive political and cultural activism, which influenced millions around the world. Serious activists must always do that which is correct and right, regardless of the consequences. Studs Terkel's *Race: How Blacks Think About the American Obsession* (1992) and Howard Zinn's masterwork *A People's History of the United States* (1980) are two necessary books to start with.

Two white media hosts and political commentators who have been in the forefront of fighting political, racial, corporate, and economic injustice for many years are Thom Hartmann and Amy Goodman. There are others, but Hartmann and Goodman have not only used their considerable skills as radio talk show hosts but they are also writers. While I cannot always listen to their daily broadcasts (generally on progressive radio stations across the nation), I can read their books, which clearly expand upon their progressive ideas explored daily on their broadcasts yet delve deeper due to the nature and medium of books.

Hartmann has been the most productive, having published over twenty-seven books including his latest nonfiction book, *The Crash of 2016: The Plot to Destroy America—and What We Can Do to Stop It* (2013). Drawing from his considerable life's work in the public and private sectors and his untiring dedication to the best of the human spirit, as well as international travel, a working and loving family life, and an unquenchable thirst for knowledge,

Hartmann uses his radio show to inform, to give voice to others, to support and highlight the many progressively democratic institutions, in addition to the movements working to make this nation and the world a better place for all. Two of his books also worth reading because of their political content are *Screwed: The Undisclosed War Against the Middle Class* (2007) and *Threshold: the Progressive Plan to Pull America Back from the Brink* (2010).

Amy Goodman is iconic among progressive media personalities. She is always accessible and uses her very popular and influential radio voice in her show, *Democracy Now!*, to expose corporate media lies and seeks global justice. Champion of the unheard voices of the majority, she is a first rate journalist who clearly records in her many books (most with her brother David Goodman) ideas that corporate media not only run from but try to hide. Her loving and extended family, both biological and cultural, allows Goodman to share her unique communication skills and wisdom with millions of listeners weekly. She takes no prisoners in her daily fight for justice. Her eyes are wide open and she does not retreat from the many political or cultural battles confronting us. Goodman is blessed with a first-rate mind, a unique ability to cut directly to the hard questions via her many guests, the famous and not-so-famous, lonely achievers, students, idea makers, international activists, climate warriors, world human rights workers, and down-right hell-raisers. She clearly is the shining example of a highly motivated, unstoppable, top-notch journalist who young people of all professions should emulate. I strongly suggest a close reading of *Exceptions to the Rulers* (2004), *Static: Government Ladies, Media Cheerleaders and the People who Fight Back* (2006), and *Breaking the Sound Barrier* (2009).

Both Hartmann and Goodman give us pause for hope. They bring to their work a genuine love of life and people, a strong activist tradition coupled with a passion for truth and justice, a willingness to engage firmly and fairly but will not take a back seat to that which they define as anti-people or anti-life. They were quick to fight against "Citizens United" and continue daily to be two people who bring light. They are on the record to be anti-racist and anti-white supremacy.

I would truly be remiss if I did not give a call out to two Black communicators who have distinguished themselves as serious activist voices for decades. Each does national call-in talk radio broadcasts daily while also giving their bodies, time, and money to local, national, and international struggles. Both, Joe Madison, "The Black Eagle," and Mark Thompson, host of "Make

47

it Plain," are featured daily and appear on Sirius XM radio. A special thanks must be given to the groundbreaking journalist, author and radio personality Tavis Smiley. He continues to make new grounds in media.

Also please check out your local Black radio stations for other voices. One Black-owned radio station in Philadelphia that must be noted for its single-mindedness of service to the Black community and others is WURD, owned by the Lomax family. My own city, Chicago, still has one of the leaders in Black radio WVON, which set the pace in the sixties and continues on today, featuring long time host and activist Cliff Kelley. Also, a mainstay of chi-town's NPR station WBEZ is the highly talented and committed friend, Richard Steele. However, the one person in the forefront of maintaining Black owned radio who must be named and honored is Bob Law of the famed *Night Talk*. He continues to this day in fighting an almost fruitless battle in the age of big money and white consolidation of communication with Clear Channel buying up formerly "Black" owned stations and employing former owners as managers. This is another book, where Black ownership of any entities that make money are going the way of the professional Negro Baseball League.

I have purposely stayed away from deeply examining religion in this book. However, there is one white priest-activist and carrier of good works from the Catholic church who needs to be highlighted: Father Michael Pfleger of St. Sabina church in Chicago. This parish is located in one of the poorest communities in the city, yet his faith community and extended family have transformed this Black community into an oasis of measurable hope that provides practical answers to both spiritual and secular problems and questions. Pfleger has been in the forefront of Black positive struggle in Chicago and the nation for decades. He truly represents the unselfish community of which Dr. King spoke and gave his life to create. Also, while teaching at Cornell University in 1968, my office was next door to Father Daniel Berrigan, another Catholic priest whom I feel was an example of a "good person" in his poetry, writing, and activism. He was also a counter-white supremacist and a positive force for all.

Consider the works of Wendell Berry, Michael Moore, Russell Banks, Robert Bly, Jonathan Kozol, Chris Hedges, Tony Judt, Frank Rich, Norman G. Finkelstein, Noam Chomsky, Ralph Nader, Bill Maher, Kevin Phillips, Greg Palast, and Lewis H. Lapham to name a very few white men—other than those referenced—who are writing and working to bring light to the world.

I have identified over fifty nationally positioned, non-Black, mostly white people working daily for the betterment of America, and the world. They are:

Naomi Aberly	Michael Lerner
Bill Ayers	Bill McKibben
Russell Banks	Rachel Maddow
Skip Bayless	Bill Maher
Robert Bly	Jane Mayer
Sherrod Brown	Michael Moore
Jimmy Carter	Ralph Nader
Priscilla Chan	John Nichols
Noam Chomsky	Sara Paretsky
Hillary Clinton	Michael Pfleger
David Corn	Thomas Piketty
Kevin Coval	Brad Pitt
Joyce Carol Oates	Frances Fox Piven
John Densmore	Matthew Rothschild
Leonardo DiCaprio	Fred Rotondaro
Barbara Ehrenreich	Mark Ruffalo
Jane Eisner	Jeffery D. Sachs
Pope Francis	Susan Sarandon
Bill Gates	Ed Schultz
Melinda Gates	Howard Schultz
Amy Goodman	Gloria Steinem
Thom Hartmann	Bernie Sanders
Jim Hightower	Hedrick Smith
Chris Hedges	Marilyn Waring
Katrina Vanden Heuvel	Elizabeth Warren
Angelina Jolie	Mary Ann Williams
Naomi Klein	William (Billy) Wimsatt
Johnathan Kozol	Tim Wise
Nicholas D. Kristof	Sheryl WuDunn
Paul Krugman	Mark Zuckerberg
Lewis H. Lapham	

I support Senator Bernie Sanders for President of the United States. I have given this selection a great deal of thought. I do think that Hillary Clinton as the first woman president, all things considered, would do a good job.

However, after listening carefully to Senator Sanders for years on the Thom Hartmann Show, examining his extensive political and voting record, reading Harvey Jafee's *Why Bernie Sanders Matters,* (2015) and Senator Sander's *The Speech,* (2011) it is clear to me that Bernie's values closely approximate my own and are essential to move the nation forward into the twenty-first century.

Senator Sanders is constantly attacked by media, right-wing pundits and a good many Democratic liberals for being a *Democratic Socialist* as if he is anti-American. I must remind readers that the Reverend Dr. Martin Luther King Jr. was a committed *Democratic Socialist,* see Michael Eric Dyson's *I May Not Get There With You: The True Martin Luther King, Jr.* (2001). Dr. King and Senator Sanders were and are Democratic Socialist in the same political reality as was President Franklin Delano Roosevelt. Also, and this is consequential for my support, according to Ted Rall's *Bernie,* (2016) his illustrated biography of the senator, he states that Sanders' net worth is $700,000, making him one of the few senators who is not a millionaire.

One of the most committed and consequential white artist working today is the film maker, writer, and activist Michael Moore. All of his work, politically and culturally, takes on the plutocrats and powers to be who are hell-bent on maintaining their control, even as they literally destroy the country and the lives of tens of millions of working and middle class people of all colors.

He is the Oscar winning filmmaker of *Bowling for Columbine* and the now classic *Roger & Me.* His many books include *Downsize This! Random Threats from an Unarmed American* (1996) *Dude, Where's My Country?* (2003) and the New York Times best seller *Stupid White Men...and Other Sorry Excuses for the State of the Nation!* (2001), with more than 4 million copies in print worldwide. However, it is his latest film *Where To Invade Next* (2015) that for me, has confirmed his greatness and brilliance. It is not only funny but an insightful slice of creative guerrilla art from an artist at the apex of his creative powers. This is a must-view-movie for those who actually care for the nation, with special concerns about education and criminal justice.

Also, Michael Moore was the first internationally known and respected artist to call for the arrest and criminal prosecution of the Governor of Michigan, Rick Snyder. Under his administration the drinking water of Flint, Michigan became lead infested and has poisoned in various degrees the people of Flint, especially the children. Governor Snyder, in his infinite right-wing wisdom, sought to save a few million dollars by changing Flint's water supply to a local source which is lead filled and undrinkable. Michael Moore took the lead in exposing this catastrophe and made it a national story.

Mr. Moore's love of America is contagious. In the February 2016 issue of *Rolling Stone*, he states, "In the end, young people, women, blacks and Hispanics are going to rule this country. That's why I'm an optimist about the future of America." In the truth-telling tradition of Black filmmakers like Haile Gerima, Spike Lee, Julie Dash and Ava DuVernay, as we say in the Black community, Michael Moore "does us proud."

Finally, he who does not do us proud, and must be loudly, accurately and forcefully called out is the republican ignorant, racist front runner for the presidency, Donald Trump. Let us not be fooled by Trump's national campaign slogan, "Make American Great Again," which is not only a frontal attack on President Barack Obama, but is *really* coded language for Make American *White* Again. This was recently confirmed in his delayed and dumbfounded reaction in not denouncing the white supremacist, David Duke and the Ku Klux Klan for their public support.

Support
Free Speech TV
Black media, and progressive radio nationwide

Violence, Poverty, and Health

Again, I charge *murder*. However, this carnage is not only police killings of Black men, boys, women, and girls, but the existence of extreme poverty and the abysmal, calculated, and abusive ignorance in most Black communities. Basic healthcare is reactive rather than preventative. The environment is poisoned from the food we consume to the air we breathe to the contaminated water we drink and clean with. The unhealthy level of *stress* that overtake our lives daily leads to high-blood pressure and obesity. Has anyone noticed the sudden proliferation of dialysis clinics popping up in and near Black communities? According to the figures from the Centers for Disease Control and a 2011 study conducted by Columbia University, over 291,000 people die each year due to poverty. The majority of deaths are Black and poor people. Such knowledge is only useful with a clear, accurate, and cold assessment of one's true relationship to the land of one's birth.

Self-knowledge leads to self-definition, which is hopefully grounded in a healthy worldview, as well as an understanding of and acknowledgement of the human, economic, political, educational, and cultural positions of Black people in America in relation to non-Blacks. For example, that Black peoples' "wealth" is one-eleventh of the wealth of white people is not an insignificant fact in our struggle for economic development. It may also be interesting to note that the combined wealth of Bill Gates of Microsoft, the Waltons of Wal-Mart, the Koch Brothers of Koch Industries, Lawrence Ellison of Oracle, and Warren Buffet eclipses that of 42 million Black people in America. I repeat, the wealth of these five families is more than that of all 42 million Black people in the United States, and one could easily include that their wealth is also greater than another 150 million white people. Their combined wealth according to the *Forbes Magazine Wealth Issue* (April 2015) is greater than the economies of many nations in the world.

Money, whether we like it or not, too often defines Black existence in America and drives our life choices. Choices for employment, education, healthcare, living space, recreation and choices of safe and risk-free environments all define who we and our children associate with on a day-to-day basis.

The perfect example of how a culture of poverty—which too often breeds a culture of low-expectation—translates to our Black youth who are often victims of a mindset that puts too low a value on the acquisition of knowledge, learning, and high reading and writing skills. If one cannot read, write, compute, think, or do math far above high school levels it is just impossible to advance or make a "livable" wage in any highly advanced, knowledge-based and technological society. That is, like it or not, the status of the majority of Black folks in America. Most Black folks often have to work two or three low-paying jobs to make ends meet. The ways this affects Black people materially, politically, and educationally are well-known. The effects of this condition on Black mental and psychological well-being is a less debated issue in the Black community.

No less important is one's psychological health. Over the last thirty years, a kind of *"learned helplessness"* or *"learned dependency"* has slowly invaded large portions of the Black community. There is a feeling of "we can't do what other people do to bring about real and lasting life-giving and life-sustaining change in our lives and communities." Nationally recognized psychiatrist, Carl C. Bell (*Sanity of Survival; Reflections on Community Mental Health*, 2004), and distinguished psychologist, Wade W. Nobles (*Seeking the Sakhu: Foundational Writing for an African Psychology*, 2006), have observed and countered this notion and have supplied medical, psychological and cultural strategies in their works. Their works amplify and build on the work of Bobby E. Wright, Amos N. Wilson, and Na'im Akbar. Black psychology, unlike white psychology, is the study of mental health of Black people and, sadly, just as Black philosophers, their work is seldom cited, referenced, acknowledged, or celebrated. The scholarly writings of Black psychologists and philosophers is barely a footnote for their white peers, which is another clear example of white supremacist domination.

Little thought is given to Black overall wellness. Black people are surrounded by anti-wellness in the form of fast food, inadequate healthcare, poor, and failing schools, and a hyper commercial culture of trying to keep up with the materially, intellectually, and morally bankrupt backwardness of the ruling and entertainment elite. This crippling and critical ignorance in the Black community starts with the most basic of all self-concepts. Few Black people, can accurately, without hesitation, culturally identify themselves. If you ask fifty randomly selected Black people in the United States to culturally identify themselves and state what it means to be Black or African American, there would be fifty different and confusing answers, even from such a small sampling. Most of their responses will be embarrassingly uninformed, shockingly simplistic, and reactive to white supremacist notions of themselves. The point is that *if you do not fundamentally know who you are, anybody can and will name you*, forcing you to start off at a serious cultural, economic, and political deficit.

FREEDOM?

This brings me to the question of American "Freedom" that the right-wing pundits preach to the nation and world constantly—that the United States is the "land of the free and home of the Brave." Considering the way we go about war in other nations, at least on the surface, our bravery could not seriously be questioned or denied. However, Black people and others continue to buy into the enormous lie that we are free when the evidence and concreteness of our daily lives loudly contradicts those ideals. The facts are: (1) a significant number of Black men and a growing number of Black women are unemployed, under-employed, incarcerated, or missing; (2) a significant number of Black children and young people are not educated, under educated, miseducated, not seeking education, and do not think that education is the answer or important; additionally, there is not a national policy, program, or movement in place for correction or alteration more than fifty years since the passage of *Brown v. Board of Education*; (3) a significant number of Black people are under housed, inadequately housed, homeless, live in restrictive communities, and intimately understand that they are not wanted in the great majority of living spaces that are not Black; (4) medical care of the youth, elderly, or clearly unhealthy among them is not a national priority, thereby forcing a growing number of Black people to self-medicate, overuse the emergency room of hospitals, or suffer quietly so as not to burden their overtaxed families—these are the people that the Affordable Care Act (ObamaCare) missed; (5) too many Black children and elderly go to bed each night hungry, "full" on junk "food" that is readily available and overly advertised, and "full" on made-up "foods" like "chicken fries"—too many young people still believe that tomatoes come from a can and do not believe that "food" that is fried, overly salted, sugared, contained in cans, or cooked in fat should be avoided; and (6) that because of color there is, in many states, restrictive voting, a Black tax on everything they buy, and that their quality of life limits serious growth, development, advancement, or options.

Black people realize their "freedom" of movement in the nation is highly monitored, and once they leave their communities they are in danger of being stopped for walking or driving while Black. They also understand that the white conservatives' use of the term "freedom" is deceptive, dishonest, disingenuous, fake, fraudulent, illusionary, mean-spirited, and clearly means "unfree" for Black people and other non-whites. Jeffrey Feldman states in *Outright Barbarous: How The Violent Language of The Right Poisons American Democracy*, "Instead of hopeful, optimistic pragmatism focused on achieving a shared future full of promise, our political debates are neck-deep in the pessimism and uncertainty that flows from violent rhetoric." These are the facts of Black life for the majority of African Americans. To continue to dismiss this as we navigate the twenty-first century is to declare stupidity, lie to our children, and loudly agree that the success we literally see right down the street, that exists among white people is illusionary.

The Police and Prison Industrial Complexes

Black and Brown boys and men are incarcerated at a rate twenty times that of white men. This fact has blunted and dismembered the Black community. When young Black men are jailed for various offenses and then released with no support systems from the state, there are few safe places for them to retreat to except back to the streets. Street culture *is not* a short- or long-term answer to our many problems.

The U.S. national policies of whole-scale criminalization and incarceration of Black men and youth have effectively removed them from the electoral, employment, education, and functional family building process. This has dangerously over-populated most state and federal prisons. These men, by and large, are illiterate. Many read below a sixth grade level and write at a mere fourth grade level, which directly impacts their articulation and speech skills. While there may be little difficulty expressing themselves in prison, beyond those walls and beyond their indigenous communities, they will run into serious communication problems. Therefore, their prospects for work remain restricted to their neighborhood streets. And, most "street" work in the Black community is in the underground economy. This economy, by definition, is generally illegal or close to it. Any rational person intrinsically understands that *if street culture was liberating, we would all be free.* Two scholars who have produced a blueprint toward understanding this critical condition in the Black community are Becky Pettit in her ground-breaking *Invisible Men: Mass Incarceration and the Myth of Black Progress* (2012) and Michelle Alexander and her over-needed study, *The New Jim Crow: Mass Incarceration in the Age of Colorblindness* (2011). However, the one activist-scholar who for over four decades has been at the forefront of prison reform and selective demolition has been Angela Davis. All of her works are a must-read, especially *Are Prisons Obsolete?* (2003),[1] and her most recent book, *Freedom Is A Constant Struggle* (2016) edited by Frank Barat.

---

[1] See four valuable studies that also supply substantive and critical analysis of Black males in America and in the criminal justice system: *Young, Black and Male in America: An Endangered Species* (1988), edited by Jewelle Taylor Gibbs; *Search and Destroy: African-American Males in the Criminal Justice System* (1996) by Jerome G. Miller; *Two Nations: Black and White Separate, Hostile, Unequal* by Andrew Hacker (1995); and *Malign Neglect: Race, Crime and Punishment in America* (1995) by Michael Tonry.

Police culture is a military culture whose members are more dedicated to those they serve with first and foremost. Three years in the United States Army taught me this and much more. The local police forces are about protecting each other, their brand, white people, and their property. Most Blacks, especially the young, view the local police as an occupying force. These newly-named "first responders" respond to Blacks differently than they respond to whites. Eric Garner's death proved this. It was shown that the "first responders," so-called emergency health workers, stood and kneeled over Mr. Garner without administering *any* emergency services. This brings back memories of Hurricane Katrina.

Institutional racism (white supremacy) is the philosophical foundation that most police departments in the United States are built upon. They do not recognize or accept any criticism from non-whites or politicians who do not tow their line. One recent example, is the highly disrespectful actions of the New York City police union and many of the officers of the NYPD, their retort to Mayor de Blasio for his response to the killing of Garner, and his discussion with his bi-racial son about how to carry himself on the streets of New York. Their behavior toward the Mayor was highly disrespectful. They turned their backs on him as he addressed them and others during a very difficult time in New York City. Unlike the postal unions and automobile unions and other private business organized labor forces, we do not see the right-wing politicians and talking heads going negative on police and fire department unions. I wonder why?

In the commons there is very little discussion of restorative justice. What are the paths, out or up for men and women who have successfully served their time and released without an elevator to the next floor of learning or work? There is talk today among Democrats and Republican lawmakers of decommissioning federal prisons; however, little money has been allocated for the serious education or employment for the recently released Black men and women. They are expected to return to their communities without skills or an education that would allow them to compete in the overground economy. Until this happens, little will change for the best. It is an open secret that Black and Brown people function in a legal system designed for our failure.

Capitalism: Gladiator Culture

One looking at European imperialism in 1900 therefore should have looked first at the depressed peoples. One would have found them also among the laboring classes in Europe and America, living in slums behind a façade of democracy, nourished on a false education which lauded the triumphs of the industrial undertaker, made the millionaire the hero of modern life, and taught youth that success was wealth. ...Out of this emerged the doctrine of the Superior Race: the theory that a minority of the people of Europe are by birth and natural gift the rulers of mankind; rulers of their own suppressed labor classes and, without doubt, heaven-sent rulers of yellow, brown, and black people.

—W.E.B. DuBois
The World and Africa (1947)

Capitalism—the fundamental benchmark that drives all aspects of North America and most of the world's economies—is not seriously discussed on the nightly news, neither written about in popular magazines nor newspapers, neither viewed nor critically discussed on the top ten television or cable news programs. Yes, capitalism. We live in a culture of predatory individual and corporation first-ness. That is, at all levels of western human development the final and determining questions are: Who is first? Who is number one? Who won? Second does not count. Charles H. Ferguson is adamant about this fact in his remarkable book, *Predator Nation,* and in his Academy Award-winning film, *Inside Job.* Another remarkable document that is a must-read is *Bailout* by Neil Barofsky. He, in no uncertain terms, indicts the federal government and corporate America for the blatant abandonment of America's people while rescuing Wall Street and the nation's banks.

The route and creation of the modern western economy goes back to the meeting of world leaders at Bretton Woods at the Mount Washington Hotel in 1944. The men and some women from primarily western economies came together during World War II to not only reshape western capitalism, but also to find and designate funds for the rebuilding of Europe after the war. Two institutions that grew out of Bretton Woods are the International Monetary Fund (IMF) and the World Bank; both institutions are functioning today and represent key corner stones in International capitalism.

The one person to emerge from Bretton Woods whose ideas are still with us is the British economist, thinker, and activist John Maynard Keynes who suffered a heart attack at the conference. Blatantly missing from that meeting were Black Africans, Black Americans, indigenous North and South Americans, and other non-white people on the planet. Two books I would highly recommend on this subject are *The Summit: Bretton Woods, 1944* (2015) by Ed Conway and *The No-Nonsense Guide to Globalization* (2006) by Wayne Ellwood. However, it must be noted that these and other world meetings surrounding the Western economies are largely white affairs, until the last forty years or so with the emergence of China and India. Yet, white supremacy still rules.

This philosophy is executed daily on Wall Street, and Capitol Hill, in addition to National and International Banks, National Mortgage and Real Estate Agencies, National Insurance Company, the military, top law firms, and lobbyist on K Street, major corporations on and off the S&P 500 list, and in local and state governments. This take-no-prisoners culture is also evident at major universities, think-tanks, media, entertainment, sports, arts, medical, and law enforcement fields. Much of this was revisited with Reaganomics of the 1980 with its huge tax cuts for the rich and super rich, and its smiling open war on the unions, total disregard for the environment, and its blatant disrespect for poor and middle-class students' inability to afford higher education. Today's economy works overtime for millionaires, billionaires, Hedge Fund opportunists and "too-big-to-jail CEOs and investors" and "too-big-to-fail banks" who continue to gamble with depositor's savings. One can measure the human and humane values of a nation by how it treats its youth. The student loan debt today is 1.4 trillion dollars, larger than the debt of credit cards and non-military foreign aid.

One cannot overstate the extent that the middle class in the United States has been wiped out, with this "greed is not enough" economy in which the one percent to five percent rulership has strategically bought themselves a Congress and state governments across the nation. They also have in their pockets the U.S. Supreme Court. The five extremely right-wing justices have exhibited unimagined injustice to the majority population of the land. The courts, in their favorable ruling in the Citizens United Case, in part mandated that "money" is "speech" and "corporations" are "people." It is a ruling that opened up the flood-gates of all kinds of secret money and private PACs of the Republican and Democratic parties to further pollute the electoral process. If you take into account a few key economic measurements, such as wealth accumulation, corporate control, education attainment and control, as well as the worthless and fraudulent for-profit "colleges" and "universities," ownership of insurance companies, hospital and healthcare facilities, you can clearly see how the one to five percent work and control the lives of the ninety-nine percent and, by extension, the nation and much of the world. David Cay Johnston, in his excellent book *Perfectly Legal*, details with shocking and shameful examples of how the rich and super rich with the help of politicians and accounting firms have hijacked the U.S. tax system and rigged it for the benefit of the few at the top of the corporate and investment classes. Also see Chuck Collins' *Numbers 99 to 1: How Wealth Inequality is Wrecking the World and What We Can Do About It* (2012), and *Looting America: Greed, Corruption, Villains and Victims* (2002) by Rosoff, Pontell and Tillman.

Why is this cultural? When a young Black boy hits the street in his community, almost from birth to his teen years, it is about watching his back and who he runs with. Gang culture in too many Black communities rules. Most, if not all, of these young men and boy's lives have been criminalized, and they have little fear of the prison system. Generally, by their teen years, too many of these young boys have been in and out of the juvenile criminal system, and their young lives have been permanently tagged by this white supremacist justice system. In fact, while legacy in many white families means a Harvard, Ivy League, or Research One University admission, legacy in too many Black families means prison and/or the military. The violence experienced in prison has been transferred to their home turf with greater, negative knowledge and effectiveness. The poet, scholar, activist, Useni Eugene Perkins' life's work is a testimony to the types of examples we need in fighting and standing strong for young men and boys. His latest effort is a paper delivered at the Deconstructing Violence: Strategies and Alternatives Conference. In his paper "Criminalization of Young Black Males," he uses over fifty years of formal and informal community knowledge to map out, in clear useable language, the many historical and political reasons for Black violence, criminalization, and incarceration.[1]

The major movers and shakers among young Black men today fall into three categories: (1) those who run the streets, especially the underground economy,

---

[1] In Useni Euguene Perkins' classic work *Home is a Dirty Street* (1975), he chronicles the day-to-day struggle of young black boys; he was one of the first to consistently do this, not only as a scholar, but also as a street worker and institution builder.

gangs; (2) those in sports—mainly basketball and football; and (3) those in popular entertainment—hip-hop and rap music. To fully comprehend any of this, requires meaningful interaction with community members beyond the barber and beauty shops and the 86,000-plus Black churches in the nation which have very little developmental cultural and political effect upon this population. Cultural capitalism invades their young years in the images projected on television, film, music, and electronic and social media; all of these, as already indicated, can be shared via personal cell phones, which are easily and often disposed of to maintain anonymity and secrecy. All digital and electronic equipment, mainly cell phones, are replaced frequently. And, like most youth with text messaging, they have created a language of their own.

As the world reaches the midpoint of the second decade of the twenty-first century, and as this country moves into its last year with its first Black president, we find ourselves entering one of the most polarizing periods since the 1960s. The "official" killing, or modern day lynching, of Black boys, teenagers, and men, and out-of-proportion incarceration of Black teenagers, women and men are now hitting the front pages of newspapers and being featured on the evening news. This is not due to any serious investigative reporting by mainstream media but by the masses of people and their strategic use of *social media*. This cannot be minimized: young peoples' use of smart phones, tablets, laptops, and other personalized media and devices has kept much of the uninformed public informed and has driven major media to try to catch up with their coverage. This is truly social citizenship. Young people may not vote consistently, as in the off-term elections, but they do organize and use their minds and feet when they are ticked-off and need to right a wrong—as in Ferguson, New York, and Cleveland.

Social media has been the game changer in sharing information and organizing at the local and national level. The nation would not have known the particulars of the Eric Garner killing without social media or the killing of twelve-year-old Tamir Rice in Cleveland, without someone with a camera phone and the courage and foresight to post it on Facebook, Twitter, Instagram, and some other forms of social media. And now we are living in a time in which we are told that what we actually saw we really did not see.

The difficulty with most of this is that young Black people are mainly communicating with each other—which is understandable. To them, however, the rest of the world remains a *gigantic mystery*. Few in the Black and poor communities across this country can accurately articulate the underlying reasons for of the 2008-2009 economic disaster. Banks and Wall Street are foreign institutions to many Black and poor people and the nation's bailout of each seldomly enters everyday conversation even though we were negatively impacted the greatest and often blamed by the right wing for their failures. The actual reasons for the wars in Iraq and Afghanistan are not serious topics of daily conversation unless a son, daughter, or family member is serving. Healthcare often remains the emergency rooms of hospitals or self-medication even with Obama Care. The majority of miseducation in the Black community is generated from under-performing public and charter schools and from Black churches. One cannot dismiss the lack of performance and ignorant comments on the part of Black politicians who are supposed to be working for the Black community. Answers to our most complicated problems remain incomplete and often based upon uninformed sources and right wing talking heads, corporate media, and ignorant and confused Negroes.

While we encourage athleticism, many young Black boys view sports as their ticket to a better life; basketball and football have taken the space that baseball used to fill in the Black community. Football has emerged as the national sport of the United States. The money it generates is almost unbelievable to the lay person. This starts at the college and university levels where the NCAA rules with a protective hand. It then escalates at each of the professional leagues—NFL, NBA, and MLB—which has grown into multi-billion dollar businesses.

The first newly-created Colleges' Football Championship was played in Dallas this year and generated hundreds of millions of dollars of revenue in and around the 1.2-billion-dollar AT&T Stadium. The new coach of the University of Michigan will reportedly be paid an excess of four million dollars a year. If a college coach is paid this kind of money, one can only imagine the money generated at the pro-level.

The scholar Thabiti Lewis, in his magnificent book *Ballers of the New School: Race and Sports in America* (2010), uncovers the many lies of sports in America. The essence of his study is that the players in the NFL and NBA are overwhelmingly Black, yet the owners, management, and officials at all levels are predominately, with few exceptions, white. This fact will not soon change. Lewis documents that the public keepers of the sports' gate are the white writers and media commentators, who are in a field of 90 percent where

Black players—most certainly in the NBA and NFL—and they are the clear majority. The college and professional use and misuse of Black athletes is not a serious topic of conversation. This is partially due to the white narrative that defines the public discourse of newspapers, magazines, television, cable, and radio. Lewis' critique of racial inequality is the driving force of this remarkable book, proving once again the power of white supremacy in dictating the lives of young Black boys and men; he writes:

> For while there is a little doubt that in the high-profile sports such as football, basketball, and baseball the presence of non-Whites speaks volumes regarding racial progress, positions of leadership beyond the playing fields are far from diverse. Contrary to popular notions, the world of sports, which has been lauded for its racial progress, is filled with discrimination, inequalities, and lack of diversity. Racism, inequality, discrimination, and nepotism in sports are real. Instead of being frustrated by repeated declarations that race is a problem, what should be more frustrating is the variety of ways discrimination exhibits itself in American sport culture. In many ways, sport culture is a reflection of our society. Further, the disenfranchisement of people of color in sport culture reinforces false notions of intellectual inferiority, ensuring a regime of racial discrimination that systematically keeps people of color out of positions of leadership.

The dominance and questions of race as it affects college athletes who do not make it to the pros seldom enter the national conversation. What happens to the young men who don't make it and do not graduate from their prospective colleges and universities? I must state rather emphatically that sports matter and are critical as a pathway out of many difficult living situations. All organized sports at the high school, college and minor leagues provide not only serious mentoring and physical skill sets, but also could eventually lead to a quality education and a pay check. However, the life lessons learned are corrupted by the almighty dollar, and the young men and women get lost in the rat race.

That which we do not know about the rich and obscenely wealthy, is that they are excellent at hiding themselves and their money. Also, it is fundamentally clear that their major goal in life is making money and putting their names on buildings at universities or city projects that they support and fight organized labor 24/7. An excellent read that gives insight to all of this and more is, *Rich People Things: Real Life Secrets of the Predator Class* by Chris Lehmann.

Haki R. Madhubuti

The only way to effectively fight Big Money and its corrupting influence is by progressive organizing, political coalition building, strategic voting, supporting and creating a vigilant and responsible fourth estate (press) and a powerful social media. Also, we the people must be in the day-to-day vanguard of strongly supporting governmental policies and laws that regulate and break up exploitative monopolies, e.g. airlines, telecommunications, etc. We still have too big to fail banks and too powerful to prosecute CEO's. Much of this was brought on by the right wing Supreme Court ruling on Citizens United. Remember, and this is central and critical to any question of power; the only entity in the United States that can effectively check-mate, contain and regulate Big Money, banks, wall street, national and international corporations is government and its people. That is why the Republicans and a significant number of Democrats from Reagan to the Tea Party are fiercely battling 24/7 at the local, state and national levels to eliminate, seriously weaken or privatize all governmental social programs or systems such as Social Security, Medicare, education, postal services, Democratic elections, union organizing, food stamps, etc.

The overwhelming influence and control of modern day Oligarchs and Plutocrats in the United States is more evident with the passing of Citizens United. With the disempowerment of the people and the recent creation over the last fifty years of the "wealth defense industry" we are now witnessing the demise of democracy as visioned by the founders, enlightened legislators, political scientists and the people. For a more informed examination of this orchestrated takeover of the peoples' government, I suggest a close reading of *Oligarchy* (2011) by Jeffrey H Winters, *Plutocrats* (2012) by Chrystia Freeland, *Future Crimes* (2015) by Marc Goodman, *The Crash of 2016* (2013) by Thom Hartmann, and the recently published *Dark Money: The Hidden History of the Billionaires Behind the Rise of the Radical Right* (2016) by Jane Mayer.

Fathers and Sons:
The Healing Call

Each generation produces its own Griots—today's griots are rappers and hip-hoppers. Young people, who see too much too early, see and experience the underside of bad breath and lies as their young minds are honoring the fires of idealism. Regardless of how strong or clear their message, it does not change the fact that boys need fathers. Tupac Shakur needed a loving daddy to check him, to curb his language, actions and aspirations. Biggie Smalls needed a baba to set parameters for him, to set goals larger than bodies draped in gold, diamonds, and bitch-talk. Tupac and Biggie needed responsible fathers and elder men in their lives who loved them enough to challenge the streets and corners in them. They needed conscientious, caring men to tattoo their history and spirit on them like the dried ink that now rots on their dead bodies.

Our sons, nation-wide, cry for love and guidance from fathers, grandfathers, adopted and cultural fathers. Their cries are tearless and muted, fearing the macho cat-calls of peers caught in the same zoo of trapped boys seeking instruction, death-spirit, and examples from older boys who dance to two laws: staying alive and getting over. Without life-affirming love, art, and actions, without supervised discipline and study, without loud examples of "can-do/ must-do" possibilities and daily diets of father-love vitamins, Tupacs and Biggies will multiply. And the word on the street is, "you ain't seen nothin, yet." A refreshing analysis of the forces directing today's youth is Bakari Kitwana's *The Hip-Hop Generation* (2002).

This call is to the fatherless nation, hip-hop and no hop, church and churchless boys of genius who have never experienced a hug or a kiss from a man, never been loved as only fathers can love. This is a call to the men who drop seeds of life in women as if that is all life is about. This is a call to rappers and the rap-less, the boys with perpetual anger in their eyes, who wear gold and silver (often to decorate their mouths) rather than use it to work for them. This message is to the fatherless nation of boys who never discovered smiles, laughter, or the wholeness of possibilities, opportunities, or a confirming wellness.

Haki R. Madhubuti

THE CALL

we the men of twenty-four-seven   at dawn
of Nat, Garvey, DuBois, Medgar, Malcolm and King,
of swift tongues, fast hands and educated ears
must rise to the answer before dawn,
we are the quiet in the fire of unforgiven streets,
we are the hands beating the come home drums,
we are the homes surrounded in father-love, yeses
& stopwatches,
we are the poetic spirit making life worth living.

this is our call,
to boys who earned their names suffering spit & fist.
scale your dreams
avoid the dust of manufactured fairy tales,
bury evil choices and mandate a working truth,
unscar your todays with a loving advocacy of tomorrow,
trust the sun, moon, grass, blooming flowers and
                    clean   water,
defeat the devil's wars, burn the torturers play pager,
write your own truths, herein lies the challenge:
how far will good go in this age of lotteries and mega churches?
how far will justice travel in the breath of polluted judges, priest, police,
lawyers and politicians? how far will peace advance in the rhetoric of clowns?
what role will wisdom play in the desert of bogus thought?
this is our call,
sponsor our sons, fill the emptiness in their questions,
this is our theology: defeat the devil's plans
answer the s.o.s., save our sons with f.o.c., fathers on call,
we are sacred answers for the deserted hearts of
boys becoming men.

Dying Of Ignorant Talk
While Taking Bullets

we do not hear the pain of others,
nor listen to the under-doings of
a people, a nation, of empire.
it is not the bullets to the head,
chokeholds on the neck,
or the piercing of the heart of a
twelve-year-old boy in cleveland.
it is not the 110 shot to death in march
by first responders across the nation
    dancing in fear,
    dying of ignorant talk,
    close-eyed to the rape of children
    pimped by prosperity ministers, politicians, bankers and wall street.

it is not the nightly news with
"if it bleeds it leads" or talk-show hosts
who can't write or speak a coherent paragraph
but can lie, throw hatred, sell sugar, used cars,
enemies list and champion the ideas of the
monied-few running in white fright and flight
miles ahead of the poor, ignorant, unheard & suffering majority.

the monied-few buy
people who vote against themselves,
people who find comfort in whiteness and witless sound blast,
multiple homes & yachts, offshore accounts,
exclusive clubs, negative taxes, private education,
triple-filtered water, beef and yes people ordering

Haki R. Madhubuti

the 47 congressional traitors to sign a letter to the
leadership of Iran against our own president and country.

bullets not only come encased in lead
they arrive as anti-intellectualism disguised as knowledge,
in legislation from ALEC[1] to legally
steal federal land, fix taxes protecting the
richest of the one percent plutocrats and as
anti-national healthcare as long as congress people are covered[2]

bullets penetrate the ugliest in
children without family, love and security,
and teenagers who only listen to each other, the
hot wind of corporate shoe makers and the
bling, bling of rappers who can't spell responsibility,
recognize the N word for what it actually is, or
acknowledge the game and gangs they've lost to

bullets eliminate the masses with a
bought, sold and compromised corporate media,
test-fixing educators,
ill informed and conflicted politicians,
doctors betraying their "do no harm" oath,
as they and the monied-few sabotage the
good in good, the yes in quality and the
fading smiles of eight-year-olds as
grandfathers and mothers greet the
unsuspected at walmart feeding their
hard worked money to the gigantic suck machine of
goods from china, india and south america as
u.s. factories close by the thousands as the leaders
blame the people for the bankruptcy of states, cities and
washed out ideas of wall street, banks and a government

---

[1] American Legislative Exchange Council

[2] Senator Ted Cruz of Texas

living on punctured rafts unable to wash itself of
lobbyists, finance, pacs and the soiled
beliefs of whiteness and the work less wealthy all
hiding in private jets, newly acquired islands and
well stocked bomb shelters from the sixties.

there is a giant hole in the u.s. constitution
written three centuries ago for a nation built on and by
enslaved africans, indentured poor whites & three-fifths of a person
clauses
benefiting the white-gods of money and property.
there is colossal hypocrisy in the nation's constitution
that protects in principal what governments deny in practice,
whose response to evil is medieval in empowering a
ruler-ship who could not find justice in a one-word dictionary and
marvels daily at their work of cloning a people
who would much rather believe than think.

Question(s)

When do we call destruction our own? When do we resist the logic of white supremacy and Black self-hatred? J. D. is a 32-year-old Black man who lives with his momma. He does not work and will not take an entry level job because he can do better on the streets. J. D. beat his momma last week for not bringing him cigarettes home. He has six children by five different women and none of them call him daddy. They call him J. D. Is he a small representation of the Black community? Some say the J. D.s and their women are a strong 25 percent. Most of our people are walking tall, working multiple jobs, carrying the weight of family, history, and the current ills and hurts of the 25 percent of J. D.s that increase daily. We cannot hide or run from a quarter of our blood and bones. They are here, in need, and dangerous—talk to bus and cab drivers, listen to the children in our schools, talk to mail carriers, policemen, doctors, social workers, barbershop owners, beauticians, and teachers who take self-defense classes because they do not teach anymore (many watch their backs and do social work). When do we say "No!" to misguided teenaged boys and young men who disrespect their elders and whose identity are multiple earrings, cell phones, Starter jackets, pants low across the cracks of their butts, their initials carved out on the back of their heads, untied sports shoes, four letter words, and faces that never smile in public? They are our sons. They are loaded weapons and most of them have never known the power of love. We have not yet become Haiti or Rwanda, but we are about to go over the cliff blindfolded. We are not the music we used to be. I grew up with the Four Tops, the Dells, the Supremes (before they became Diana Ross and the Supremes), the Miracles, the Temptations, Marvin Gaye, Aretha Franklin, The Intruders, and Black love music of self-love and Black responsibility. We did not kill each other to gain a street corner or a reputation. When do we call destruction our own?

These questions, which were first published in my 1994 book *Claiming Earth: Race, Rage, Rape Redemption, Blacks Seeking a Culture of Enlightened Empowerment*, are reprinted here only because we still face the same internal problems. The major problem remains: too many of our young boys are being raised without love, protection, confirming knowledge, a working family and extended families, or institutional support. Most importantly, there are too many missing and functioning fathers, grandfathers, and uncles.

Stop Corporate Sovereignty and the Trans-Pacific Partnership

As with occupied Wall Street (2011) the Vancouver, B.C. magazine *Adbusters* again takes the lead in fighting the passage of the Trans-Pacific Partnership trade deal. If passed, the TPP will do more harm to people, states, and countries than all of the other trade agreements combined. From *Adbuster's* (3/16) issue:

> The Trans-Pacific Partnership is the largest trade deal in history; 6,000 pages. 7 years of secret meetings. 40% of global GDP. 500 trans-national corporate interest. 9,000 foreign-owned companies. 18,000 US-owned companies. Investor-State Dispute Mechanisms allowing corporations to sue governments. To challenge state, federal, and local court rulings in "special tribunals" – World Bank Kangaroo Courts that could, once and for all, succeed in putting profits before people. Profits before governments. Profits before federal legislation, or fair use guidelines, or intellectual property provisions, or environmental protection, or temporary foreign worker restrictions, or any of those other pesky freedoms that get in the way of shareholder returns. It's the creation of an alternative, parallel universe for corporations alone, one which has its own charter, its own rules, its own Bill of Rights, one which gives them the ability to crush anyone – people, states, countries – who refuse to comply with their vision.

All of our political, cultural, and human resources should be used to stop this international corporate giveaway of the public commons and our human rights. President Obama, in his outsized advocacy of the TPP is clearly on the wrong side of history. We, citizens of the US and the world must support Senator Bernie Sanders and others in their battle against TPP. Also, we must enlarge our support of *Adbusters, The Nation, In These Times, Mother Jones, The Progressive, The New Internationalist, The Populist, Extra!, The Hightower Lowdown, The Final Call, The New Yorker, The New York Review of Books, International Socialist Review, Z Magazine*, and other progressive voices – print and web. This is a call to resist, disrupt, undermine, and to organize from neighborhood block clubs to student campuses against this travesty which will, in effect complete the destruction of the working and middle classes in the United States and internationally.

Money: Owning Self, Community, Business, and Our Tomorrows

Two economic indicators slapped me squarely in the face. First, there is the pimp-cry of Pastor Creflo Dollar of Atlanta, Georgia, as exposed by *The Root's* Kirsten West Savlai, calling for 200,000 people to contribute $300 each toward his purchase of a new Gold stream G-650 jet. Of course, this is to support his worldwide ministry of "prosperity gospel" which espouses that God rewards the truly righteous believers *now* and with their "God-given" affluence and new riches. They are required to not only support him but walk the red carpet of God's chosen people themselves.*

The second financial indicator is the March 2015 issue of *Forbes* magazine highlighting its twenty-ninth annual almanac of world wealth. This issue clearly makes my point regarding the United States as the only modern day functioning empire on the planet. Of the 1,826 billionaires worldwide, 536 of them are Americans, and out of the top 50 richest people, 24 are Americans with Bill Gates (79.2 billion dollars) and Warren Buffett (72.7 billion dollars) coming in at numbers one and three, respectively. To get into this club one has to have a minimum of 18.1 billion dollars. No, there are no Blacks in this club. However, there are a few Black billionaires—as if that really mattered. This fact has no constructive meaning to Black people and our economic condition in America and worldwide.

One of the more knowledgeable and committed Black men on the economy of African Americans is Dr. Claud Anderson. Anderson's deeply researched, culturally focused, and heartfelt thesis on economics, *PowerNomics: The National Plan to Empower Black America* (2001), is required reading in understanding the current economic, political, and cultural state of Black America. I write this after a lifetime of building Black businesses and schools in the United States. I came at this subject with both a practical and theoretical knowledge base.

---

* I would donate ten dollars if he would get in his jet and not come back

Dr. Anderson in his work comes the closest to my ideas and what I have been trying to do my entire adult life. Read his words:

> Blacks are the only group of people forced to practice capitalism without capital in the richest and most capitalistic nation on earth. These facts, coupled with the majority of society's total unwillingness to approve corrective action and reparations for descendants of Black slaves reveal the true nature of racism against Black people.
>
> Racism and other legacies of slavery predetermine the success of Black Americans as a group. One of the most glaring examples of inherited inequalities is wealth distribution. Black America's percentage of ownership of the nation's wealth remains where it was in the 1860s on the eve of the Civil War. At that time, when nearly every Black person in America was either in full slavery or semi-slavery, Blacks owned one-half of one percent of this nation's wealth. The emancipation of enslaved Blacks in no sense rendered social justice and economic recompense.
>
> Today, more than 140 years later, we are "100 percent" free, yet Black Americans still own only one-half of one percent of this nation's wealth. Today, the income of Blacks as compared to Whites has regressed to the level it was at the end of the 1960s.
>
> Approximately 38 percent of the Black population is beneath the poverty line and another one-third is marginal, just above the poverty line. The limited assets that Black Americans most often have such as automobiles and personal effects, depreciate rather than appreciate in value.

Claud Anderson goes on to state that the "three major impediments to Black competitiveness" are:

- Mal-distribution of wealth and resource powers
- Inappropriate behavior patterns
- Lack of a national plan for empowerment

In the body of his study, he gives further explanation and weight to these three areas. Throughout his study he refers to "structured racial inequalities" of wealth and resources. He goes back time and time again to elaborate on how the "life chances and rewards" are rigged against Black people. And that "historical origins of white control of wealth, resources and power" are not at the top of the civil rights agenda. Anderson's definition of wealth is critical to his argument:

What is wealth? Wealth refers to the net value of a person, group or community less than their liabilities or debt at a given point in time. It is inbred value. Income, in contrast, refers to a flow of dollars over a period of time. With rare exceptions, most Blacks are so marginalized that they own and control little wealth or resources anywhere, including their own neighborhoods. The ancestors of enslaved Blacks were forced to concentrate simply on surviving, pursuing civil rights and integration. They had little to bequeath to their descendents. Even though they succeeded in their social and civil rights efforts, these children cannot inherit welfare, food stamps, public housing or a "good" job.

He clearly believes, as I do, that if any group made up of tens of millions of any people—in this case African people—were not controlled from sun-up to sun-down as an enslaved population, then that people could build a nation, too. He writes:

White society will not publicly admit that its powerful self-interests perpetuate the legacy of slavery and Jim Crow semi-slavery. The critical contributions of Black people to the development of this nation and the Western civilization are largely hidden. To admit Black people's contributions is to trigger White guilt and a sense of responsibility for Black people's predicament.

According to records, the majority society compiled its wealth by using a simple economic principle: the industry of slavery produced a 1500 percent return on investment without the burden of wages, employee benefits, and taxes. The lifetime profits produced by slaves were passed on to the slaveholders' heirs and their heirs' heirs. Wealth accumulated for White society while poverty accumulated for Blacks.

Our nation claims to be an equal opportunity, color-blind society, after more than a century of mal-distributing the nations land and wealth-producing resources to everyone but Blacks. Even after Jim Crow segregation ended in the 1960s, and this nation formally became a "just society," the White society committed only $15 billion to conduct a "War on Poverty." Since this program included every group in America, it is unclear how this limited effort was supposed to correct the centuries of abuse inflicted specifically on Black people. Social conservatives argue that seven years of the Great Society programs fulfilled all responsibilities that White society had to Blacks for 400 years of slavery and Jim Crow semi-slavery.

I cannot do justice to this profound work. It must be read by all serious Black folks and others who wish to make substantial economic changes in the lives of Black people. I can only add that after over fifty years on the frontlines of institution building that one does not have to be Adam Smith, John Maynard Keynes, Karl Marx, Robert Heilbroner, or John Kenneth Galbraith to understand that the international and most national economies are not working for the great majority of people. In my youth, Marxism was the answer for heaven on earth. At best, a Marxist analysis is helpful in understanding the inequities in market economies. It is not the answer to the powerful pull of capitalism and the embarrassing downfall and failure of Communism in Eastern Europe.

Economics is a foreign subject to most of us, myself included. Yet as a poet-businessman, I have had to soil and wash my hands because every two weeks my co-workers do not want a poem but a check for their labor. To state categorically that I understand the "art" of making money is to infer a falsehood that I most readily admit to. My understanding of market economies is about as substantive as my reflections on quantum physics or any math beyond algebra. However, I have always possessed a deep desire to be independent. Because of the poet, politics, and color in me, I will never be a major player in the money game. It is not that money does not interest me; it does, but there are many more important concerns that take up what little time I have *outside of writing*, working, and studying—such as family and extended family development, teaching, editing, publishing, and maintaining my health and moral state of mind. I believe it is extremely unhealthy and unethical to misuse, exploit, or take advantage of any people for personal or "collective" profit. There are many, many acts that I will not perform for money or wealth. However, there are many ideas about general wealth and power that cannot be missed:

1. The making of a great deal of money is not a fair game, nor is it open to all who may understand best how to use it. Money-making is not an equal opportunity employer.

2. Very few working people will have any serious money over their lifetime, including managers and small business owners. If one works for a weekly check, he or she will be less likely to be able to save enough money to move into the investment class, where one's money works for one, rather than one working for one's money.

3. People with big money generally have had some help: (a) inherited wealth; (b) stolen wealth; (c) idea wealth, yours or somebody else's;

(d) entertainment wealth—tap dancing on the art of other people; (e) retail wealth—Wal-Mart/Sam's Club; (f) real estate wealth—building Disneylands and strip malls on all the farm lands available; (g) advertising wealth—the key is to sell to as many people, as possible, objects that they do not need or want; (h) law firm wealth—finding the loopholes to keep the money with the people who have money; (i) investment wealth—avoid junk bonds and men like Michael Milken and Ivan Boesky (j) sports wealth—be like Mike and men like him; and (k) media wealth—to make us think that the Mikes are major players in the wealth game, and, that you, too can be rich (that's why lotteries exist).

4. One of the reasons capitalism works in America is because most people do not realize that it does not work. The great secret is that there is socialism for the rich, near rich, and recent Pentagon graduates. For wanna-be lobbyists, the best experience on a resume is "former Congressperson" The incestuous relationship between government and business is obscene. Who you know *and what* you know about them is as important as having a *good lawyer*. For example, that much of the large farming business is subsidized in America says a lot about power and political friendships. Few would call a farmer lazy or nonproductive (that does not explain why small family farms are going the way of the dinosaur). However, the subsidizing for the dairy and tobacco farms would put most "welfare queens" to shame. The waste in the federal budget could possibly finance several small nations into the next millennium with some change left over.

5. People with big hearts do not have money. That is why foundations and grant-giving agencies are named for and financed by the fortunes of dead men. Men like the Rockefellers, Morgans, Fords, and others who built their wealth on the bodies of others. Foundations were created by their families and friends to give some of the "blood money" away in order to help create positive memories of them.

6. The greed factor in a capitalist economy is the fuel that runs the engine and cannot be underestimated. When people love money first

and foremost, children generally suffer. The people who take economic risks against unhealthy odds do not understand the game. Big capitalism is risky, yes. The winners are always those inside the loop who have the inside track on the next trade, however, for the middle player, capitalism is like a lottery game. Often, it is a roll of the dice or fall of the ball. The higher one is in the game, the fewer the balls one has to contend with. After all, the higher-ups are generally making the balls and machines that operate the game.

7. The saying that "it takes money to make money" is a truism that is timeless in most cultures. Also, there is the saying, "nothing is parted quicker than a fool and his money." Most people with serious money do not buy lottery tickets, gamble on riverboats, or wager on horse races, sports games, or prize fights. The seriously rich own riverboats, sports teams, race tracks and horses, boxers, and the hotels where the middle class and poor can stay in comfort while they lose their underwear.

8. The reality that "money makes money" means that most people—and I do mean literally the great majority of the world's people: Black, White, Red, Brown, and Yellow—will not be able to join the monied class. Most rich people keep their secrets to themselves and do not welcome new members without a great deal of consideration and investigation.

9. You can always tell who the people are without money. They generally wear overpriced, poorly-made clothes that are valued more for their label than for the quality. Many drive expensive cars that cost one-half of their yearly salary and carry large amounts of money around with them. People who have real money keep it to themselves because they do not want more of us to know about it for obvious reasons: (a) they think that we may ask/beg for some; (b) they think that we may try to steal it from them; (c) all kinds of charitable and not-for-profit groups would be camping on their doorstep; and (d) it may attract too many reporters who write for *The Nation, The Progressive, Mother Jones* and *In These Times.*

10. Ask a family member to explain NAFTA (North American Free Trade Agreement) and GATT (General Agreement on Tariffs and Trade) to you. If they do not know, try to explain it to them. If ignorance is victorious, call a Congressperson and really get confused. Just remember, the first rule of NAFTA and GATT is: someone is going to make BIG money and it won't be you. Oh, here are some more letters that you need to think about: BCCI (Bank of Commerce and Credit International) and the newly called -for TPP (Trans-Pacific Partnership).

WHAT SHOULD MONEY-LESS PEOPLE DO?

Part of our dilemma is that many of us do not understand the value of family, extended family, and community in relationship to wealth. I have always felt that family is as important as participating in a quality pension plan. Therefore, very human relationships, built around life-giving, life-saving, and life-sustaining values, are a crucial part of the bottom line for a healthy life.

This can be translated in a number of ways:

1. Black churches have always been secondary homes for most of us. Where is the "wealth" of the church—which is a collective wealth—being invested? It should be invested back into the community it serves in a number of ways, including (a) credit unions; (b) food co-ops; (c) rehabilitating and building new homes in their communities; (d) elderly apartments; (e) restaurants with low-cost, high-quality food; (f) chain grocery stores using local farmers as a base; (g) bulk buying of the items the church members use the most (e.g., stoves, refrigerators, etc.); (h) children-centered activities (e.g., after-school programs, boys and girls clubs, etc.); and (i) the idea that whatever we need, we should be able to buy in our own communities and, therefore, re-circulate the money.

2. Support a national Black bank. African Americans are 40 million strong in this country. If the 18 million adults among us put one dollar per week in a national bank, there is great potential for re-investment and growth. Part of the problem here is that we don't know who we would trust to administer $18 million a week of our money? This is a moral/value problem; a trust problem.

3. Do not be afraid of starting small businesses. This country was built on the backs of indigenous people, the backs of enslaved Africans, and and on the backs of indentured Asians, Latinos, and Europeans. Small businesses still employ the majority of the people. We have to get into the business of business. Our children need to be nurtured and educated in the self-reliant occupations. While it is true that we must make, a profit, we must never lose sight of the human side of the equation. If we have to work for large multi-national corporations, we must never forget who we are. In fact, Black folks must become guerrilla warriors in the boardrooms, state buildings, universities, and playing fields of the business world. We must work, often undercover, to bring more quality Blacks into our work places. That is what culturally focused guerrilla warriors do; they help their own as they fight against evil.

4. Support small farmers. Local farmers need us and we need them. Part of our health problems could be minimized if we had fresh food. The closer the crop is to the market, the better it is for the consumer. What about the Black rural-urban connection?

5. Organize and study. Work with like-minded people. Practice good values. Oppose all forms of greed; teach our children frugality and productivity skills. Do not be afraid to fight big-monied interests, whether private or governmental.

6. In a highly competitive world, ideas about increasing efficiency and quality while cutting costs to maintain and develop one's business are critical. A number of years ago, Federal Express, Kinkos, personal and business fax machines and personal computers were just ideas. Today, we do not know how we would get along without them. Black colleges and universities with business schools should think of ways to make the community that surrounds them empowerment zones. How can professors and students take the classroom to the streets and revitalize at least the neighborhoods nearby?

7. Most of the mom-and-pop stores in Black communities in urban areas are owned and controlled by other cultures—primarily Arabs,

Asians, and East Indians. They use a system of families and extended families, which is financed internally. It is something like a tri-circle, a small circle inside a larger circle, inside an even larger circle: the center (smallest) circle represents old-line families or new families with money. They loan money to the second circle of families who have been here for a while and worked their way up from retail to distribution. The third (outer) circle represents the new arrivals and/or the poorer individuals within that cultural/ethnic circle. They borrow money from the center at very low interest and buy retail storefronts and go head-to-head with Black businesses. The center circle family loans the money to the third circle family on the condition that they (a) buy their products from the second circle family who are distributors, (b) employ mainly family and extended family only, (c) help to develop the third circle concept, and (d) keep outsiders out.

8. The ultimate goal is for our culture to control at least a sector of the national economy. If we supply fruit, vegetables, a specific labor market, or shoe strings to the nation we would be in much better shape than we are now. Our consumer dollars need to be directed mainly to those businesses that support us by, (a) employment, (b) supporting our service organizations and institutions, (c) invest their resources in our businesses and communities, and (d) consider our ideas in their own development.

9. Move to control the real estate in our communities with a strategy of going beyond the African American community. This work entails new building starts and rehabs. Black people who are architects, construction workers, contractors, or suppliers should be involved in all the construction that takes place in African American communities.

10. We have to be mindful of the global economy with a special eye on Africa. In too many of the future economic forecasts, Africa is not even considered as a viable player at the conservation or investment levels except by the newly-minted capitalists from China and Japan

(see Howard W. French's *China's Second Continent: How a Million Migrants are Building a New Empire in Africa*, 2014).

11. We need to understand and use the United States tax code more strategically. Poor people receive food stamps, and the rich, near rich, well off, and corporations have lower tax rates. The level of government benefits that exist for the rich and corporations is really welfare disguised as tax cuts. This is made clear in David Cay Johnston's, *Perfectly Legal*, (2003). He explains in detail how the rich evade taxes, profit off taxes, take advantage of tax loopholes and much more. In essence, the U.S. tax code is a hidden gift to the rich, corporations and non-profit organizations to the sum of over $900 billion each year.

12. We need "Independent Black Institutions" at every level of human existence. Not merely to copy white institutions, but to function as advocates, supporters/support systems, and direction givers to a population that has been written off the political, cultural, and economic map of this country and world.[1] If the white fundamentalist (religious right) taught us anything from their success, it is that to not organize and struggle for our ideas only puts us in the position of reacting to the ideas, cultures, and movements of others. This hard and fundamentalist Christianity, as documented in *Kingdom Coming: Rise of Christian Nationalism* by Michelle Goldberg and *The Baptizing of America* by Rabbi James Rudin makes it patently clear that the United States is nowhere near socialism or communism, but too many whites and Blacks are so captured by extreme Christian nationalism that they feel it is actually more important than and supersedes all human law, including the Constitution of the United States.

---

[1] The Jewish people in America and the world, most certainly after the Holocaust, have been very effective in their development of Jewish institutions that not only work for them, but for others, too. However, when a people (Jews) have close to a 100 percent voting record in Congress for most—if not all—of its concerns, I would state rather emphatically that they as a people are functioning in their best interests. The Jewish people have many lobbying entities other than individual Congress men and women and one of their most effective lobbies is AIPAC. Who lobbies for Black people 24/7? To understand the extent and influence that the Black rich and near rich have in the Black community read *The Boule's Journal* the official publication of Sigma Pi Phi fraternity, and *Black Enterprise Magazine*. *Ebony* and *Essence* magazines always give insight into the Black middle class and their aspirations.

Haki R. Madhubuti

When we consider the world's population in relation to usable land and water, any thinking person can see that we are in trouble. Everything of value that we need in order to maintain a quality life comes from land and water. Conscientious people, groups, organizations, churches, etc., need to buy land and maintain it. There is something about living close to the land and water that enables one to maintain a more human perspective.

Any people who are in control of their own cultural, economic, political, and educational imperatives should be about the healthy replication of themselves at every level of human activity. And, the larger questions for any people, and especially for the formerly enslaved Africans/Black people are: What do we own? What area of the nation's economy do we control? Who works for the benefit of Black children and adults 24/7? When will our best and brightest in the world of finance pool their brain-power and resources to create wealth for Black people's benefit?

Will we see a wealth change in the black community in our lifetime? Only and only if Black people as a people decide to make such a change, a radical change themselves. In an editorial in the *New York Times* (9/15/15), "Segregation Destroys Black Wealth" highlighting the work of the National Fair Housing Alliance"s fight for fair housing in the United States. The answer is unlikely. After 50 years of the Fair Housing Act, there is little progress and this "toxic" problem is still with us and stops black wealth development according to the editorial:

> Throughout history, ethnic groups have been able to translate economic gains into housing in better neighborhoods and advantages for their children. But for African Americans, the researchers write, that transition has been "thwarted by segregation and the prejudice and discrimination that create and maintain it." In other words, the damage reaches across generations and continues today.

A deep and rewarding quality of life for the majority of the nation's peoples looking and working toward a bright future is in doubt. However, the real gift of the united states is its size and its diversity: people, land mass and natural resources. One can actually lose oneself in this vast country, especially if one has money and/or unique skills and, this is critical – if you are not Black.

Reparations /Restitutions:
A Part of the Answer

New laws are not enough. The emergency we now face is economic.
And it is a desperate and worsening situation. For the 35 million poor
people in America ... there is a kind of strangulation in the air. In our
society it is murder, psychologically, to deprive a man of a job or an
income. You are in substance saying to that man that he has no right
to exist.

—Rev. Dr. Martin Luther King Jr.

At the heart of America's inability to be taken seriously as the champion
of Western moral and ethical values, and its attempt to export democracy
and human rights to Asia, Africa, South America, and Eastern Europe is its
historical treatment of Native American/Indians and African Americans/Black
people. Most people of the United States are abysmally ignorant of this
nation's genocidal destruction of the indigenous populations during this nation's "founding and creation." That same ignorance of the brutal and inhuman
enslavement and use of Africans in the development of the nation and its enormous wealth has been viewed by too many as simply "divine intervention."

One of the burning issues capturing public and private dialogue and debate of the twenty-first century is whether the descendants of Africans, now
in America, are due any restitution for their foreparents'-250-plus years of
great suffering and slave labor. This is no small matter. American history, as
taught in the nation's schools, arrives with an extreme contempt 'for facts,
which are arranged to always favor the "founders" and their stories. Fortu-
nately the works of Lerone Bennett Jr., Howard Zinn, Chancellor Williams,
Carter G. Woodson, James W. Loewen, Molefi Kete Asante, Marimba Ani,
and others exist to counter popular lies, fabrications, inventions, and outright fairy tales disguised as historical truths.[1] Charles W. Mills in his critical

---

[1] *Before the Mayflower: A History of African America* by Lerone Bennett Jr., *The Destruction of Black Civilization* by Chancellor Williams, *The Mis-Education of the Negro* by Carter G. Woodson, *A People's History of the United States 1492-Present* by Howard Zinn, *Lies My Teacher Told Me* by James W. Loewen, *Erasing Racism* by Molefi Kete Asante and *Yurugu: An African-Centered Critique of European Cultural Thought and Behavior* by Marimba Ani. Also see the works of John Henrik Clarke, Yosef ben Jochannan, Maulana Karenga, and Cheikh Anta Diop.

Haki R. Madhubuti

study, *The Racial Contract*, defines this clouding of historical reality as "illusory idealizing abstraction." If one truly understands the emergence of the United States' dominance in the international arena as the most powerful economic, political, cultural, and military force in world history, the question must be asked: What role did people of African ancestry, who now number over forty-two million, contribute to this creation?

The enslavement of African people by Europeans and Americans, and the wealth acquired as a result, can be argued and documented as the principal act that propelled the economies of Western governments, and primarily the United States, into becoming the uncontested super-power in the world. Currently, the United States' influence, wealth, and military power is so great that it does not seek permission from friends or foe for its adventures around the world; Iraq is the latest and best example. The wealth of the United States as exhibited by individuals, corporations, institutions, foundations, and government is so exceptional that only a few nations can compete economically or militarily with it without serious disruptions and depletions of resources; for example, the former USSR. I emphasize, without fear of contradiction, that the basis for much of this wealth can be directly linked to the inhuman and unrestricted free use of African people's labor and intelligence for over 300 years.

The enslavement of African people positioned the United States to jump-start its economy, and in less than 350 years to overtake all of Europe, Asia, the Caribbean, South America, and of course, Africa. The depopulation of Africa of its people and resources through the Transatlantic Slave Trade (Maafa)[2] is the under-discussed reason that Africa as a continent has not been able to develop at the same pace of other continents like Asia and South America. In 1860, the combined net worth of Blacks in America was half of one percent of the wealth of white America. Surprisingly, in 2005, this disparity hovered around the same percentage. Also, wherever African people exist, especially within the United States, their economic development as a people is in a frozen state of despair and anger.

Today's call for reparations, nationally and internationally, must not be confused with welfare, food stamps, affirmative action, the great society programs, grants, or some re-invented charity thought up by the Neo-cons at the American Enterprise Institute. The demand for reparations /restitutions is not recent or new. From 1865 to today, there has been a constant drumbeat for the redress

---

[2] Maafa (pronounced Ma-Ah-Fa): a Kiswahili word meaning disaster or great tragedy used to give greater clarity to the enslavement and colonialism of African people. See *Yurugu: An African, Centered Critique of European Cultural Thought and Behavior* by Marimba Ani.

and compensation for the descendants of the formerly enslaved Africans. The distinguished scholar Raymond A. Winbush's book, *Should America Pay? Slavery and the Raging Debate on Reparations* (2003), documents three distinct stages of reparation activity: (1) in 1898, we see the work of Callie House with the establishment of the Ex-Slave Mutual Relief, Bounty and Pension Association; (2) then from 1920 through 1968, we witnessed the work of Marcus Garvey, Queen Mother Audley Moore, and the Black Nationalist Press; and (3) from 1968 to the present, the founding of Black Nationalist formations including the Republic of New Africa (1968), The National Coalition of Blacks for Reparations in America (1987), the December 12th Movement, The National Black United Front, and The Reparation Coordinating Committee all working in harmony with the likes of Congressman John Conyers (D-Michigan), attorneys Charles Olgetree, Willie Gary, Randall Robinson, and the late Johnnie Cochran.

Randall Robinson's *The Debt: What America Owes to Blacks* (2000) is a persuasive thesis in favor of reparations. He, as an advocate, takes no prisoners in his argument and documentation of the absolute horror of the enslavement of African people and the lasting psychological scars branded on the enslaved and their descendants. However, it was James Forman of the Student Nonviolent Coordinating Committee (SNCC) who in 1969 delivered the *Black Manifesto* before the National Black Economic Development Conference in Detroit, which was adopted by the body. In a very condensed manner, this manifesto was a progressive and revolutionary rallying call for action and accountability. On May 4, 1969, James Forman interrupted a service at New York's Riverside Church to present the *Black Manifesto* and demand $500 million in reparations for Blacks.

The Black Manifesto to the White Christian Churches and the Jewish Synagogues in the United States of America and All Other Racist Institutions demanded funding for education and economic initiatives, the establishment of Southern land banks, publishing and printing industries, communication and media industries, and a National Black Labor Strike and Defense Fund. It was an International Black Appeal that would link Black struggles in Africa and other parts of the Black Diaspora and much more. Arnold Schuchter's *Reparations* (1970) and Boris I. Bittner's *The Case for Black Reparations* (1973) both take an outsiders view on the subject and are worth reading as reactions to the *Manifesto* and the growing movement.

In a *Chicago Tribune*/WGNTV poll conducted between May 3 and May 7, 2001, reporters Gary Washburn and Celeste Garrett wrote that "as debate intensifies across the nation over compensating African Americans for the evils of slavery, the views of Illinois residents on the concept split sharply along racial lines. Only six percent of whites surveyed across the state said they favored the idea of having the federal government pay reparations to blacks... while eighty-four percent said they were opposed. At the same time, sixty-six percent of blacks said they favored reparation payments, while only fifteen percent did not." Much of the objections to reparations by Blacks and whites have to do with the passage of time. One hundred and fifty years since the legal abolition of slavery, the questions are: who should receive reparations, and how does one identify the descendants of enslaved Africans?

Unlike the Jewish Holocaust of World War II or the Japanese American internment in the United States during the same war in which compensation and/or reparations to survivors have been paid, identifying survivors was not a dismissive concern. Randall Robinson in *The Debt* and most of the contributors to Raymond A. Winbush's *Should America Pay?* view the time passed and who to pay as a technicality that intelligent minds could easily solve. I agree.

Montombi Tutu, the daughter of Nobel Laureate Archbishop Emeritus Desmond Tutu and a delegate to the 2001 United Nations World Conference on Racism, writes in *Should America Pay?*: "The establishment of the State of Israel is based on biblical claims to that land as the homeland given by God to the Jewish people. It is a claim based on something that happened over two thousand years ago. I am not here calling for a debate on the legitimacy of the State of Israel. I am merely arguing that the same western governments that claim slavery happened too long ago for compensation by people of African descent accept as legitimate the right of European Jews to claim land based on theological interpretations that happened even longer ago. If one claim can be legitimately made, why not the other?" Is it because one people is African, another European?

I think that the larger problem here is one of will and the fear of opening up a nest of rats. For me the issue is not giving each Black person in America a reparation check. I feel that such action will only debase and demean the entire struggle. In fact, the best way for the U.S. to make the problem go away is to give checks out. This would not only quiet some of the activists, but would greatly stimulate the national economy. It is a known fact that money that arrives in the Black community generally stays there for about four hours. Such cash allotments to individuals would be, as far as I am concerned, a travesty of justice. Most people who have worked in this movement for years are not seeking handouts, charity, loans, grants, affirmative actions, or "feel good" tokens from the United States and the west. All are illusions of progress and payments in which we are locked down, locked out, and locked in to scramble for pennies among the penniless. There has been and continues to this day to be a highly effective hidden cost of being African American. The killing question which the rulership does not want to entertain, is how the wealth generated by the enslavement of African people has aided in perpetuating inequality and modern scientific enslavement and oppression. Again, I reference Claud Anderson's *PowerNomics: The National Plan to Empower Black America* (2001).

In 1995, Melvin L. Oliver and Thomas M. Shapiro published a groundbreaking study titled *Black Wealth, White Wealth: A New Perspective on Racial Inequality.* The authors poke holes in the so-called power of the "new Black middle class" who possess only fifteen cents for every dollar of wealth held by middle-class whites and document how most working Blacks live close to paycheck-to-paycheck. They document the nation's racial inequality that is based upon a deep and penetrating analysis of private and corporate wealth. To illustrate the validity of their argument, two white men, Bill Gates of Microsoft and Larry Elision of Oracle, have a combined wealth that exceeds the combined wealth of all 42 million Blacks in the United States. Oliver and Shapiro effectively argue that it is impossible for Black people—due to systematic economic barriers—to accumulate wealth. Most are confined to urban cotton-picking labor and the underground economy.

Thomas M. Shapiro in his 2004 book, *The Hidden Cost of Being African American,* argues that even though some African Americans have crossed the railroad tracks and enjoy the pleasures and riches of America, the vast majority under the current economic system will never acquire such opportunity. His thesis is that fundamental levels of racial inequality persist, particularly in the area of *asset accumulation*—inheritance, savings accounts, stocks, bonds, trusts, home equity, and other investments. Professor Shapiro states that wealth "perpetuates racial inequality" as well as "class inequality among both whites and African Americans." His three big ideas are: (1) Family inheritance and racial discrimination are linked and impact Black people negatively in homeownership, money passed at death, and paying for college, stating that few Black families have any start-up or catch-up monies to compete. He states that "it is virtually impossible for people of color to earn their way to equal wealth through wages...They cannot preserve their occupational status for their children; they cannot out-earn the wealth gap;" (2) Inheritances are what he calls "transformative assets," which is "unearned, inherited wealth" which helps to lift families "economically and socially beyond where their own achievements, jobs and earnings would place them;" and (3) "The way families use head-start assets to transform their own lives" have racial and class consequences. He makes it very clear that a great many "whites continue to reap advantages from the historical, institutional, structural and personal dynamics of racial inequality, and they are either unaware of these advantages or deny they exist." His study confirms that Black people pay a "very steep tax for this uneven playing field." We call it a Black Tax.

However, we must make known that reparations/restitutions* are not only due from the U.S. government, but also from national and international corporate structures as well as religious institutions, especially the Catholic church. Chicago's former Alderman Dorothy Tillman had been in the forefront of the reparations fight in Chicago. When she was in office, she was the lead alderman to force the city to pass a law that mandated that corporations must prove that they had no ties to the enslavement of Africans in order to do business with the city. Deadria Farmer-Paellmann, considered the Rosa Parks of the reparations litigation movement, is the lead plaintiff in a class-action suit against Fleet Boston Financial Corporation, Aetna Inc., Cox, and their predecessors and others. Later she added more companies that had been documented to have financial ties to slavery, including Bayou Lehman Brothers Holdings, Brown Brothers Harrison, American International Group, Lloyd's of London, Loews Corporation, Union Pacific, Norfolk Southern, West Point Stevens, R.J. Reynolds Tobacco Holdings, Brown and Williamson Tobacco, and Liggett Group. *The Wall Street Journal* of May 10, 2005 reported on the links between J.P. Morgan and slave ownership. That which cannot be minimized is that corporate, banking, insurance, financial companies, and others not only helped to finance the enslavement of Africans, but after the abolition of slavery continued in any number of ways to take advantage of the poor and uneducated Blacks. Michael Hudson in his book, *Merchants of Misery*, details how corporate America continued to profit from poverty and the fragile lives of poor Black people and others. Ted Nace, in his book *Gangs of America: The Rise of Corporate Powers and the Disabling of Democracy* (2003), writes about the "brutal history of The Virginia Company (1607-1624)" and names it

---

*Do not forget hundreds of years of bank and mortgage companies redlining. The Clinton Administration's three strikes and mandatory sentencing laws that removed over 100,000 Black and brown men from their communities. If, indeed we can bail out the "too big to fail banks," and Wall Street, why not the millions of Black, brown and poor people who were economically and emotionally destroyed by said banks and Wall Street?

"as the starting place for the 244-year holocaust of African slavery."

Finally, and this is crucial, our first priority is that we must support the Reparations Movement; and we must use our current resources and the supplemental allocations to create wealth as a whole within the African American community. Yes, African Americans should receive reparations for the 250 years of chattel enslavement, the 110 years of brutal disfranchisement throughout the South and other parts of the country, and for the nationwide segregation enforced through the "Black Codes" and "Jim and Jane Crow" laws. And yes, we would appreciate an apology from the President and the U.S. Congress. However for me, this is minor. What is major is for the federal government and corporations to seriously move toward corrective actions and that means investments in Black community institutions, its children, and its people.

I believe as does Robert Westley, according to his essay, "Many Billions Gone: Is it Time to Reconsider the Case for Black Reparations?" that reparations should be provided for a people since we are not enslaved individually but as a people. Professor Westley writes, "Blacks have been and are harmed as a group. That racism is a group practice: I am opposed to individual reparations as a primary policy objective. Obviously, the payment of group reparations would create the need and the opportunity for institution building that individual compensation would not." The point is that to a great extent white wealth was created as a result of the brutal enslavement of Africans, and therefore, we must understand that the national "racial wealth gap" and "wealth inequality" that exist between Blacks and whites can only be corrected by an infusion of resources for serious economic development and wealth building for the majority of Black people and not just for the faint few. I do not need reparations. Russell Simmons and Oprah Winfrey do not need reparations. I (and they), under great odds, have been able to "succeed" in America. Mr. Simmons and Ms. Winfrey, through their respective companies, have emerged as two of the wealthiest people in the world. There exists in this country a small, yet significant Black middle class who are not living paycheck-to-paycheck. These Blacks would not be the first in line for reparations. Reparations should first go to the most-needy of our people. Anything less is an insult to the millions of Africans whose lives were snatched from them as they, under the most horrible of conditions, worked from sun-up to sun-down for hundreds of years in making the United States the wealthiest nation in the world. It is payback time!

Meaningful Change

Here are a few examples of meaningful change that do work:

1. The acquisition of life-giving and life-sustaining knowledge and skill should be a priority, this country's industries should be "out or in-sourced" to Black and poor communities, rather than to China and India. I'm not against globalization but first let's make our own citizens a global work force.

2. Each house, apartment, and living space must become a mini-learning institution. I can walk into to your home and define where you are culturally and educationally. Reading, writing, and thinking critically about the important issues that confront Black people and the world need to be central to one's existence. If parents or caregivers read, generally children will read. Books and other learning materials must be a fixture in all of our lives.

3. *Children first.* From birth our children must be viewed as potential geniuses. We must accept the fact of their young brilliance and be prepared to nurture them by providing cultural, spiritual, educational, political, healthcare, and financial structures that will help in nurturing their natural gifts. Children must be loved and nurtured in a secure, motivating, clean, orderly, serious, and playful environment. All, if not most, children are born at genius level. The culture that they are born into either develops the genius in them or cuts it off by the age of six. Children need to be nurtured into a love of learning and be taught that learning is lifelong, often difficult and boring, but absolutely necessary. Boys becoming men must learn how to be good mates, husbands and fathers. They must think and act progressively toward Black women and all women.

4. Always know more about your own culture than others. Black cultural knowledge and critical thinking about oneself, people, and

the world is vital. A university education or advanced technological knowledge is imperative in today's political and economic climate. However, seldom will African American students receive an enlightened Black education at most Euro-American institutions of higher education. And sadly, this includes many Black colleges and universities. [1]

5. Black women have become the backbone of the Black community. In a world ruled by men, we are losing Black boys and men like poor people's dollars in a state lottery. We must always be in the forefront of demanding and protecting the equality of women and men; however, since not enough Black men exist, and most certainly functional and responsible Black men exist in the market place of relationahips, too many Black women continue to battle alone.

6. Over 1.5 million Black and Brown boys are incarcerated in the nation's prisons, jails, parole, and court systems. Millions more are dysfunctional and exist outside of most economic and political structures. Too many others have bought into the lies and fantasy of the Euro-American establishment. If nothing else, Hurricane Katrina, and Iraq and Afghanistan wars should have made very clear the racial divide in the nation. Black, Latino, and poor white people who fight the nation's wars must learn to work politically together. The Democrats take us for granted and the Republicans don't take us at all. We need a Black Congress. Dr. Ron Daniels of The Institute of the Black World of the 21st Century has been calling for such a formation. These times demand that we become intimately involved in

---

[1] Make yourself aware of these writers and thinkers: Chinua Achebe, Claud Anderson, Delores P. Aldridge, Marimba Ani, Molefi Kete Asante, Houston A. Baker Jr., Amiri Baraka, Lerone Bennett Jr., Herb Boyd, Carl C. Bell, Gwendolyn Brooks, Anthony T. Browder, Jacob H. Carruthers, Chinweizu, John H. Clarke, Patricia Hill Collins, Ellis Cose, George E. Curry, Angela Davis, Ossie Davis, Ruby Dee, Cheikh Anta Diop, Manthia Diawara, Errol A. Henderson, W.E.B. DuBois, Marcus Garvey, Mari Evans, Frantz Fanon, John Hope Franklin, Beverly Guy-Sheftall, Marc Lamont-Hill, Asa Hilliard, bell hooks, Fred Hord, Earl Ofari Hutchinson, Diane Turner, Brenda Greene, Regina Jennings, Maulana Karenga, Woody King Jr., Bakari Kitwana, Carol D. Lee, Audre Lorde, Sonia Sanchez, Kalamu ya Salaam, Thabiti Lewis, Mumia Abu-Jamal, Toni Morrison, Walter Mosley, Wade Noble, Ishmael Reed, Adolph Reed Jr., Paul Robeson, Barbara A. Sizemore, Keith Gilyard, Quincy Troupe, Susan Taylor, Khephra Burns, Zora Neale Hurston, Ida B. Wells, Howard Thurman, Gloria Wade-Gayles, Alice Walker, Tavis Smiley, Eugene B. Redmond, Ngugi wa Thiong'o, Ronald W. Walters, John Edgar Wideman, Michael Simanga, Lita Hooper, Raymond A. Winbush, Cornel West, Chancellor Williams, August Wilson and Carter G. Woodson, Paula Giddings, Edmund Gordon, Charles Ogletree, Derrick Bell, Vincent Harding, and Danielle Allen to name a very few writers whose work you'll be interestingly nurtured by. Once you taste the maturing words of these writers and others, you will be angry for not knowing, and at the same time, elated for finding this goldmine in our community. Nothing will stop you now.

politics at the local, state, national and international levels. This also demands that our relationship with women and girls must change radically and substantively. Equality of the sexes is much more than a word, but must be creative, enlightened, and measurable actions. We also must become conscious of, respectful and supportive of other family structures such as gay, lesbian, bisexual, and transgender communities, which we must accept as natural and necessary. Such communities must reside naturally in all current Black families with support given, especially in today's political and cultural climate.

7. The Black rich and wealthy must step up to the plate. When we look at other cultures, most certainly the Irish, Jewish and Polish, in Chicago, and Germans internationally, they have created institutions in their respective areas to aid their people that government structures miss. The Black rich among us must understand we are living in critical times and our young people need financial, cultural, and family support now. It is not enough just to share ones' wealth with ones' immediate family and extended family; we must think of national and international—or better yet, Diaspora Blacks—as family. If the Black rich and wealthy among us concentrated some of their money, time, and energy into local Black schools, helping to make the schools in their cities—in terms of quality, excellence, and resources—a place that all students would want to stand in line to get into, then we are on the right track.

8. It is not enough for us to just make sure that our biological children receive all that is needed. For those of us who understand the world we live in, we also have cultural Black children. Walter Lomax Jr, MD, during his lifetime, understood this need and acted on the national stage quietly to change this condition positively for young people. You can look at the works of Andrew Billingsley, Derrick Bell, Carol D. Lee, Barbara Ann Sizemore, Angela Davis, Paul Adams, Useni Eugene Perkins, Father Michael Pfleger, Susan Taylor, and countless others who went beyond their educational and career callings to do cultural work outside of that which they

were paid to do by their respective institutions. My call is for Black people with resources to now share those resources in terms of one's time and monies to make a loving change now. I am not interested in how many cars you own, how many houses you have, how large your yachts are, or where you do your timeshares. What I am interested in is how you reach out to help develop, save, and love young Black people.

9. In the empire there must be, by those affected, many responses to its negative reach. However, it is clear that the one act that would get the attention of current rulership is a national boycott of a major retailer or enterprise, be it banking system, credit cards, transportation (airlines), hotels, department stores, etc. A good test for young activists is to take on a national retailer like Wal-Mart or Papa John's and organize something like a national "don't buy" campaign for a designated time frame.

We must be active in creating a modernized nation-wide, progressive movement for political, economic, and cultural change. Such a national movement must be sophisticated and strategic, as the institutions we are confronting are the current billion-dollar classes that fund the right; we will be out-spent, out maneuvered, and out organized by money. The only answer to that is to organize millions of people across the nation. We have people. Also, for the most part, we have what is good and right on our side. And there is nothing more powerful in a direct-actions struggle than a fired-up grandmother or young people responding to actions and policies they consider wrong, unfair, and anti-poor people. All of us need to study "movement" literature and individuals. We must not be afraid of the awesome and complicated power of corporate systems and their unlimited resources that will be thrown at us. A key concept of movement organizing is to start in your own family: mothers, fathers, sisters, brothers, grandparents, aunts, uncles, and of course, students, wherever they can be found. We must not forget that most serious political and social change in our lifetime must involve millions of young people from all cultures, especially young Blacks and whites, and, young whites who have been able to subordinate their own white skinned privileges.

Liberating Men on the
Issues of Women

There is not one of us who should not feel pain in our hearts for the sexual oppression of young women and girls that occurs in all nations.[1] We should all be outraged. But how does one shake loose a medieval consciousness? I say a consciousness because I truly believe that it is just that basic. Yes, I am aware that violence against women is historical, psychological, and cultural on a global level, but I am also aware that change often starts in one's mind, with one person at a time.

We live in a world where patriarchal leadership in most cultures is the norm; where a man—a father, a grandfather, a brother, an uncle, or a son in a family, almost any family—rules. As a man, if you truly love the women-folk of your families, you must ask yourself several critical questions. "Do I love, care for, and respect the females of my family at the same deep level that I love, care for and respect the males of my family?" If the answer is yes, then the next question is: "Am I willing to make the same and often greater commitment to the females of my family that I have made to the males?" Then ask: "Am I willing to encourage them to reach for their dreams and to assist them, to the best of my ability, in developing their minds, bodies, and spirits, to assist them in nurturing their natural talents in a supportive family environment that is free, open, and encouraging? Am I willing to be a vocal advocate of women's equality and liberation inside the family and publicly when I am with men and boys on the job, the basketball court, or in the clubs and centers of men's entertainment and power?"

Outdated and nonfunctioning customs and traditions exist in most, if not all, cultures dominated by men. In far too many cultures, women and children are still viewed as property to be put on the table of deals that guarantee for most of them a life of suffering, pain, unhappiness, and servitude. The same must be said for the male-dominated hip-hop culture. These cultures must

---

[1] A version of this essay was published in *Tough Notes: A Healing Call For Creating Exceptional Black Men*, Third World Press, Chicago, 2002

94

be questioned and, if necessary, confronted wherever they exist. Much of this anti-women nonsense has a western biblical origin, starting with the story of Adam and Eve, with Eve tempting Adam with the forbidden fruit. Women have not recovered from this male-created story, even in 2015.

Whether the oppressive communities are religious, secular, or a combination, their outright denial of women the equal protection under the law, as well as access to the institutions of intellectual development is truly a travesty. The Black church, as a primary spiritual center and the defining institution of the Pan-African and Black Nation, must be in the forefront of redefinition and leadership in reference to Black women.

It is easy to publicly condemn the oppression of women on a grand scale, talking to the masses. However, such condemnation often falls on deaf ears unless coming from a powerful voice in government, the corporate world, religious communities, or major academic institutions. And when change is initiated, it must be at a national policy level if it is to affect local customs and traditions that have guided the lives of women and men for centuries.

Young men must understand that it is indeed within their power to make significant social and cultural advances. However, change only starts when individuals operating within families, communities, block clubs, fraternities, institutions, cultures, etc. realize that certain actions within Black culture, ethnic groups or the nation are out of step with progressive thought and development.

Each of us must first examine our own hearts, minds, and actions toward women and girls. That is, as men in all of our relationships—personal and professional—do we accord the same regard to women that we give to men? Second, we must all question the status-quo. Just because "we've always done it that way" does not make it right, correct, or good for the development of young men and women. To that end, I strongly recommend the following books to help you on the road to developing an intellectual basis for equality among the genders:

Black Authenticity: A Psychology for Liberating People of African Descent – Marcia Sutherland
Words of Fire – Beverly Guy-Sheftall (editor)
Focusing: Black Male-Female Relationships – Delores P. Aldridge
Black Women, Feminism and Liberation: Which Way? – Vivian Gordon
When and Where I Enter – Paula Giddings
Don't Play in the Sun – Marita Golden
Saving our Sons – Marita Golden

Haki R. Madhubuti

The Rooster's Egg – Patricia J. Williams
We Should Be Feminists – Chimamanda Ngozi Adichie
Ain't I a Woman: Black Women and Feminism – bell hooks
Deals with the Devil and other Reasons to Riot – Pearl Cleage
Strategies for Resolving Conflicts in Black Male-Female Relationships –
   LaFrancis Rodgers-Rose
The Black Feminist Reader – T. Denean Sharpley-Whiting
Technical Difficulties – June Jordan
Any of the works of Alice Walker, Angela Davis, Toni Morrison,
   Sonia Sanchez, and Nikki Giovanni

These books are jump-starts to open you up to a whole new world of original Black thinkers on the question of gender equality. If you are truly ready for revolutionary transformation, start here. And always remember, stopping the women stops the future.

Black boys and men, honor Black women because they have carried the weight, baggage, and criticism, and nurtured the children of our people and provided backbone to our struggle when there were no other backs or bones. Honoring Black women is not some romantic illusion about momma and grandmomma always being there to heal a cold, fix a meal, keep the church open, and provide hard-earned pennies and dollars for life-sustaining essentials. No indeed. Black women did and continue to clean their babies' behinds, breast- or bottle-feed them, educate them, and use their hands rather forcefully on their children's legs and butts when they (we) stray too far off track. Black women have been our answers, no matter the questions. They have been the period and exclamation points in our many paragraphs of life. Honor Black women because they are the "yes" and "can do" in the midst of crippling denials, mistaken visions, demeaning history in the politics and economy of illusion. Honor Black women because we understand and appreciate the sacrifices and commitments they have made to be nurses, doctors, teachers, engineers, scientists, professors, lawyers, judges, university presidents, PhDs, entrepreneurs, carpenters, policewomen, professional basketball players, tennis players, track and field athletes, artists, writers, poets, wives, mothers, and good and productive women. Honor Black women because, simply put, Black men would not be here if women had not said yes to Black families. That commitment fundamentally is the first and most lasting fact of our reality.

Violence Against Women

violence against women in a violent nation(s),
violence against women in a football nation(s),
violence against women in an offensive war nation,
> where patriarchy is manliness and the bible is law
> in the name of god, nation and man as head of home, workplace and
earth.
violence against women in a basketball nation,
violence against women in a 24/7 war on women nation where authorities
> give a wink, smile and nod to domestic and anti-abortion violence
> where 90 percent of
> police and military are men and rape kits go untested and the culture
is anti-women
where combat is hand to head in the home and on the battlefield
violence against women in a baseball nation,
violence against women in a male decision making nation and world
> where war is made for insulting a president's father and oil
> where man is made in the image of god and is a man's man.
violence against women in a world where men run it without question or opposition,
violence against women in a husbands and fathers beat wife, wives and children nation,
> where men sell women and children, trade and barter women,
violence against women in a male S & P 500 (ceo and money first nation)
violence against women where congress and the supreme court are bought
and sold in
a monied white men nation,
violence against women in its war on the LGBT* communities where lies, fab-
rication,
> money and more money talks, rules and legislates.

---

* Lesbian, Gay, Bisexual, and Transgendered communities

Haki R. Madhubuti

violence against women in the culture, workplace, bedroom, kitchen, speech,
social media, art, psychology, television, film, radio, video, classroom,
politics, literature, history, sport, courts, print media, fraternities, sororities,
churches, mosques,
temples, synagogues, families and everywhere violence is expected, accepted,
encouraged and
elevated as answer and loudly excused solution.
violence against women with fist, knives, guns, chain saws, poison,
penises, and all acts of terror waiting to be invented and thought of by
each and future generations of men.

violence against women as in "she made me do it" or in *blame the victim*
violence against women world where our greatest misgiving is our own

silence.

our own revisions.

One Hundred and More Reasons to Believe in Women's Liberation

Gwendolyn Brooks, Margaret G. Burroughs, Safisha Madhubuti, Shirley Graham DuBois, Mary McLeod Bethune, Barbara A. Sizemore, Rosa Parks, Margaret Walker Alexander, Grace Lee Boggs, Darlene Clark Hine, Betty Carter, Geneva Smitherman, Mari Evans, Lucille Clifton, Gayle Jones, Alice Walker, Elizabeth Catlett, Harriet Tubman, Johari Amini Hudson, Anita Hill, Thulani Davis, Arundhati Roy, Patricia J. Williams, Toni Morrison, Aretha Franklin, Maxine Graves, Betty Shabazz, Toni Cade Bambara, Tiamoyo Karenga, Judy Richardson, Delores P. Aldridge, Anna Julia Cooper, Sonia Sanchez, Shirikiana Aina Gerima, Beverly Guy-Sheftall, Paula J. Giddings, Johnnetta B. Cole, Diane Nash, Nina Simone, Sandra E. Gibbs, Coretta Scott King, Octavia Butler, Frances Curtis Frazier, Inez Hall, Susan L. Taylor, Cynthia Cooper, Pearl Cleage, Nikki Giovanni, Maya Angelou, Assata Shakur, Naomi Long Madgett, Audre Lorde, Wilma Rudolph, Beverly Lomax, the WNBA, Willalyn Fox, Myrlie Evers, Charshee McIntyre, Jayne Cortez, Sara Lomax, Erykah Badu, Ella Baker, Laini Mataka, Jackie Taylor, Marita Golden, Cicely Tyson, Imani Humphrey, Sweet Honey In The Rock, Val Gray Ward, Joanne Gabbin, June Jordan, Queen Mother Moore, bell hooks, Ruby Dee, Lolita Green, Gloria Joseph, Sherley Ann Williams, Shirley Chisholm, Zora Neale Hurston, Vivian V. Gordon, Abena Joan Brown, Mary Church Terrell, Barbara Ehrenreich, Estella Conwill Majozo, Andrea L. Taylor, Lisa Lee, Marge Piercy, Adrienne Rich, Bernardine Dohrn, Brenda Greene, Asha Bandele, Marie Brown, Diane Turner, Barbara Lee, Jessica Care Moore, Edwidge Danticat, Katrina Vanden Heuvel, Naomi Klein, Regina Jennings, Eleanor Traylor, Angela Jackson, Dorothy Irene Height, Joycelyn Elders, Rose Perkins, Gwendolyn Mitchell, Mary Mitchell, Regina Taylor, Frances Cress Welsing, Katherine Dunham, Angela Davis, Mariama Richards, Laini N. Madhubuti, Regina Alcantor, Janet Hutchinson-Lee, Janeen Lee, Winnie Mandela, Kimya Moyo, Lorraine Hansberry, Madam C.J. Walker, Marimba

Haki R. Madhubuti

Ani, Amina Baraka, Msiba Ann Grundy, Bessie Head, Julianne Malveaux, Jane Addams, Roxane Gay, Elizabeth Alexander, Rufaro Lawrence, Soyini Walton, Julia Hare, Aneb Gloria House, Ava DuVernay, Denise Borel Billups, Chimamanda Ngozi Adichie, Nora Brooks Blakely, Cassandra Wilson, Nicole Mitchell, Julianna Richardson, Michelle Alexander, Lita Hooper, Becky Pettit, Claudette Marie Muhammad, Nell Irvin Painter, Venus E. Evans-Winters, Yvette Jackson Moyo, Michelle Obama, Dawn Turner, Black mothers and grandmothers, and the unknown women whose waters we drink and learn from.

Are you aware of and understand the wonderment and power of these women? Do you believe that your life has been enriched as a result of their work and their presence among us? Can you walk and communicate with these women without fear? Do you believe that most women have the capacity for greatness in them? Do you believe that your mother, sister, grandmothers, aunts, female relatives, and friends have received the nurturing and education necessary to fulfill their dreams? Do the Black men that you associate with have any knowledge of these women? Do you really believe that all women should be able to fight for their dreams, enjoy equal rights, and have open doors to institutions that can assist them in achieving their potential? Are you afraid of intelligent, assertive, beautiful, athletic, culturally focused, and highly competent women? If you can answer positively to the above questions, believe in the power of women and plan to act in the affirmative toward them; go tell your mother, and add her name and the names of other significant women in your life to this list.

The White, Dark Secret

In America, Black people are no longer needed as a critical labor force. Our 40-million-plus population is not significant to the continued development of the United States with the minor exception of fighting in foreign and domestic wars (yes, we will kill our own people). We are not needed to pick cotton, vegetables or fruit (Latinos), as skilled labor (Eastern Europeans), to rebuild the nation's infrastructure, (the trade unions are still highly tribal and racist to the bone). The current population of the United States as of 2014 is about 310.1 million making it the third largest in the world far behind China and India. The white poor in the U.S. is about 10 percent of the population, which makes it in real numbers about 31 million. The Black poor is approximated to be 10.9 million, about 28 percent of the Black population. The Hispanic percentage of poor people is 25 percent, its population which roughly translates into about 10 million. The point I'm making here is that the white poor, if we look closely at their voting records in 2010 and 2014, voted against their own self-interest, casting their votes in concert with the Republican party, the Tea Party, the Libertarians, in essence, with the likes of the Koch Brothers, corporate classes, and big banks, this should tell us exactly what we need to see and hear. Black people, by and large in the economic sphere beyond consumers do not matter in the United States other than as uninformed consumers.

If we seriously look at who runs the United States in all of the determinant areas of human activity, we see white people. Or we may see a measured and manageable number of Blacks and others who think and often act white. If we survey the universities and colleges that many white and Black people graduate from such as the Ivy Leagues, the Big Ten, Pac-12, the Top Southern schools like Duke and Emery, the top state schools, the standalone independents like Chicago, Stanford, Massachusetts Institute of Technology, and several state schools like University of California-Berkeley and Los Angeles and hundreds of others you will notice that the Black students and teaching faculty have significantly receded. This should tell us something.

Deep and honest knowledge of one's culture is an absolute necessity especially as we all fight to navigate our lives in an ever-evolving and increasingly difficult world. Any people who are anchored in their own cultural imperatives: visual arts, literature, history, science, music, religion, politics, and economics, surely will walk more confidently than a people with little or negative knowledge of themselves. The harm and damage that the state does to its own people (whites) means that it is capable of doing a greater harm to others (non-whites). The collective intelligence or cultural memory of our best minds have not been passed on to the majority of our people. Mind you, I did not say, the great majority, but 50.1 percent or, to be realistic, less than half of our people have an accurate cultural and liberation knowledge base.

Critical self-knowledge, historical memory and respect for world knowledge starts with an introduction to the best that one's own culture and other cultures have to offer. Such knowledge should, more likely than not, produce a people who are about, first and foremost, the healthy replication of themselves to thereby stimulate those affected toward a level of enlightened empowerment in all areas of human activity. Remember, Black people by the mass are not going anywhere; in so many ways, we fundamentally help to build this nation and are still owed a serious debt. (See Ta-Nehisi Coates "The Case for Reparations," the *Atlantic Magazine,* June 2014 and "The Black Family in the Age of Mass Incarceration" the *Atlantic,* October 2015)

Too often we—Blacks—victimize ourselves by buying into the white analysis of Black problems. The one statement that is quoted too often is "Black on Black Crime exists fundamentally because of white on Black crime." It is indeed a problem, but it is nowhere in the universe of the daily crimes committed against Black people by white people and their many "laws and policies" which are *unknown* to most Blacks. One major example is the unreported crimes and deaths committed against Black men and women in prison. Too often others write about Black people as if they/we do not feel hurt, loved, have children, worry, get stressed and sick, over-eat, work two jobs, help children with homework, cook meals, pray, smile and laugh, play sports, and regularly do human things.

In closing, I will only add that we—those who love life and beauty, those who smile daily at the beautiful laughter of children of all cultures and understand the power of breath, family, love, sharing, and beneficial production— remain *realistic optimists.* We must practice daily among each other a defining trust as well as display unconditional love, unconditional courage, i.e. a deep willingness for organized struggle against all injustice and an unquenchable thirst for life-long learning in search of life-giving, life-affirming, and life-saving knowledge. We must be the best that our talents and abilities will allow— and be an example of the direction we need to go, especially for our youth.

Standing as an African Man:
Black Man in a Sea of Whiteness

Where do I belong and what is the price I have to pay for being where and who I am?

Study the faces of children who look like you. Walk your streets. Count the smiles and bright eyes, and make a mental note of their ages. At what age do our children cease to smile naturally, smile full-teeth, uninhibited, expecting full life? At what age will memory of lost friends, and lost relatives, deaden their eyes? Where does childhood stop in much of our community? At seven, eight? How many killings, rapes, beatings, verbal and mental abuse, hustles, get-over programs, drug infestations, drive-by-shootings/drive-by leaders must they witness before their eyes dry up for good and their only thought is, "Will I make it to the age of twenty-five?" When the life in the eyes of our children does not gleam brightly with future and hope, we cease being nurturers and become repairers of broken spirits and stolen souls. This is the state we are now in and too often it is too late.[1]

Where do I belong and what is the price I have to pay for being where and who I am?

If you don't know, you can't do.

From whom do we buy our food? From whom do we rent our apartments? From whom do we buy our clothes, furniture, cars, and life-bettering needs? On whose land do we walk, sleep, live, play, work, get high, chase women, lie, steal, produce children, and die? Why is it that over a million Black men and 100,000 Black and brown women populate the nation's prisons? Is race a factor in a land where white people control most things of value? Is race a factor in a country where young Black boys and men are dying quicker than their birth rate? When do we declare war on our own destruction? Why is it that the Blacker one is the worse it is? Who taught Black people that killing Black people is alright and sometimes honorable?

---

[1] An earlier version of this essay was published in *Claiming Earth: Race Rage Rape, Redemption—Blacks Seeking a Culture of Enlightened Empowerment*, Third World Press, Chicago, 1994.

Haki R. Madhubuti

This is Our Charge!

Study the landscape. Read the music in your hearts, Remember the beauty of mothers, sisters, and the women in our lives who talked good about us. Remember when we talked good about us. Remember when we talked good about them. Understand the importance of ideas.

This is Our Mission!

Pick up a book. Challenge the you in you. Rise above the limited expectations of people who do not like you and never will like you. Rise above the self-hatred that slowly eats your heart, mind, and spirit away. Find like-minded brothers (and sisters). Study together. Talk together. Find each other's heart. Ask the right questions. Why are we poor? Why are our children not educated? Why are our children dying at such an unbelievable rate? Why are we landless?

What does land ownership have to do with race? What does wealth have to do with race? Why do we hate being called African and Black? What does Africa mean to me, us? Why is Africa in a state of confusion and civil war? Why is there no work in our communities? What is the difference between a producer and a consumer? What do we produce that is sold and used worldwide? Whose knowledge is most valuable for the development of Black (African) people? Would I kill myself and others who look like me if I loved myself and those who look like me? From where does self-love come? Who taught me, us, self-hatred? Is self-hatred an idea? Is self-love an idea? To whose ideas do we tap dance? With whose ideas do we impress each other? Are African (Black) ideas crucial to our discourse and development? Can a Black person be multicultural if he/she does not have his/her culture first? When do we declare war on ignorance, intellectual beggar mentalities, and white world supremacy? Is race an idea? When will we use the race idea to benefit us?

Where do I belong and what is the price I have to pay for being where and who I am?

We belong among the people worldwide who look like us. We belong to a world where we produce rather than consume. We belong to a world where the measurement of Black beauty and worth is internal, cultural, and confirming. We belong where our education is not anti-us. We belong among African men who are brothers and brothers who are Africans.

#BlackLivesMatter, And!

Between hurricanes and volcanoes that encase the "Black Lives Matter" movement nothing happens unless Black lives matter. If we do not love, care, educate and protect ourselves, especially our children, the world for us literally stops. The next all-demanding steps are that Black families, Black institutions, Black communities, Black businesses and Black visions matter. As we fight the exterior, the interior must be created, supported, fortified and expanded.

Where are our great Black institutions? Where are the high achieving schools, colleges, universities, museums, medical centers, think tanks and centers of learning that great civilizations require? There are only a few left in our communities. All others, and I do mean all of them, are in deep, deep financial and organizational trouble bordering on severe breakdown, bankruptcy or irrelevancy. The critical, life giving and life saving institutional structures that feed into and sustain a people are fastly disappearing from Black communities. That which is not acknowledged nationally is that the *Negroes are back in charge*, and black lives matter movement is toady's young people's answer to the failure of current Negro leadership.

The major institutions that have survived and thrived among us are the Black churchs. And, I categorically, state without reservation that Black churches are clearly not enough. Its weakness is not found in their traditional mission of providing spiritual guidance, bonding traditions, family rituals, psychological support and a vision of Black tomorrows. They fail when they are expected to supply everything that our communities need for survival, growth and success on a local, national and world stage.

Black lives matter, just as Black families, communities, schools, colleges universities, graduate schools (law, medicine, business, engineering, humanities, science, technology, the arts, self-defense, psychology, etc.) matters. A Black mindset not only states and defines what matters, but digs deep each second, minute, hour and days of each month and years to do the necessary work that our fore parents—mothers and fathers who proceeded us or left to us to complete the tasks. The larger goal is always justice. Not only in recognizing our own suffering but that of others. Thereby erasing the fears that keep us apart rather than joining of hands to solve problems.

We have become refugees in our own land, not citizens in the country built on the backs of Black people. Today, because we are alive and questioning whether Black lives matter or not, there are also the buts? It is always the buts, the genuine, heartfelt, overworked buts. If we could just get past the buts in our individual and collective lives; maybe, just maybe, we will cease to be a marginalized and dependent people and rise to the occasion and excel in doing the possible and impossible whatever the mission may be. And I am not talking about a *movie*.

Sixteen Shots in Fifteen Seconds

These are the defining questions. What on earth have we done as Black people to deserve the horrific treatment that we have received from white people over the last three centuries? What major transgression have we—Black people, African American, people of African ancestry—committed against white people, European Americans, that has relegated the clear majority of us to a state of total dependency?

For centuries we have suffered deep injustices at the hands of those in power, white power. This white war against Black people in America has never ended. Individual white violence, organized group violence, institutional violence, commercial violence, military violence, and state sponsored violence all add up to the unceasing acts of national terrorism that have crippled and stopped most serious Black acts of liberation.

The city of Chicago represents one of the major centers of such violence against Black people. Over the last decade the city has paid out over 500 million dollars to settle police misconduct and lawsuits. On October 20, 2014, Officer Jason Van Dyke shot teenager Laquan McDonald 16 times in less than 15 seconds. A recent video revealed that most of the bullets were shots into his young body as he lay unmoving on the pavement. For over a year, the whole criminal justice system from the mayor's office, police department to the Cook County State's Attorney office attempted to suppress this information.

The video was officially released in November of 2015. Prior to that time, however, the city paid five million dollars to Laquan McDonald's family without a lawsuit, Officer Van Dyke was put on desk duty at $80,000 a year, other incriminating tapes were confiscated and erased, the mayor's office, under the guise of letting the federal investigators take the lead stopped everything locally, hoped that the murder would go away. They—Mayor Rahm Emanuel, Police Superintendent Garry McCarthy, and Cook County State's Attorney Anita Alvarez—realized that if the video was released Emanuel may not have been re-elected, because as we all know, his re-election greatly depended upon the Black community, whom he ended up betraying time and time again.

We are now in our defining hour. Why do they hate us? Why has being Black in America, first and foremost defined our reality before anything else? Charles M. Blow the columnist and author writes of the killing of 17-year-old Laquan McDonald in the *New York Times* (11/30/15). He states: "The only reason that these killings keep happening is because most of American society tacitly approves or willfully tolerates it. There is no other explanation. If America wanted this to end, it would end."

Chicago remains the most segregated city in the United States. The daily violence perpetuated externally and internally is so enormous that it too often falls on deaf ears. And any measurable social indicators Black people in Chicago and across the nation are at the bottom. A recent report from the University of Illinois at Chicago's Great City Institute confirms that young Black men in Chicago between the ages of 20-to-24 represent over 47 percent of out-of-work and out-of-school population and 44 percent in Illinois. This is compared to 20 percent of Hispanic men and 10 percent of white men in Chicago in the same age group. This was reported by Alexia Elejalde-Ruiz on the front page of *Chicago Tribune* of January 26, 2016. Take my word for it, our situation is far worse than reported.

This is why *Black Lives Matter* to us. If we do not see and love the value of our own lives, we by our silence have joined our enemies. I will state it one final time—we must have *unconditional love for Black people.* If this becomes an undeniable fact everything else will fall into place and the traitors among our own people will finally realize the treachery of their own ways. And those who rally against us will see that we are indeed, one people—Black, self-defined and ready.

Art as Answer

That which has the power to save lives, to change lives, to give birth to imagination that can power questions from unknown spaces of one's expanded brain, while unlocking the mystery of misunderstood relationships and loves, all while celebrating the highs and lows of one's undisciplined, careless, clueless, narrowly focused vision until it truly becomes a vision, thereby, humanizing all future growth of a person's production is art.

Art is harmonized voices and instruments, it is painted oils on canvas, clothing, public walls; or it is feet of young dancers and yoga bodies using the air, wind and open spaces to tell a story with each curvature of one's body or bodies; not forgetting the immense power of language artfully combined to visit the strange cultures of one's inclusiveness, now able to burst into the public's commons with metaphors and ideas of likeness, unlikeness and formality of spiritual and secular experiences—all expanded and explained on paper or screen in the unique and written original poems, fictions, literary non-fictions, plays, indigenous urban or rural stories, narrations, epics, histories, memoirs or fables that are indefinable but easily and early recognized as art.

Young Black boys and men, girls and women too—exposed early and often to the magic and discipline of art-making—can and will see another world and other possibilities. Art, in the many forms and cultural rooms of making a life, can also give a life. To be young and in the grips of creation, after all is said, done, and acknowledged, is to be in search of something self-directing that is forever thirsting for beauty, breath, and truth while fighting hourly the many temptations leading Black boys and girls towards ordinariness, sameness, and predictable failure all accompanied by the loneliness and isolation of having lived ones' life on the assembly line of anti-knowing and anti-wanting to know.

Art opens the avenues of the unasked questions and denied gifts and fuels life's energies in ones' ability to say yes to tomorrow and yesterday. We can be saved and elevated by the unique beauty of a child's—any child's smile— running toward full laughter having viewed, read, experienced, listened to, showed and located something wonderful and at peace with itself, Art. Art works and illuminates.

More Powerful than God?

More powerful than Christianity, Islam, Judaism,
    Hinduism, Buddhism, Sikhism, Jainism and love.

More powerful than Shintuism, Ancestor Veneration,
    Evolutionism, decency, Creationism, Monotheism,
    Freedom, Atheism, Philosophy, Science and fear.

More powerful than Spirituality, Sociology, Marxism,
    Secularism, Zionism, Nationalism, Climate change,
    Democracy, Humanism, and the lives of children.

More powerful than Confucianism, morality, Communism,
    logic, Yoruba and Zulu beliefs, The Commons,
    Black Theology, Native American-First Nations People's beliefs,
    Egyptology, psychology, joy and truth.

More powerful than peace, prayers and all of the United States'
    cultural, political, financial systems,
    and reigns as *the God* of cowardly politicans,
    without a close second and *untouchable* is:

The National Rifle Association

Remember

The lifelong acquisition of knowledge is essential and first love
We must develop young people who understand nuance, quality growth
and are skilled at analysis in our ever changing
and complex world, ways, wills and whys
we must erase the fear of learning—thereby embracing
the process of questioning and seeking answers that
allow and encourage sound music and maturation at every
level of human creation, this fundamentally requires
deep thinking, the love of studying, effective altrism,
social intelligence and an unquenchable desire to know the art of healing.
This must lead to:
correct thoughts
good thoughts
exceptional thoughts
protective thoughts
preventive thoughts
questioning thoughts
just thoughts
right thoughts
solution and wisdom thoughts
a whole people thinking and acting for themselves,
in their own and the world's best interest forever
ripening.

The Four Unconditionals

Clearly, all people and especially formerly enslaved Black people, *do what we've been taught to do*, whether such instruction is formal, informal, at the point of a gun, at the end of a whip–lash, in the dungeons of the nation's prisons, its classrooms of mis-education and anti-self or as sugar in all of its capitalist disguises. This speaks volumes to our current condition.

Our predicament, this national state of affairs that Black people struggle with each day, is man-made. The international philosophy of white national-ism, constructed and practiced as white supremacy and white skin privilege, are the white power trains driving this world view, this culture. To this end, all 86,000 black churches must again become *liberated zones* for self-definition, self-defense, quality education, economic development, political understand-ing and enrichment, family and extended family inclusiveness, and spiritual enlightenment that is not anti-self or based upon a fiction that is realized in some distant future and some other *world*. The time is *now* for the four uncon-ditionals:

1. Unconditional Love – for self, one's family, one's people and *all* children. Deep caring for the environment, the planet and justice. An allegiance to all that is good, right, just and correct – preserved with integrity and a morality encased in life-giving and life-saving vision, health, wellness, and peace.

2. Unconditional Courage – to always question authority, injustice, greed, dishonesty and corruption. To struggle against the accepted grain of copy corporate culture. To be creative, innovative and encourage artists and their art, to fight destructive weather of ill gotten influence, wealth, power, and unquenchable greed.

3. Unconditional Search – for knowledge, hard facts, enlightenment, hidden answers, truth within the truth, moral questions within the deadly noise of corporate consumerism of a buy and sell culture. To put scholars and scholarship and academic achievement at the center

of our continued quest for liberation. To teach and believe that learn-ing and daily studying are the heartbeats of all enlightened and inde-pendent people. We must understand the absolute necessity for strong and outstanding schools, colleges and universities, that they are essen-tial to our core existence in building a knowledge based culture and civilization.

4. Unconditional Will – to appreciate and be aware of the power of *one*, creative individualism. Comprehend the necessity of organizations in the ongoing struggles for political, social and economic justice. Authenticity, fairness, quality, merit and excellence should be central to where we want to be. Foundational to all existence is the quality and place of *work*, from the collecting of garbage from urban streets, the harvesting of fruits, vegetables, and the production of food on rural family farms to the building of cities, mass transportation systems, healthy living spaces, medical centers, businesses, institutions, sports centers, libraries, art, music, dance, theaters, and relaxation venues. We need all of this and much more with the critical task of creating psychologically and physically whole-peoples. We must never doubt the power or capacity of the human spirit in each person to be creative and to do good. This understanding should be at the apex of our thinking, work, actions and memory in actively resisting the Americanization and westernization of the world.

Afterword

This is my response to an unevenly shared planet, where one fights daily for the right to be recognized as a full person, viewed in the light of real possibilities in an impossible world. Too few Black people have been exposed to or conceptualized the beauty and responsibility of private thought, healing thought, or meditative thought. We, as most people, have not learned the benefits of quiet contemplation or of thinking beyond our daily fight for survival. This is a serious debilitating condition.

This is why reading, thinking, studying, debating, and listening and dialogue are all critical to whole-person growth. This is also why organized struggle against anti-human activities is absolutely necessary for healing growth. It is crucial to include the qualitative understanding of the life-affirming aspects of one's culture, as it is equally important to understand the cultures of others—why Germans are different from the French, Nigerians from South Africans, Jews from Arabs, Japanese from Chinese, and so on and so on. Young people need to be taught these truths early as they learn the fundamental connections to their own heritage.

What I am suggesting in these few closing paragraphs is that the average person from all cultures—Black or white, Native American or Asian American, or others do not contribute adequate time for thinking, reading, study, or acts of rejuvenation, growth, and knowledge acquisition as life-affirming acts. What about stillness and quite time, without media—social or otherwise? We must be moral agents of our own tomorrows that lead us toward bright health for ourselves and our children. Fundamentally, this requires a knowledge-base derived from cultural wisdom passed down from one's elders and others, yet, we must be realistic optimists about life and its promises. No one is giving us anything—history teaches that, and the one percent white ruler-ship confirms it.

All people regardless of current circumstances have unique possibilities in the United States that do not exist elsewhere. We—Black folks, African Americans, people of African ancestry—have thousands of years of history, bonding traditions, civilization building, scholarship, art, politics, and all that is necessary in creating and sustaining a whole people; we just need to effectively pull from our traditions as well as others and organize for that which is good, just, correct, and right as defined and practiced by a liberating culture.

Most of us do not have material wealth—which is critical and needed—however, we do have wisdom-wealth. We just have to search for it, and upon finding, use it, and share it with others in building political and economic wealth. And, in doing so, walk daily among green vegetation, mainly trees, drink plenty of clean water, move toward a plant-based diet, and exercise. Continue to question injustices and fortify yourself to fight for social, political, and economic justice as a lifelong battle. Take time to love yourself and family as you seek mental clarity, liberating light, and material security. Gather in community, listen to the heartbeats of our young, smile, and give them hope and more than they need to develop. Go to war for your own mind, create and engage a working and creative brain. Always promote wellness, deep breathing, and healthy possibilities. Remember, we must recapture a healthy memory. No long-term tomorrows can exist without a people willing to forsake the quick-fix culture. We need quiet, deep illumination travelling toward a vision that includes: (1) our children, (2) the best minds of all generations, (3) a sharing philosophy of life, (4) a knowledge based culture that leaves few behind, (5) erase fear factor as an argument for war, (6) recalibrated money, its many negative uses and cease praising billionaires and millionaires as examples for all, and (7) free education from preschool to graduate school. The real hope for the United States and others rests almost entirely on the minds and actions of the young of all cultures. Support #BlackLivesMatter and all organized efforts to save, improve, and advance Black life.

Final words: we are up against the empire, and the empire does not have a soul or a conscious; thereby, I agree with Arundhati Roy from her book, *War Talk*:

> Our strategy should be not only to confront Empire, but to lay siege to it. To deprive it of oxygen. To shame it. To mock it. With our art, our music, our literature, our stubbornness, our joy, our brilliance, our sheer relentlessness—and our ability to tell our own stories. Stories that are different from the ones we're brainwashed to believe.
>
> The corporate revolution will collapse if we refuse to buy what they are selling—their ideas, their version of history, their wars, their weapons, their notion of inevitability.
>
> Remember this: We be many and they be few. They need us more than we need them.

A Note on the Bibliography

I started to seriously think about empire after reading W.E.B. DuBois's *The World and Africa* in 1962 while serving in the United States Army. That year I also began volunteering at the first Black museum in the country, which was then named The Ebony Museum of Negro History (later renamed The DuSable Museum of African American History). The military helped to instill in me a discipline about life and its many challenges that remains with me and drives me in my reading, travels, and work. My volunteer work at the museum and day-to-day association with its founders helped me to understand the importance of history, memory, and building Black institutions.

Having taught in the academy for over 43 years, I've learned the critical importance of structured and random lifelong reading, studying, inquiry, conversation, and debate. I have acquired an enormous respect for language and its many uses, both positive and negative. I am primarily a poet but realized early in my writing career that writing prose in the form of the essay is absolutely necessary and required in enlarging one's readers. In all of my prose books there are extensive bibliographies, primarily because many of my ideas are built upon the thinking, research, and published works of others.

This bibliography represents a lifetime of reading, study, travel, and organized struggle, and is still very much incomplete. Very seldom do we take into account the vastness of this nation, the bigness of this country, blessed with prairies, mountains, great lakes, farms that are family-based and corporate-based, state and federal parks and lands protected for our youth by the government. This vast land bordered by two oceans on the east and west and independent nations at the north and south who do not threaten us very seldom enters the conversation of ordinary people. Here is the tip of the iceberg of my reading for this book and in no way is conclusive, authoritative, or complete.

Bibliography

Abramoff, Jack. *Capital Punishment: The Hard Truth About Washington Corruption From America's Most Notorious Lobbyists.* Washington, D.C.: WND Books, 2011.

Abu-Jamal, Mumia, and Marc Lamont-Hill. *The Classroom and the Cell: Conversations on Black Life in America.* Chicago: Third World Press, 2012.

Acemoglu, Daron, and James A. Robinson. *Why Nations Fail: The Origins of Power, Prosperity, and Poverty.* New York: Crown Publishing Group, 2012.

Achebe, Chinua. *The Education of a British-Protected Child: Essays.* New York: Alfred A. Knopf, 2009.

Ahamed, Liaquat. *Lords of Finance: The Bankers Who Broke the World.* New York: The Penguin Press, 2009.

Ahmad, Eqbal. *Confronting Empire.* Cambridge, MA: South End Press, 2000.

Alexander, Michelle. *The New Jim Crow: Mass Incarceration in the Age of Colorblindness.* New York: The New Press, 2011.

Allen, Theodore W. *The Invention of the White Race: Racial Oppression and Social Control,* Vol 1. 2nd ed. New York: Verso, 2012.

Alterman, Eric. *What Liberal Media?: The Truth About BIAS and the News.* New York: Basic Books, 2003.

Anderson, Claud. *Dirty Little Secrets About Black History, Its Heroes, and Other Troublemakers.* Bethsda, MD: PowerNomics Corporation of America, Inc., 1997.

——. *PowerNomics: The National Plan to Empower Black America.* Bethsda, MD: PowerNomics Corporation of America, Inc., 2001.

Arvedlund, Erin. *Too Good to Be True: The Rise and Fall of Bernie Madoff.* New York: Portfolio, 2009.

116

Asante, Molefi Kete. *Erasing Racism: The Survival of the American Nation.* New York: Prometheus Books, 2003.

Asante. *The Afrocentric Idea.* Philadelphia: Temple University Press, 1998.

Asim, Jabari. *The N Word: Who Can Say It, Who Shouldn't, and Why.* Boston: Houghton Mifflin Harcourt, 2007.

Atlas, James, ed. *How They See Us: Meditations on America.* New York: Atlas & Co., 2010.

Ayers, Bill, and Bernadine Dohrn. *Race Course Against White Supremacy.* Chicago: Third World Press, 2009.

Ayers, Bill. *Public Enemy: Confessions of an American Dissident.* Boston: Beacon Press, 2013.

Bacevich, Andrew J. *The Limits of Power: The End of American Exceptionalism.* New York: Metropolitan Books, 2008.

——. *Washington Rules: America's Path to Permanent War.* New York: Metropolitan Books, 2010.

Baker, Houston A. *Betrayal: How Black Intellectuals Have Abandoned the Ideals of the Civil Rights Era.* New York: Columbia University Press, 2008.

Baldwin, James. *The Cross of Redemption: Uncollected Writings.* Ed. Randall Kenan. New York: Pantheon, 2010.

——. *The Price of the Ticket: Collected Nonfiction 1948-1985.* New York: St. Martin's Press, 1985.

——. *James Baldwin: Collected Essays.* Ed. Toni Morrison. New York: The Library of America, 1998.

Baldwin, James. *The Evidence of Things Not Seen.* New York: Henry Holt and Company, 1995.

Bandele, Asha. *Something Like Beautiful: One Single Mother's Story.* New York: Harper Collins, 2009.

Banks, Russell. *Dreaming Up America.* New York: Seven Stories Press, 2009.

Bibliography

Baptist, Edward E. *The Half Has Never Been Told: Slavery and the Making of American Capitalism.* New York: Basic Books, 2014.

Baraka, Amiri. *Razor: Revolutionary Art for Cultural Revolution.* Chicago: Third World Press, 2012.

Barber, Benjamin R. *Fear's Empire: War, Terrorism, and Democracy.* New York: W. W. Norton & Company, 2003.

Beinart, Peter. *The Crisis of Zionism.* New York: Picador, 2013.

Bell, Carl C. *The Sanity of Survival: Reflections on Community Mental Health and Wellness.* Chicago: Third World Press, 2004.

Bell Jr., Derrick A. *Afrolantica Legacies* Third World Press, 1998

——. *Ethical Covenants: Brown v. Board of Education and the Unfulfilled Hopes for Racial Reform,* Oxford University Press, 2004

Bender, Thomas. *A Nation Among Nations: America's Place in World History.* New York: Hill & Wang, 2006.

Bennett, Lerone. *Before the Mayflower: A History of Black America.* 6th ed. Chicago: Johnson Publishing Company, 1992.

——. *Forced into Glory: Abraham Lincoln's White Dream.* Chicago: Johnson Publishing Company, 2000.

Berger, Maurice. *White Lies: Race and the Myths of Whiteness.* New York: Farrar, Straus and Giroux, 1999.

Berrigan, Daniel. *America Is Hard to Find: Notes from the Underground and Letters from Danbury Prison.* New York: Doubleday, 1972.

Berry, Wendell. *The Hidden Wound.* San Francisco: North Point Press, 1989.

Birnbaum, Jeffrey H. *The Lobbyists: How Influence Peddlers Get Their Way in Washington.* New York: Times Books, 1992.

Black, William K. *The Best Way to Rob a Bank Is to Own One: How Corporate Executives and Politicians Looted the S&L Industry.* Austin: University of Texas Press, 2005.

Bloom, Joshua, and Waldo E. Martin, Jr. *Black Against the Empire: The History and Politics of the Black Panther Party.* Berkeley: University of California Press, 2013.

Blow, Charles M. *Fire Shut Up in My Bones: A Memoir*. Boston: Houghton Mifflin Harcourt, 2014.

Blumenthal, Max. *Goliath: Life and Loathing in Greater Israel*. New York: Nation Books, 2013.

Bly, Robert. *Iron John: A Book About Men*. Reading, MA: Addison-Wesley Publishing Company, Inc., 1990.

Bogle, John C. *Enough: True Measures of Money, Business, and Life*. Hoboken, NJ: John Wiley & Sons, Inc., 2009.

Bonifaz, John C. *Warrior-King: The Case for Impeaching George W. Bush*. New York: Nation Books, 2003.

Bouza, Tony. *The Decline and Fall of the American Empire: Corruption, Decadence, and the American Dream*. New York: Plenum Press, 1996.

Boyd, Herb. *Baldwin's Harlem: A Biography of James Baldwin*. New York: Atria Books, 2008.

Boyd, Herb, and Ilyasah Al-Shabazz, eds. *The Diary of Malcolm X: El-Hajj Malik El-Shabazz, 1964*. Chicago: Third World Press, 2013.

Boyd, Herb, Ron Daniels, Maulana Karenga, and Haki Madhubuti, eds. *By Any Means Necessary: Malcolm X: Real, Not Reinvented: Critical Conversations on Manning Marable's Biography of Malcolm X*. Chicago: Third World Press, 2012.

Brembeck, Howard S. *In Search of the Fourth Freedom*. 2nd ed. Notre Dame: University of Notre Dame Press, 1998.

Brock, David. *Blinded by the Right: The Conscience of an Ex-Conservative*. New York: Crown Publishing Group, 2002.

——. *The Republican Noise Machine: Right-Wing Media and How It Corrupts Democracy*. New York: Crown Publishing Group, 2004.

Brockman, John, ed. *This Idea Must Die: Scientific Theories that Are Blocking Progress*. New York: Harper Perennial, 2015.

Brodkin, Karen. *How the Jews Became White Folks & What That Says About Race in America*. New Brunswick, NJ: Rutgers University Press, 1998.

Bibliography

Brooks, Gwendolyn. *Primer for Blacks.* Chicago: Third World Press, 1991.

——. *Blacks.* Chicago: Third World Press, 1991.

Brzezinski, Zbigniew, and Brent Scowcroft. *America and the World: Conversations on the Future of American Foreign Policy.* New York: Basic Books, 2008.

Buchanan, Patrick J. *Suicide of a Superpower: Will America Survive to 2025?* New York: Thomas Dunne Books, 2011.

Buck-Morss, Susan. *Thinking Past Terror: Islamism and Critical Theory on the Left.* New York: Verso, 2006.

Bugliosi, Vincent. *The Betrayal of America: How the Supreme Court Undermined the Constitution and Chose our President.* New York: Nation Books, 2001.

——. *The Prosecution of George W. Bush for Murder.* Cambridge, MA.: Vanguard Press, 2008.

Burrell, Tom. *Brainwashed: Challenging the Myth of Black Inferiority.* 5th ed. New York: Smiley Books, 2010.

Butler, Smedley D. *War Is A Racket.* Los Angeles: Feral House, 1939, 2003.

Cahill, Kevin with Rob McMahon. *Who Owns The World.* New York: Grand Central Publishing, 2010.

Carroll, James. *House of War: The Pentagon and the Disastrous Rise of American Power.* Boston: Houghton Mifflin Harcourt, 2006.

Carruthers, Jacob H. *Intellectual Warfare.* Chicago: Third World Press, 1999.

Carter, Jimmy. *Palestine: Peace Not Apartheid.* New York: Simon & Schuster, 2006.

Chafetz, Gary S. *The Perfect Villain: John McCain and the Demonization of Lobbyist Jack Abramoff.* Groton, MA.: Martin and Lawrence Press, 2008.

Chayes, Sarah. *Thieves of State: Why Corruption Threatens Global Security.* New York: W. W. Norton & Company, 2015.

Chideya, Farai. *The Color of Our Future: Race in the 21st Century.* New York: William Morrow, 1999.

Chinni, Dante, and James Gimpel. *Our Patchwork Nation: The Surprising Truth About the "Real" America.* New York: Gotham Books, 2010.

Chinweizu. *The West and the Rest of Us: White Predators, Black Slavers, and the African Elite.* New York: Vintage Books, 1975.

Chomsky, Noam. *9-11: Was There an Alternative?* New York: Seven Stories Press, 2011.

—. *Hopes and Prospects.* New York: Hamish Hamilton, 2010.

—. *Interventions.* New York: Hamish Hamilton, 2007.

—. *Occupy: Reflections on Class War, Rebellion, and Solidarity.* 2nd ed. Westfield, NJ: Zuccotti Park Press, 2013.

—. *Power Systems: Conversations with David Barsamian on Global Democratic Uprisings and the New Challenges to U.S. Empire.* London: Hamish Hamilton, 2013.

—. *Because We So.* San Franciso: City Lights Books, 2015.

—. *What Kind of Creatures Are We?* New York: Columbia University Press, 2016.

Chomsky, Noam, and Ilan Pappé. *On Palestine.* Chicago: Haymarket Books, 2015

Chorover, Stephan L. *From Genesis to Genocide: The Meaning of Human Nature and the Power of Behavior Control.* Cambridge, MA: The MIT Press, 1979.

Chua, Amy. *Day of Empire: How Hyperpowers Rise to Global Dominance—and Why They Fall.* New York: Anchor Books, 2009.

Churchill, Ward. *A Little Matter of Genocide: Holocaust and Denial in the Present Americas 1492 to the Present.* San Francisco: City Books, 1997.

—. *Kill the Indian, Save the Man: The Genocidal Impact of American Indian Residential Schools.* San Francisco: City Light Books, 2004.

Clarke, John Henrik. *Notes for an African World Revolution: Africans at the Crossroads.* Trenton, NJ: African World Press, Inc., 1991.

—. *Who Betrayed the African World Revolution? and Other Speeches.* Chicago: Third World Press, 1994.

Bibliography

Clarke, Peter. *The Last Thousand Days of the British Empire: Churchill, Roosevelt, and the Birth of the Pax Americana.* New York: Bloomsbury Press, 2008.

Clements, Jeffrey D. *Corporations Are Not People: Why They Have More Rights Than You Do and What You Can Do About It.* San Francisco: Berrett-Koehler Publishers, Inc., 2012.

Coates, Ta-Nehisi. *Between The World and Me.* New York; Spiegel & Gray, 2015.

Cobb, Charles E. *This Non-Violent Stuff'll Get You Killed.* New York: Basic Books, 2014.

Cockburn, Alexander. *A Colossal Wreck: A Road Trip Through Political Scandal, Corruption, and American Culture.* New York: Verso, 2014.

Cockburn, Alexander, and Jeffrey St. Clair. *Whiteout: The CIA, Drugs, and the Press.* New York: Verso, 1998.

Coetzee, J. M. *Diary of a Bad Year.* Melbourne: Text Publishing, 2012.

Cole, Ellis. *The Envy of the World: On Being A Black Man in America.* New York: Washington Square Press, 2002.

Collins, Chuck. *99 to 1: How Wealth Inequality Is Wrecking the World and What We Can Do About It.* San Francisco: Berrett-Koehler Publishers, Inc., 2012.

Collins, Chuck, and Felice Yeskel. *Economic Apartheid in America: A Primer on Economic Inequality & Insecurity.* New York: The New Press, 2005.

Conway, Ed. *The Summit: Bretton Woods, 1944: JM Keynes and the Reshaping of the Global Economy.* New York: Pegasus Books, 2015.

Cooper, Frederick. *Africa in the World: Capitalism, Empire, Nation-State.* Cambridge, MA: Harvard University Press, 2014.

Cowan, Paul. *The Tribes of America: Journalistic Discoveries of Our People and Their Cultures.* New York: Doubleday, 1979.

Cramer, Richard Ben. *How Israel Lost: The Four Questions.* New York: Simon & Schuster, 2004.

Cruse, Harold. *Crisis of the Negro Intellectual.* New York: Morrow, 1967.

Daniels, Cora. *Ghetto Nation: A Journey into the Land of Bling and the Home of the Shameless.* New York: Doubleday, 2007.

Danticat, Edwidge. *Create Dangerously: The Immigration Artist at Work.* Princeton: Princeton University Press, 2010

Darwish, Mahmoud, and Ibrahim Muhawi, trans. *Memory for Forgetfulness: August, Beirut, 1982.* Berkeley: University of California Press, 1995.

Davis, Angela Y. *Freedom Is A Constant Struggle.* Chicago: Haymarket Books, 2016.

Davis, Kenneth C. *A Nation Rising: Untold Tales of Flawed Founders, Fallen Heroes, and Forgotten Fighters from America's Hidden History.* New York: HarperCollins Publishers, 2010.

Davis, Mike. *Planet of Slums.* New York: Verso, 2007.

DeGruy, Joy. *Post Traumatic Slave Syndrome: America's Legacy of Enduring Injury and Healing.* Portland: Joy DeGruy Publications Inc., 2005

Delacoste Frédérique, and Priscilla Alexander, eds. *Sex Work: Writings by Women in the Sex Industry.* 2nd ed. San Francisco: Cleis Press, 1998.

Delgado, Richard, and Jean Stefancic, eds. *The Derrick Bell Reader.* New York: New York University Press, 2005.

Derber, Charles. *Regime Change Begins at Home: Freeing America from Corporate Rule.* San Francisco, Berret-Koehler Publishers, Inc., 2004.

Dezell, Maureen. *Irish America Coming Into Clover: The Evolution of a People and a Culture.* New York: Doubleday, 2001.

Diaz, Tom, *Making A Killing. The Business of Guns in America.* New York:T6 New Press, 1999.

Douthat, Ross. *Bad Religion: How We Became a Nation of Heretics.* New York: The Free Press, 2012.

Dower, John N. *Culture of War: Pearl Harbor/Hiroshima/9-11/Iraq.* New York: W. W. Norton & Company/The New Press, 2010.

Draper, Robert. *Do Not Ask What Good We Do: Inside the U.S. House of Representatives.* New York: Free Press, 2012.

DuBois, W. E. B. *The Black Reconstruction: An Essay Toward a History of the Part Which Black Folk Played in the Attempt to Reconstruct Democracy in America, 1860-1880.* New York: Russell & Russell, 1935.

Bibliography

——. *The World and Africa: An Inquiry into the Part Which Africa Has Played in World History*. New York: The Viking Press, 1947.

Duneier, Mitchell. *Slim's Table: Race, Respectability, and Masculinity*. Chicago: The University of Chicago Press, 1992.

Dyson, Michael Eric. *Come Hell or High Water: Hurricane Katrina and the Color of Disaster*. New York: Basic Civitas Books, 2005.

——. *I May Not Get There With You: The True Martin Luther King Jr.* New York: The Free Press, 2000.

——. *Race Rules: Navigating the Color Line*. Reading, MA: Addison-Wesley Publishing Company, Inc., 1996.

Ehrenreich, Barbara. *Nickel and Dimed: On (Not) Getting By in America*. New York: Metropolitan Books, 2001.

——. *This Land is Their Land: Reports from a Divided Nation*. New York: Metropolitan Books, 2008.

Eisler, Riane. *The Real Wealth of Nations: Creating a Caring Economics*. San Francisco: Berrett-Koehler Publishers, Inc., 2007.

Ellerbe, Helen. *The Dark Side of Christian History*. Windermere, FL: Morningstar and Lark, 1995.

Elliott, Paul. *Brotherhoods of Fear: A History of Violent Organizations*. London: Blandford Press, 1998.

Ellison, Keith. *My Country 'Tis of Thee: My Faith, My Family, Our Future*. New York: Gallery Books/Karen Hunter Publishing, 2014.

Ellwood, Wayne. *The No-Nonsense Guide to Globalization*. 2nd ed. Oxford: New Internationalist, 2006.

Emmott, Stephen. *Ten Billion*. New York: Vintage Books, 2013.

Entman, Robert M., and Andrew Rojecki. *The Black Image In the White Mind: Media and Race in America*. Chicago: The University of Chicago Press, 2001.

Epping, Randy Charles. *A Beginner's Guide to the World Economy: Eighty-One Basic Economic Concepts That Will Change the Way You See the World.* 3rd ed. New York: Vintage Books, 2001.

Evans, Mari. *Clarity as Concept.* Chicago: Third World Press, 2006.

Evans-Winter, and Magaela C. Bethune, eds. *(Re) Teaching Trayvon: Education for Racial Justice and Human Freedom.* Rotterdam: Sense Publishers, 2014.

Faber, Eli. *Jews, Slaves and the Slave Trade: Setting the Record Straight.* New York: New York University Press, 1998.

Falk, Richard. *Palestine: The Legitimacy of Hope.* Charlottesville: Just Word Books, 2014

Fallows, James. *Breaking the News: How the Media Undermine American Democracy.* New York: Pantheon Books, 2006.

Faludi, Susan. *The Terror Dream: Fear and Fantasy in Post-9/11 America.* New York: Metropolitan Books, 2007.

Fanon, Frantz. *The Wretched of the Earth.* New York: Grove Weidenfeld, 1963.

Farmer, Paul. *Pathologies of Power: Health, Human Rights, and the New War on the Poor.* Berkeley: University of California Press, 2003.

Feagin, Joe R. *Racist America: Roots, Current Realities, and Future Reparations.* New York: Routledge, 2000.

Feagin, Joe R., Hernån Vera, and Pinar Batur. *White Racism.* 2nd ed. New York: Routledge, 2001.

Feldman, Jeffrey. *Outright Barbarous: How The Violent Language of The Right Poisons American Democracy* Brooklyn: IG Publishing, 2008.

Feldman, Keith P. *A Shadow over Palestine: The Imperial Life of Race in America.* Minneapolis: University of Minnesota Press, 2015.

Ferguson, Charles H. *No End In Sight: Iraq's Descent into Chaos.* New York: Public Affairs, 2008.

Finkelstein, Norman G. *The Holocaust Industry: Reflections on the Exploitation of Jewish Suffering.* New York: Verso, 2000.

Bibliography

Firestein, Stuart. *Ignorance: How It Drives Science*. New York: Oxford University Press, 2012.

Fishman, Charles. *The Wal-Mart Effect: How the World's Most Powerful Company Really Works—and How It's Transforming the American Economy*. New York: The Penguin Press, 2006.

Forman, Seth. *Blacks in The Jewish Mind: A Crisis of Liberalism*. New York; New York University Press, 1998.

Foner, Eric. *Who Owns History?: Rethinking the Past in a Changing World*. New York: Hill & Wang, 2002.

Fox, Loren. *Enron: The Rise and Fall*. Hoboken, NJ: John Wiley & Sons, Inc., 2003.

Frank, Thomas. *The Wrecking Crew: How Conservatives Rule*. New York: Metropolitan Books, 2008.

—. *What's the Matter With Kansas?: How Conservatives Won the Heart of America*. New York: Metropolitan Books, 2004.

Freeland, Chrystia. *Plutocrats: The Rise of the New Global Super-Rich and the Fall of Everyone Else*. New York: The Penguin Press, 2012.

Freire, Paulo. *Pedagogy of the Oppressed*. New York: The Continuum Publishing Company, 2000.

Friedman, Thomas L., and Michael Mandelbaum. *That Used to Be Us: How America Fell Behind in the World It Invented and How We Can Come Back*. New York: Farrar, Straus and Giroux, 2011.

Fuller, Jack. *What Is Happening to News: The Information Explosion and the Crisis in Journalism*. Chicago: The University of Chicago Press, 2010.

Galbraith, Peter W. *The End of Iraq: How American Incompetence Created a War Without End*. New York: Simon & Schuster, 2006.

Garey, Diane. *Defending Everybody: A History of the American Civil Liberties Union*. New York: TV Books, 1998.

Genovese-Fox, Elizabeth, and Eugene D. Genovese. *The Mind of the Master Class: History and Faith in the Southern Slaveholder's Worldview*. Cambridge, MA: Cambridge University Press, 2005.

Giddings, Paula J. *Ida: A Sword Among Lions: Ida B. Wells and the Campaign Against Lynching.* New York: Amistad, 2009.

Ginzburg, Ralph. *100 Years of Lynchings: A Shocking Documentary of Race Violence in America.* New York: Lancer Books, 1962.

Giovanni, Nikki. *Chasing Utopia: A Hybrid.* New York: William Morrow and Company, 2013

Gitlin, Todd. *The Intellectuals and the Flag.* New York: Columbia University Press, 2006.

Glantz, Aaron. *How America Lost Iraq.* New York: Jeremy P. Tarcher/Penguin, 2005.

Gold, Dore. *Hatred's Kingdom: How Saudi Arabia Supports the New Global Terrorism.* Washington, D.C.: Regnery Publishing, Inc., 2003.

Goldberg, J. J. *Jewish Power: Inside the American Jewish Establishment.* Reading, MA: Addison-Wesley Publishing Company, Inc., 1996.

Golden, Marita. *Don't Play in the Sun: One Woman's Journey Through the Color Complex.* New York: Doubleday, 2004.

—. *Saving Our Sons: Raising Black Children in a Turbulent World.* New York: Anchor Books, 1995.

Goodman, Amy, and David Goodman. *Standing Up to the Madness: Ordinary Heroes in Extraordinary Times.* New York: Hyperion, 2008.

—. *The Exception to the Rulers: Exposing Oily Politicians, War Profiteers, and the Media that Love Them.* New York: Hyperion, 2004.

—. *Static: Government Liars, Media Cheerleaders, and the People Who Fight Back.* New York: Hyperion, 2006.

Goodman, Amy, and Denis Moynihan, ed. *Breaking the Sound Barrier.* Chicago: Haymarket Books, 2009.

Goodman, Marc. *Future Crimes.* New York: Doubleday, 2015

Gordon, John Steele. *An Empire of Wealth: The Epic History of American Economic Power.* New York: Harper Perennial, 2004.

Bibliography

Grandin, Greg. *The Empire of Necessity: Slavery, Freedom, and Deception in the New World.* New York: Metropolitan Books, 2014.

Greenwald, Glenn. *Great American Hypocrites: Toppling the Big Myths of Republican Politics.* New York: Crown Publishing Group, 2008.

——. *No Place to Hide: Edward Snowden, The NSA, and the U.S. Surveillance State.* New York: Metropolitan Books, 2014.

Greer, John Michael. *Decline and Fall: The End of Empire and the Future of Democracy in 21st Century America.* Canada: New Society Publishers, 2014.

Gross, Ariela. *What Blood Won't Tell: A History of Race on Trial in America.* Cambridge, MA: Harvard University Press, 2008.

Grunwald, Michael. *The New Deal: The Hidden Story of Change in the Obama Era.* New York: Simon & Schuster, 2012.

Hacker, Andrew. *Two Nations: Black and White, Separate, Hostile, Unequal.* New York: Ballantine Books, 1995.

Hacker, Jacob S. and Paul Pierson. *Winner Take All Politics: How Washington Made the Rich Richer and Turned Its Back on the Middle Class.* New York: Simon & Schuster Paperbacks, 2011.

Hagedorn, Ann. *The Invisible Soldiers: How America Outsourced Our Security.* New York: Simon & Schuster, 2014.

Haley, Alex. *The Autobiography of Malcolm X.* New York: Ballantine Books, 1999.

Hamill, Pete. *News Is a Verb: Journalism at the End of the Twentieth Century.* New York: Ballantine Books, 1998.

Hanson, Victor Davis. *Carnage and Culture: Landmark Battles in the Rise of Western Power.* New York: Doubleday, 2001.

Harding, Vincent. *Hope and History: Why We Must Share the Story of the Movement.* New York: Orbis Books, 1990.

Hardt, Michael, and Antonio Negri. *Empire.* 10th ed. Cambridge, MA.: Harvard University Press, 2001.

——. *Multitude: War and Democracy in the Age of Empire.* New York: The Penguin Press, 2004.

Harford, Tim. *The Undercover Economist.* New York: Random House, 2007.

Harper, Hill. *Letters to a Young Brother: MANifest Your Destiny.* New York: Gotham Books, 2006.

Harris, Fredrick C. *The Price of the Ticket: Barack Obama and the Rise and Decline of Black Politics.* New York: Oxford University Press, 2012.

Harris, Marvin. *Cannibals and Kings: The Origins of Cultures.* New York: Vintage Books, 1977.

—. *Cows, Pigs, Wars, and Witches: The Riddles of Culture.* New York: Vintage Books, 1978.

—. *Our Kind: Who We Are, Where We Came From & Where We Are Going.* New York: Harper & Row Publishers, 1989.

Hart, Carl L. *High Price: A Neuroscientist's Journey of Self-Discovery that Challenges Everything You Know About Drugs and Society.* New York: Harper, 2013.

Hartmann, Thom. *Screwed: The Undeclared War Against the Middle Class—and What We Can Do About It.* San Francisco: Berrett-Koehler Publishers, 2007.

—. *Rebooting the American Dream: 11 Ways to Rebuild Our Country.* San Francisco: Berrett-Koehier Publishers, Inc., 2010.

—. *Threshold: The Progressive Plan to Pull America Back from the Brink.* New York: Plume, 2010.

—. *The Crash of 2016: The Plot to Destroy America—and What We Can Do to Stop It.* New York: Twelve, 2013.

Headrick, Daniel R. *The Tools of Empire: Technology and European Imperialism in the Nineteenth Century.* Oxford: Oxford University Press, 1981.

Hedges, Chris. *Wages of Rebellion: The Moral Imperative of Revolt.* New York: Nation Books, 2015.

—. *Empire of Illusion: The End of Literacy and the Triumph of Spectacle.* New York: Nation Boons, 2009.

Henderson, Errol Anthony. *Afrocentrism and World Politics: Towards a New Paradigm.* Westport, CT: Praeger Publishers, 1995.

Bibliography

——. *African Realism?* Lanham, Md: Rowman & Littlefield, 2015.

Herbert, Bob. *Losing Our Way: An Intimate Portrait of a Troubled America.* New York: Doubleday, 2014.

Herman, Edward S., and Noam Chomsky. *Manufacturing Contest: The Political Economy of the Mass Media.* New York: Pantheon Books, 1988.

Hertz, Noreena. *The Silent Takeover: Global Capitalism and the Death of Democracy.* New York: The Free Press, 2001.

Heuvel, Katrina Vanden. *The Change I Believe In: Fighting for Progress in the Age of Obama.* New York: Nation Books, 2011.

Hightower, Jim. *If Gods Had Meant Us to Vote They Would Have Given Us Candidates.* New York: HarperCollins Publishers, 2000.

Hitchens, Christopher. *No One Left to Lie To: The Triangulations of William Jefferson Clinton.* New York: Verso, 1999.

Hodgson, Godfrey. *The Myth of American Exceptionalism.* New Haven: Yale University Press, 2009.

Hoffman, Nicholas Von. *Hoax.* New York: Nation Books, 2004.

hooks, bell. *We Real Cool: Black Men and Masculinity.* New York: Routledge, 2004.

Hooper, Lita. *Art of Work: The Art and Life of Haki R. Madhubuti.* Chicago: Third World Press, 2007.

Howard, Philip K. *The Death of Common Sense: How Law is Suffocating America.* New York: Random House, 1994.

Hubbard, Glenn, and Tim Kane. *Balance: The Economics of Great Powers from Ancient Rome to Modern America.* New York: Simon & Schuster, 2013.

Hudson, Michael, ed. *Merchants of Misery: How Corporate America Profits From Poverty.* Monroe, ME: Common Courage Press, 1996.

Huffington, Arianna. *Pigs at the Trough: How Corporate Greed and Political Corruption Are Undermining America.* New York: Crown Publishing Group, 2003.

Ivins, Molly, and Lou Dubose. *Shrub: The Short but Happy Political Life of George W. Bush.* New York: Random House, 2000.

Ivry, Bob. *The Seven Sins of Wall Street: Big Banks, Their Washington Lackeys, and the Next Financial Crisis*. New York: Public Affairs, 2014.

Jaffe, Harry, *Why Bernie Sanders Matters*. New York: Regan Arts., 2015.

Jahoda, Gloria. *The Trail of Tears: The Story of the American Indian Removals 1813-1855*. New York: Wings Books, 1975.

Jamail, Dahr. *Beyond the Green Zone: Dispatches from an Unembedded Journalist in Occupied Iraq*. Chicago: Haymarket Books, 2007.

Jennings, Regina. *Malcolm X and the Poetics of Haki Madhubuti*. Jefferson, NC: McFarland & Company, Inc., Publishers, 2006.

Jett, Joseph, and Sabra Chartrand. *Black and White on Wall Street: The Untold Story of the Man Wrongly Accused of Bringing Down Kidder Peabody*. New York: William Morrow, 1999.

Johnson, Chalmers. *Blowback: The Costs and Consequences of American Empire*. New York: Henry Holt and Company, 2000.

——. *Dismantling the Empire: America's Last Best Hope*. New York: Metropolitan Books, 2010.

——. *Nemesis: The Last Days of the American Republic*. New York: Metropolitan Books, 2006.

——. *The Sorrows of Empire: Militarism, Secrecy, and the End of the Republic*. New York: Metropolitan Books, 2004.

Johnston, David Cay. *Perfectly Legal: The Covert Campaign to Rig Our Tax System to Benefit the Super Rich—And Cheat Everybody Else*. New York: Portfolio, 2005.

Jones, Van. *Rebuild the Dream*. New York: Nation Books, 2012.

Judt, Tony. *Ill Fares the Land*. New York: The Penguin Press, 2010.

Judt, Tony, and Timothy Snyder. *Thinking the Twentieth Century*. New York: The Penguin Press, 2012.

——. *When The Facts Change: Essays 1995-2010*. New York: Penguin Press, 2015.

Kaiser, Robert G. *So Damn Much Money: The Triumph of Lobbying and the Corrosion of American Government*. New York: Vintage Books, 2010.

Bibliography

Kapuściński, Ryszard. *The Other*. New York: Verso, 2008.

Karabell, Zachary. *The Leading Indicators: A Short History of the Numbers that Rule Our World*. New York: Simon & Schuster, 2014.

Karcher, Stephen. *The Elements of the I Ching*. Rockport, MA.: Element Books, 1995.

Karenga, Maulana. *Introduction to Black Studies*. 3rd ed. Los Angeles: University of Sankore Press, 2002.

——. *Kwanzaa: A Celebration of Family, Community, & Culture*. Los Angles: University of Sankore Press, 2008.

——. *Maat: The Moral Ideal in Ancient Egypt*. Los Angeles: University of Sankore Press, 2006.

Kassir, Samir. Being Arab. London: Verso, 2013

Kelley, Robin D. G. *Freedom Dreams: The Black Radical Imagination*. Boston: Beacon Press, 2002.

——. *Yo Mama's Disfunktional!: Fighting the Culture Wars in Urban America*. Boston: Beacon Press, 1997.

Khalidi, Rashid. *Brokers of Deceit: How the US Has Undermined Peace in the Middle East*. Boston: Beacon Press, 2013.

——. *The Iron Cage: The Story of the Palestinian Struggle for Statehood*. Boston: Beacon Press, 2006.

Kibbe, Matt. *Don't Hurt People and Don't Take Their Stuff: A Libertarian Manifesto*. New York: William Morrow, 2014.

Kick, Russ, ed. *You Are Still Being Lied To: The Remixed Disinformation Guide to Media Distortion, Historical Whitewashes and Cultural Myths*. New York: Disinformation, 2009.

Kilstein, Jamie, and Allison Kilkenny. *#NEWSFAIL*. New York: Simon & Schuster, 2014.

King, Coretta Scott, ed. *The Words of Martin Luther King, Jr*. New York: William Morrow, 2014.

King, Thomas. *The Inconvenient Indian: A Curious Account of Native People in North America.* Minneapolis: University of Minnesota Press, 2012.

Kitty, Alexandra. *Don't Believe It: How Lies Become the News.* New York: Disinformation, 2005.

Kitwana, Bakari. *The Hip-Hop Generation: Young Blacks and the Crisis in African-American Culture.* New York: Basic Civitas Books, 2003.

——. *The Rap on Gangsta Rap: Who Run It? Gangsta Rap and Visions of Black Violence.* Chicago: Third World Press, 1994.

——. *Why White Kids Love Hip Hop: Wanksta, Wiggers, Wannabes, and the New Reality of Race in America.* New York: Basic Civitas Books, 2006.

Klein, Naomi. *This Changes Everything: Capitalism vs. the Climate.* New York: Simon & Schuster, 2014.

——. *The Shock Doctrine: The Rise of Disaster Capitalism.* New York: Picador, 2008.

Korten, David C. *When Corporations Rule the World.* West Hartford, CT: Kumarian Press, 1996.

Kotkin, Joel. *Tribes: How Race, Religion and Identity Determine Success in the New Global Economy.* New York: Random House, 1993.

Kristof, Nicholas D., and Sheryl WuDunn. *Half the Sky: Turning Oppression Into Opportunity for Women Worldwide.* New York: Alfred A. Knopf, 2009.

Krugman, Paul. *End This Depression Now.* New York: W. W. Norton & Company, 2012.

——. *The Great Unraveling: Losing Our Way in the New Century.* New York: W. W. Norton & Company, 2003.
——. *The Return of Depression Economics and the Crisis of 2008.* New York: W. W. Norton & Company, 2009.

Lando, Barry M. *Web of Deceit: The History of Western Complicity in Iraq, from Churchill to Kennedy to George W. Bush.* New York: Other Press, 2007.

Lee, Carol D. *Culture, Literacy, and Learning: Taking Bloom in the Midst of the Whirlwind.* New York: Teachers College Press, 2007.

Bibliography

Lefevre, John. *Straight to Hell: True Tales of Deviance, Debauchery, and Billion-Dollar Deals.* New York: Atlantic Monthly Press, 2015.

Lehmann, Chris. *Rich People Things: Real Life Secrets of the Predator Class.* Chicago: Haymarket Books, 2011.

Lerner, Michael, ed. *Tikkun Reader: Twentieth Anniversary.* Lanham, MD: Rowman & Littlefield Publishers, Inc. 2007.

Leovy, Jill. *Ghettoside.* New York: Spiegel & Grue, 2015.

Lewis, Anthony. *Freedom for the Thought We Hate: A Biography of the First Amendment.* New York: Basic Books, 2009.

Lewis, Michael. *Flash Boys: A Wall Street Revolt.* New York: W. W. Norton & Company, 2014.

——. *The Big Short.* New York: W.W. Norton, 2010.

Lichtenstein, Nelson, ed. *Wal-Mart: The Face of Twenty-First-Century Capitalism.* New York: The New Press, 2006.

Lichtman, Allan J. *White Protestant Nation: The Rise of the American Conservative Movement.* New York: Atlantic Monthly Press, 2008.

Lindorff, Dave, and Barbara Olshansky. *The Case for Impeachment: The Legal Argument for Removing President W. Bush from Office.* New York: Thomas Dunne Books, 2006.

Lingeman, Richard. *The Nation. Guide to the Nation.* New York: Vintage Books, 2009.

Lipsitz, George. *The Possessive Investment in Whiteness: How White People Profit from Identity Politics.* Philadelphia: Temple University Press, 2006.

Litwack, Leon F. *How Free is Free?: The Long Death of Jim Crow.* Cambridge, MA: Harvard University Press, 2009.

Long, David E. *The Anatomy of Terrorism.* New York: The Free Press, 1990.

Looman, Mary D. and John D. Carl. *A Country Called Prison.* Cambridge: Oxford University Press, 2015.

Lubiano, Wahneema, ed. *The House that Race Built: Black Americans, U.S. Terrain.* New York: Pantheon Books, 1997.

Lui, Meizhu, et al. *The Color of Wealth: The Story Behind the U.S. Racial Wealth Divide.* New York: The New Press, 2006.

Lynn, Barry C. *Cornered: The New Monopoly Capitalism and the Economics of Destruction.* Hoboken, NJ.: John Wiley & Sons, 2010.

Maddow, Rachel. *Drill: The Unmooring of American Military Power.* New York: Crown Publishing Group, 2012.

Madhubuti, Haki R. *Black Men: Obsolete, Single, Dangerous? The Afrikan American Familiy in Transition.* Chicago: Third World Press, 1991.

——. *Claiming Earth: Race, Rage, Rape, Redemption: Blacks Seeking a Culture of Enlightened Empowerment.* Chicago: Third World Press, 1994.

——. *Enemies: The Clash of Races.* Chicago: Third World Press, 1978.

——. *From Plan to Planet: Life Studies: The Need for Afrikan Minds and Institutions.* Chicago: Broadside Press, 1973.

——. *Tough Notes: A Healing Call for Creating Exceptional Black Men.* Chicago: Third World Press, 2002.

Madrick, Jeff. *Age of Greed: The Triumph of Finance and the Decline of America, 1970 to the Present.* New York: Alfred A. Knopf, 2011.

Maher, Bill. *New Rules: The Polite Musings From a Timid Observer. ? Rodale Publishing,* 2015.

Mallaby, Sebastian. *More Money Than God: Hedge Funds and the Making of a New Elite.* New York: The Penguin Press, 2010.

Mandela, Nelson. *Long Walk to Freedom.* Boston: Little, Brown and Company, 1994.

Mander, Jerry. *The Capitalism Papers: Fatal Flaws of An Obsolete System.* Berkeley: Counterpoint, 2012.

Mann, Thomas E., and Norman J. Ornstein. *It's Even Worse Than It Looks: How the American Constitutional System Collided with the New Politics of Extremism.* New York: Basic Books, 2012.

Marazzi, Christian. *The Violence of Financial Capitalism.* Los Angeles: Semiotext(e), 2010.

Bibliography

Marcial, Gene G. *Secrets of the Street: The Dark Side of Making Money.* New York: McGraw-Hill, 1995.

Marks, Stephen. *Confessions of a Politician Hitman: My Secret Life of Scandal, Corruption, Hypocrisy, and Dirty Attacks that Decide Who Gets Elected (and Who Doesn't).* Naperville, IL: Sourcebooks, Inc., 2007.

Massey, Douglass S., and Nancy A Denton. *American Apartheid: Segregation and the Making of the Underclass.* Cambridge, MA.: Harvard University Press, 1993.

Matthiessen, Peter. *End of the Earth: Voyages to Antartica.* Washington, D.C.: National Geographic, 2003.

Mayer, Jane. *Dark Money.* New York: Doubleday, 2016.

Mayer, Jane, and Jill Abramson. *Strange Justice: The Selling of Clarence Thomas.* Boston: Houghton Mifflin Company, 1994.

Mazzetti, Mark. *The Way of the Knife: The CIA, a Secret Army, and a War at the Ends of the Earth.* New York: Penguin Books, 2013.

McChesney, Robert W., and John Nichols. *The Death and Life of American Journalism: The Media Revolution That Will Begin the World Again.* New York: Nation Books, 2010.

McElvaine, Robert S. *Grand Theft Jesus: The Hijacking of Religion in America.* New York: Crown Publishing Group, 2008.

McGuire, Danielle L. *At the Dark End of the Street: Black Women, Rape, and Resistance—a New History of the Civil Rights Movement from Rosa Parks to the Rise of Black Power.* New York: Alfred A. Knopf, 2010.

McKibben, Bill. *Deep Economy: The Wealth of Communities and the Durable Future.* New York: Times Books, 2007.

McKoy, Sheila Smith. *When Whites Riot: Writing Race and Violence in American and South African Cultures.* Madison: The University of Wisconsin Press, 2001.

McLean, Bethany, and Joe Nocera. *All the Devils Are Here: The Hidden History of the Financial Crisis.* New York: Portfolio/Penguin, 2010.

Mearsheimer, John J. *Why Leaders Lie: The Truth About Lying in International Politics.* New York: Oxford University Press, 2011.

Mearsheimer, John J., and Stephen M. Walt. *The Israel Lobby and U.S. Foreign Policy.* New York: Farrar, Straus and Giroux, 2007.

Mendelssohn, Kurt. *The Secret of Western Domination: How Science Became the Key to Global Power, and What This Signifies for the Rest of the World.* New York: Praeger Publishers, 1976.

Miller, E. Ethelbert. *Fathering Words: The Making of an African American Writer.* New York: St. Martin's Press, 2000.

Miller, Jerome G. *Search and Destroy: African-American Males in the Criminal Justice System.* New York: Cambridge University Press, 1996.

Mills, Charles W. *The Racial Contract.* New York: Cornell University Press, 1999.

Mnookin, Seth. *Hard News: The Scandals at The New York Times and Their Meaning for American Media.* New York: Random House, 2004.

——. *The Republican War on Science.* New York: Basic Books, 2005.

Mooney, Chris. *Storm World: Hurricanes, Politics, and the Battle Over Global Warming.* Orlando: Harcourt, Inc., 2007.

Moore, Michael. *Dude, Where's My Country?* New York: Warner Books. 2003.

Morris, Monique W. *Black Stats: African Americans by the Numbers in the Twenty-First Century.* New York: The New Press, 2014.

Morrison, Toni. *God Help the Child.* New York: Alfred A. Knopf, 2015.

——. *Playing in the Dark: Whiteness and the Literary Imagination.* Cambridge, MA: Harvard University Press, 1992.

Moyers, Bill. *Moyers on America: A Journalist and His Times.* New York: The New Press, 2004.

Moyo, Dambisa. *Dead Aid: Why Aid Is Not Working and How There Is a Better Way for Africa.* New York: Farrar, Straus, and Giroux, 2009.

——. *How the West Was Lost: Fifty Years of Economic Folly and the Stark Choices Ahead.* New York: Farrar, Straus, and Giroux, 2011.

Bibliography

—. *Winner Take All: China's Race for Resources and What it Means for the World.* New York: Basic Books, 2012.

Muhammad, Khalil Gibran. *The Condemnation of Blackness: Race, Crime, and the Making of Modern Urban America.* Cambridge, MA.: Harvard University Press, 2011.

Murray, Charles. *Coming Apart: The State of White America, 1960-2010.* New York: Crown Forum, 2012.

Nader, Ralph. *Only the Rich Can Save Us.* New York: Seven Stories Press, 2009.

Nash, George H. *The Conservative Intellectual Movement in America Since 1945.* New York: Basic Books, 1976.

Nelson, Jack. *Terror in the Night: The Klan's Campaign Against the Jews.* New York: Simon & Schuster 1993.

NewHouse, John. *Imperial America: The Bush Assault on the World Order.* New York: Alfred A. Knopf, 2003.

Nichols, John, and Robert W. McChesney. *Tragedy & Farce: How the American Media Sell Wars, Spin Elections, and Destroy Democracy.* New York: The New Press, 2005.

Niose, David. *Fighting Back the Right: Reclaiming America from the Attack on Reason.* New York: Palgrave Macmillan, 2014.

Nobles, Wade W. *Seeking the Sakhu: Foundational Writings for an African Psychology.* Chicago: Third World Press, 2006.

The Nobel Prize Literature Laureates Foundation. *Nobel Lectures: From the Literature Laureates, 1986 to 2006.* New York: The New Press, 2007.

Nunberg, Geoffrey. *Talking Right: How Conservatives Turned Liberalism Into a Tax-Raising, Latte-Drinking, Sushi-Eating, Volvo-Driving, New York Times-Reading, Body-Piercing, Hollywood-Loving, Left-Wing Freak Show.* New York: Public Affairs, 2006.

Oakes, James. *The Ruling Race: A History of American Slaveholders.* New York: W. W. Norton & Company, 1998.

Ogletree, Charles J., and Austin Sarat, eds. *From Lynch Mobs to the Killing State: Race and the Death Penalty in America.* New York: New York University Press, 2006.

Ogletree, Charles. *The Presumption of Guilt: The Arrest of Henry Louis Gates Jr. and Race, Class, and Crime in America.* 2nd ed. New York: Palgrave Macmillan, 2012.

Oliver, Melvin L., and Thomas M. Shapiro. *Black Wealth/White Health: A New Perspective on Racial Inequality.* New York: Routledge, 1995

Oren, Michael B. *Ally: My Journey Across the American-Israeli Divide.* New York: Random House, 2015.

Ortiz-Dunbar, Roxanne. *An Indigenous Peoples' History of the United States.* Boston: Beacon Press, 2014.

Painter, Nell Irvin. *The History of White People.* New York: W. W. Norton & Company, 2010.

Palast, Greg. *The Best Democracy Money Can Buy: The Truth About Corporate Cons, Globalization, and High-Finance Fraudsters.* New York: Plume, 2003.

Pardue, Mary Jane. *Who Owns the Press: Investigating Public vs. Private Ownership of America's Newspapers.* Portland: Marion Street Press, 2010.

Parenti, Christian. *Lockdown America: Police and Prisons in the Age of Crisis.* New York: Verso, 1999.

Parenti, Michael. *Dirty Truths: Reflections on Politics, Media, Ideology, Conspiracy, Ethnic Life and Class Power.* San Francisco: City Lights Books, 1996.

—. *Inventing Reality: The Politics of the Mass Media.* New York: St. Martin's Press, 1986.

—. *Super Patriotism.* San Francisco: City Lights Books, 2004.

Paretsky, Sara. *Writing In An Age of Silence.* New York: Verso, 2009.

Parks S., Gregory, and Matthew W. Hughey, eds. *Twelve Angry Men: True Stories of Being a Black Man in America Today.* New York: The New Press, 2010.

Pelton, Robert Young. *Licensed to Kill: Hired Guns in the War on Terror.* New York: Three Rivers Press, 2006.

Pepper, William F. *An Act of State: The Execution of Martin Luther King.* New York: Verso, 2003.

Bibliography

Perkins, John. *Confessions of an Economic Hit Man.* San Francisco: Berrett-Koehler Publishers, Inc., 2004.

Perkins, Useni Eugene. *Home is a Dirty Street.* Chicago: Third World Press, 1996.

—. *Harvesting New Generations.* Chicago: Third World Press, 2005.

Peters, Joel. *Israel and Africa.* London: The British Academic Press, 1992

Peters, Ralph. *Endless War.* Mechanicsburg, PA: Stackpole Books, 2010.

Pettit, Becky. *Invisible Men: Mass Incarceration and the Myth of Black Progress.* New York: Russell Sage Foundation, 2012.

Pfaff, William. *The Irony of Manifest Destiny: The Tragedy of America's Foreign Policy.* New York: Walker & Company, 2010.

Phillips, Kevin. *Bad Money: Reckless Finance, Failed Politics, and the Global Crisis of American Capitalism.* New York: Viking Penguin, 2008.

Phillips, Peter, et al. *Censored 2010: The Top 25 Censored Stories of 2008-09.* New York: Seven Stories Press, 2009.

Pickney, Darryl. *Blackballed: The Black Vote and US Democracy.* New York: New York Review Books, 2014.

Pierce, Charles P. *Idiot America: How Stupidity Became a Virtue in the Land of the Free.* New York: Doubleday, 2009.

Pieterse, Jan Nederveen. *White on Black: Images of Africa and Blacks in Western Popular Culture.* New Haven: Yale University Press, 1992.

Piketty, Thomas, and Arthur Goldhammer, trans. *Capital in the Twenty-First Century.* Cambridge, MA.: The Belknap Press of Harvard University Press, 2014.

Pilger, John, ed. *Tell Me No Lies: Investigative Journalism that Changed the World.* New York: Thunder's Mouth Press, 2005.

Pitt, William Rivers, and Scott Ritter. *War on Iraq: What Team Bush Doesn't Want You To Know.* New York: Context Books, 2002.

Piven, Frances Fox. *Lessons for Our Struggle.* Chicago: Haymarket Books, 2011.

—. *The War at Home: The Domestic Costs of Bush's Militarism.* New York: The New Press, 2004.

Porter, Bernard. *Empire and Superempire: Britain, America and the World.* New Haven: Yale University Press, 2006.

Posner, Richard A. *A Failure of Capitalism: The Crisis of '08 and the Descent Into Depression.* Cambridge, MA: Harvard University Press, 2009.

Poulson-Bryant, Scott. *Hung: A Meditation on the Measure of Black Men in America.* New York: Doubleday, 2005.

Prashad, Vijay. *The Poorer Nations: A Possible History of the Global South.* New York: Verso, 2012.

Quindlen, Anna. *How Reading Changed My Life.* New York: Ballantine Books, 1998.

Rai, Milan. *War Plan: Ten Reasons Against War on Iraq.* New York: Verso, 2002.

Rall, Ted. *Bernie.* New York/Oakland: Seven Stories Press, 2016.

Rank, Mark Robert. *One Nation, Underprivileged: Why American Poverty Affects Us All.* New York: Oxford University Press, 2005.

Rashid, Ahmed. *Descent into Chaos.* New York: Viking, 2008.

Ray, Schaap, Van Meter and Wolf, eds. Dirty Works 2: The CIA in Africa. Secausus: Lyle Staurt Inc., 1979.

Raymond, Allen, and Ian Spiegelman. *How to Rig an Election: Confessions of a Republican Operative.* New York: Simon & Schuster, 2008.

Reed, Ishmael. *The Complete Muhammad Ali.* Montreal: Baraka Books, 2015.

—. *Black Hollywood Unchained: Commentary on the State of Black Hollywood.* Chicago: Third Word Press, 2015.

Rees, Martin. *From Here to Infinity: A Vision for the Future of Science.* New York: W. W. Norton & Company, 2012.

Rich, Adrienne. *Arts of the Possible: Essays and Conversations.* New York: W. W. Norton & Company, 2001.

Bibliography

Richardson, Ken. *The Making of Intelligence.* New York: Columbia University Press, 2000.

Risen, James. *Pay Any Price: Greed, Power, and Endless War.* Boston: Houghton Mifflin Harcourt, 2014.

——. *State of War: The Secret History of the CIA and the Bush Administration.* New York: Free Press, 2006.

Ritholtz, Barry, and Aaron Task. *Bailout Nation: How Greed and Easy Money Corrupted Wall Street and Shook the World Economy.* Hoboken, NJ: John Wiley & Sons, Inc., 2009.

Roberts, Gene, and Thomas Kunkel. *Breach of Faith: A Crisis of Coverage In the Age of Corporate Newspapering.* Fayetteville: The University of Arkansas Press, 2002.

Robinson, Randall. *The Debt: What America Owes to Blacks.* New York: Dutton, 2000.

Rodriguez, Richard. *Brown: The Last Discovery of America.* New York: Viking Penguin, 2002.

Roediger, David R. *Working Towards Whiteness: How America's Immigrants Became White.* New York: Basic Books, 2005.

Rogers, Toby. *Ambushed: Secrets of The Bush Family, The Stolen Presidency, 9-11 and 2004.* Oregon: Trineday, 2004.

Rosenberg, Alfred, and Robert Poise, ed. *Race and Race History and Other Essays.* New York: Harper & Row Publishers, 1970.

Rosoff, Stephen, Henry N. Pontell, and Robert H. Tillman. *Looting America: Greed, Corruption, Villains, and Victims.* New Jersey: Prentice Hall, 2003.

Ross, Lawrence C. *The Divine Nine: The History of African American Fraternities and Sororities.* New York: Dafina Books, 2000.

Rossi, Melissa. *What Every American Should Know About Who's Really Running America and What You Can Do About It.* New York: Plume, 2007.

——. *What Every American Should Know About Who's Really Running the World: The People, Corporations, and Organizations that Control Our Future.* New York: Plume, 2005.

Roy, Arundhati. *Field Notes on Democracy: Listening to Grasshoppers.* Chicago: Haymarket Books, 2009.

——. *War Talk.* Cambridge, MA: South End Press, 2003.

Ruiz, Don Miguel. *The Four Agreements: A Toltec Wisdom Book.* San Rafael, CA: Amber-Allen Publishing, 1997.

Russo, Gus. *SuperMob.* New York: Bloomsbury, 2006.

Rutherford, Paul. *Weapons of Mass Persuasion: Marketing the War Against Iraq.* Toronto: University of Toronto Press, 2004.

Sachar, Howard M. *A History of Israel from the Rise of Zionism to Our Time.* 3rd ed. New York: Alfred A. Knopf, 2007.

Sachs, Jeffrey D. *The End of Poverty: Economic Possibilities for Our Time.* New York: The Penguin Press, 2005.

——. *The Price of Civilization: Reawakening American Virtue and Prosperity.* New York: Random House, 2011.

Sage, Jesse, and Liora Kasten, eds. *Enslaved: True Stories of Modern Slavery.* New York: Palgrave Macmillan, 2006.

Said, Edward W., and Christopher Hitchens. *Blaming the Victims: Spurious Scholarship and the Palestinian Question.* New York: Verso, 2001.

Said, Edward W. *Culture and Imperialism.* 3rd ed. New York: Alfred A. Knopf, 1993.

——. *From Olso to Iraq and the Road Map: Essays.* New York: Pantheon Books, 2004.

——. *Orientalism.* New York: Vintage Books, 1979.

——. *Reflections on Exile and Other Essays.* Cambridge, MA: Harvard University Press, 2000.

——. *Representations of the Intellectual: The 1993 Reith Lectures.* New York: Vintage Books, 1996.

Sander, Peter. *Madoff: Corruption, Deceit, and the Making of the World's Most Notorious Ponzi Scheme.* Guilford, CT: The Lyons Press, 2009.

Bibliography

Sanders, Bernie. *The Speech.* New York: Nation Books, 2011.

Scahill, Jeremy. *Blackwater: The Rise of the World's Most Powerful Mercenary Army.* New York: MJF Books, 2008.

——. *Dirty Wars: The World Is a Battlefield.* New York: Nation Books, 2013.

Scheer, Robert. *The Pornography of Power: How Defense Hawks Hijacked 9/11 and Weakened America.* New York: Twelve, 2008.

Schoen, Douglas E. *American Casino: The Rigged Game That's Killing Democracy.* New York: Velocity Press, 2012.

Schulman, Daniel. *Sons of Wichita: How the Koch Brothers Became America's Most Powerful and Private Dynasty.* New York: Grand Central Publishing, 2014.

Schultz, Ed. *Killer Politics: How Big Money and Bad Politics Are Destroying the Great American Middle Class.* New York: Hyperion, 2010.

Schweizer, Peter. *Throw Them All Out: How Politicians and Their Friends Get Rich Off Insider Stock Tips, Land Deals, and Cronyism That Would Send the Rest of Us to Prison.* Boston: Houghton Mifflin Harcourt, 2011.

Shabecoff, Philip, and Alice Shabecoff. *Poisoned Profits: The Toxic Assault on Our Children.* New York: Random House, 2008.

Shapiro, Thomas M. *The Hidden Cost of Being African American: How Wealth Perpetuates Inequality.* New York: Oxford University Press, 2004.

Sharpley-Whiting, T. Denean. *Pimps Up, Ho's Down: Hip Hop's Hold on Young Black Women.* New York: New York University Press, 2007.

Shavit, Ari. *My Promised Land: The Triumph and Tragedy of Israel.* New York: Spiegel & Grau, 2013.

Shaw, Randy. *The Activist's Handbook: A Primer for the 1990's and Beyond.* Berkeley: University of California Press, 1996.

Shipler, David K. *The Working Poor: Invisible in America.* New York: Alfred A. Knopf, 2004,

Sim, Stuart. *Fundamentalist World: The New Dark Age of Dogma.* Lanham, MD: Totem Books, 2004.

Simanga, Michael. *Amiri Baraka and the Congress of African People: History and Memory.* New York: Palgrave Macmillan, 2015.

Simons, Suzanne. *Master of War: Blackwater USA's Erik Prince and the Business of War.* New York: HarperCollins Publishers, 2009.

Sims, Norman, and Mark Kramer, eds. *Literary Journalism: A New Collection of the Best American Nonfiction.* New York: Ballantine Books, 1995.

Smiley, Tavis, and Cornel West. *The Rich and the Rest of Us: A Poverty Manifesto.* New York: Smiley Books, 2012.

Smith, David Livingstone. *Less Than Human: Why We Demean, Enslave, and Exterminate Others.* New York: St. Martin's Griffin, 2011.

Smith, Glenn W. *The Politics of Deceit: Saving Freedom and Democracy from Extinction.* Hoboken, NJ: John Wiley & Sons, Inc., 2004.

Smith, Hendrick. *Who Stole The American Dream?* New York: Random House, 2013.

Smith, Robert C. *We Have No Leaders: African Americans In the Post-Civil Rights Era.* Albany, NY: State University of New York Press, 1996.

Sontag, Susan. *Regarding the Pain of Others.* New York: Farrar, Straus and Giroux, 2003.

—*Styles of Radical Will.* New York: Farrar, Straus and Giroux, 2002.

—. *Under the Sign of Saturn.* New York: Farrar, Straus and Giroux, 1980.

Sorkin, Andrew Ross. *Too Big to Fail: Inside the Battle to Save Wall Street.* London: Allen Lane, 2009.

—. *The Age of Fallibility: Consequences of the War on Terror.* New York: Public Affairs, 2006.

—. *The Bubble of American Supremacy: The Costs of Bush's War in Iraq.* New York: Public Affairs, 2004.

Soros, George. *Financial Turmoil: In Europe and the United States.* New York: Public Affairs, 2012.

Bibliography

——. *The New Paradigm for Financial Markets: The Credit Crisis of 2008 and What It Means.* New York: Public Affairs, 2008.

——. *Open Society: Reforming Global Capitalism.* New York: Public Affairs, 2000.

Sowell, Thomas. *Migrations and Cultures: A World View.* New York: Basic Books, 1996.

——. *Race and Culture: A World View.* New York: Basic Books, 1994.

Steele, Claude M. *Whistling Vivaldi and Other Clues to How Stereotypes Affect Us.* New York: W. W. Norton & Company, 2010.

Steinzor, Rena. *Why Not Jail?* New York: Cambridge University Press, 2015.

Stephen, Elliot, ed. *Where To Invade Next.* San Francisco: McSweeney's, 2008.

Stephens, Mitchell. *The Rise of the Image the Fall of the Word.* New York: Oxford University Press, 1998.

Stewart, Rory. *The Places in Between.* Orlando: Harcourt, Inc., 2004.

Stiglitz, Joseph E. *The Price of Inequality: How Today's Divided Society Endangers Our Future.* New York: W. W. Norton & Company, 2012.

Stiglitz, Joseph E., and Linda J. Bilmes. *The Three Trillion Dollar War: The True Cost of the Iraq Conflict.* New York: W. W. Norton & Company, 2008.

Stiglitz, Joseph E. *Globalization and Its Discontents.* New York: W. W. Norton & Company, 2002.

Stone, Oliver, and Peter Kuznick. *The Untold History of the United States.* New York: Gallery Books, 2012.

Straus, Scott. *The Order of Genocide: Race, Power, and War in Rwanda.* Ithasca: Cornell University Press, 2006

Sundquist, Eric J. *Strangers in the Land: Blacks, Jews, Post-Holocaust America.* Cambridge, MA: The Belknap Press of Harvard University, 2005.

Sutherland, Marcia. *Black Authenticity: A Psychology for Liberating People of African Descent.* Chicago: Third World Press, 1993.

Swain, Carol M. *The New White Nationalism in America: Its Challenge to Integration.* New York: Cambridge University Press, 2002.

Swanson, David. *War Is a Lie.* Charlottesville, VA: David Swanson, 2010.

Sztorman, Elana Maryles. *The War on Women in Israel.* Naperville, IL: SourceBooks, 2015

Taibbi, Matt. *Griftopia: Bubble Machines, Vampire Squids, and the Long Con That Is Breaking America.* New York: Spiegel & Grau, 2010.

——. *The Divide: American Injustice in the Age of the Wealth Gap.* New York: Spiegel & Grau, 2014.

Talbot, David. *The Devil's Chessboard.* New York: Harper, 2015.

Tawfiq, Idris. *Understanding Islam: A Primer.* Northampton, MA: Olive Branch Press, 2009.

Teachout, Zephyr. *Corruption in America: From Benjamin Franklin's Snuff Box to Citizens United.* Cambridge, MA.: Harvard University Press, 2014.

Telushkin, Joseph. *Jewish Literacy.* New York: Morrow, 2001.

Tifft, Susan E., and Alex S. Jones. *The Trust: The Private and Powerful Family Behind The New York Times.* Boston: Little, Brown and Company, 1999.

Thomas, Helen. *Front Row at the White House: My Life and Time.* New York: Scribner/A Lisa Drew Book, 1999.

Thompson, Carlyle Van. *Black Outlaws: Race, Law, and Male Subjectivity in African American Literature and Culture.* New York: Peter Lang Publishing, 2010.

Timmerman, Kenneth R. *Shakedown: Exposing the Real Jesse Jackson.* Washington, D.C.: Regnery Publishing, Inc., 2002.

Todd, Emmanuel, and C. Jon Delogu, trans. *After the Empire: The Breakdown of the American Order.* New York: Columbia University Press, 2003.

Todd, Richard. *The Thing Itself: On the Search for Authenticity.* New York: Riverhead Books, 2008.

Tucker, Frank H. *The White Conscience: An Analysis of the White Man's Mind and Conduct.* New York: Frederick Ungar Publishing Co., 1968.

Bibliography

Unger, Craig. *House of Bush, House of Saud: The Secret Relationship Between the World's Two Most Powerful Dynasties.* New York: Scribner, 2004.

Vaca, Nicolás C. *The Presumed Alliance: The Unspoken Conflict between Latinos and Blacks and What it Means for America.* New York: Rayo, 2004.

Varoufakis, Yanis. *The Global Minotaur: America, Europe, and the Future of the Global Economy.* London: Zed, 2015.

Vollman, William T. *Imperial.* New York: Viking Books, 2009.

——. *Riding Toward Everywhere.* New York: Ecco, 2008.

——. *Rising Up and Rising Down: Some Thoughts on Violence, Freedom, and Urgent Means.* New York: Harper Perennial, 2005.

Walsh, Joan. *What's the Matter With White People?: Why We Long for a Golden Age that Never Was.* Hoboken, NJ: John Wiley & Sons, Inc., 2012.

Walt, Stephen M. *Taming American Power: The Global Response to U.S. Primacy.* New York: W. W. Norton & Company, 2005.

Walters, Ronald W. *White Nationalism, Black Interests: Conservative Public Policy and the Black Community.* Detroit: Wayne State University Press, 2003.

Walton, Hanes. *African American Power and Politics: The Political Context Variable.* New York: Columbia University Press, 1997.

Warren, Elizabeth. *A Fighting Chance.* New York: Metropolitan Books, 2014.

Washington, Harriet A. *Medical Apartheid: The Dark History of Medical Experimentation on Black Americans from Colonial Times to the Present.* New York: Harlem Moon, Broadway Books, 2006.

Waters, T.J. *Class 11: My Story Inside the CIA'S First Post-9/11 Spy Class.* New York: Plume, 2007.

Watson, Clifford, and Geneva Smitherman. *Educating African American Males: Detroit's Malcolm X Academy Solution.* Chicago: Third World Press, 1996.

Weiner, Eric J. *The Shadow Market: How a Group of Wealthy Nations and Powerful Investors Secretly Dominate the World.* New York: Scribner, 2010.

Weiss, Gary. *Born to Steal: When the Mafia Hit Wall Street.* New York: Warner Books, 2003.

Welsing, Frances Cress. *The Isis Papers.* Chicago: Third World Press, 1991.

Wendel, Janine R. *Shadow Elite: How the World's New Power Brokers Undermine Democracy, Government, and the Free Market.* New York: Basic Books, 2009.

West, Cornel, and Christa Buschendorf, ed. *Black Prophetic Fire.* Beacon Press, 2014.

—. *Democracy Matters: Winning the Fight Against Imperialism.* New York: The Penguin Press, 2004.

—. *Race Matters.* New York: Vintage Books, 2001.

—, ed. *The Radical King: Martin Luther King, Jr.* 2nd ed. Boston: Beacon Press. 2015.

Westad, Odd Arne. *Restless Empire: China and the World Since 1750.* New York: Basic Books, 2012.

Wexler, Laura. *Fire In A CaneBrake: The Last Mass Lynching in America.* New York: Scribner, 2003

White, Deborah Gray, ed. *Telling Histories: Black Women Historians in the Ivory n Tower.* Chapel Hill: University of North Carolina Press, 2008.

Whittacker, David J. *Terrorism: Understanding the Global Threat.* Harlow: 2007.

Wicker, Tom. *Tragic Failure: Racial Integration in America.* New York: William Morrow, 1996.

Wideman, John Edgar. *Fatheralong: A Meditation on Fathers and Sons, Race and Society.* New York: Pantheon Books, 1994.

Williams, Chancellor. *The Destruction of Black Civilization: Great Issues of a Race from 4500 B.C. to 2000 A.D.* 3rd ed. Chicago: Third World Press, 1989.

Williams, Patricia J. *Seeing a Color-Blind Future: The Paradox of Race.* New York: The Noonday Press, 1998.

—. *The Rooster's Egg: On the Persistence of Prejudice.* Cambridge, MA.: Harvard University Press, 1995.

Williams, William Appleman. *Empire as a Way of Life: An Essay on the Causes and Character of America's Present Predicament Along with a Few Thoughts About an Alternative.* New York: Oxford University Press, 1980.

Bibliography

Wilson, Amos N. *Blueprint for Black Power: A Moral, Political and Economic Imperative for the Twenty-First Century.* New York: African World InfoSystems, 1998.

——. *The Falsification of African Consciousness: Eurocentric History, Psychiatry, and the Politics of White Supremacy.* 5th ed. New York: African World InfoSystems, 2002.

——. *Black on Black Violence: The Psychodynamics of Black Self-Annihilation in Service of White Domination.* Brooklyn: Afrikan World Infosystems, 1990.

Winbush, Raymond A. *Should America Pay?: Slavery and the Raging Debate on Reparations.* New York: Amistad, 2003.

Winters, Jeffrey A. *Oligarchy.* Cambridge: Cambridge University Press, 2011.

Winters-Evans, Venus, and Magaela C. Bethune, eds. *(Re)Teaching Trayvon: Education for Racial Justice and Human Freedom.* The Netherlands: Sense Publishers, 2014.

Wise, Tim. *Colorblind: The Rise of Post-Racial Politics and the Retreat from Racial Equity.* San Francisco: City Lights Books, 2010.

——. *White Like Me: Reflections on Race from a Privileged Son.* 3rd ed. Berkeley: Soft Skull Press.

Wolff, Michael. *The Man Who Owns the News: Inside the Secret World of Rupert Murdoch.* New York: Broadway Books, 2008.

Woodiwiss, Michael. *Gangster Capitalism: The United States and the Global Rise of Organized Crime.* New York: Carroll & Graf Publishers, 2005.

Wright, Bobby E. *The Psychopathic Racial Personality and Other Essays.* Chicago: Third World Press, 1984.

Wright, Bruce. *Black Justice in a White World.* New York: Barricade Books, Inc., 1996.

——. *Black Robes, White Justice: Why Our Justice System Doesn't Work for Blacks.* Secaucus, NJ: Lyle Stuart Inc., 1987.

Wright, Lawrence. *The Looming Tower: Al-Qaeda and the Road to 9/11.* New York: Vintage Books, 2007

Yancy, George. *Black Bodies, White Gazes: The Continuing Significance of Race.* Lanham, MD: Rowman & Littlefield Publishers, Inc., 2008.

Yette, Samuel F. *The Choice: The Issue of Black Survival in America.* New York: G. P. Putnam's Sons, 1971.

Younge, Gary. *A Stranger in a Strange Land: Encounters in the Disunited States.* New York: The New Press, 2006.

Zakaria, Fareed. *In Defense of a Liberal Education.* New York: W. W. Norton & Company, 2015.

Zinn, Howard. *A People's History of the United States 1492-Present.* New York: HarperCollins, 1999.

——. *Artists in Times of War.* New York: Seven Stories Press, 2003.

——. *On War.* New York: Seven Stories Press, 2001.

——. *The Other Civil War: Slavery and Struggle in Civil War America.* New York: Harper Perennial, 2011.

Zweig, Jason. *The Devil's Financial Dictionary.* New York: Public Affairs, 2015.

Appendix

'White on Black' indicates a relationship, and the order of the terms identifies the dominant partner, the producers and consumers of the images in question.' Africans did not traffic in European slaves for three hundred years, nor have they occupied the dominant place in the world's political, economic and cultural system. Several hundred years of western hegemony lends western images a range, complexity and historical weight which images stemming from Africa and from blacks do not possess.

The question that keeps arising is, what interests of whites are being served by these representations? This refers not merely to measurable economic and political interests but also to relations of a subtler nature in cultural, emotional and psychological spheres, and to the various ways in which these relations figure in the phenomenon of subordination. Generally, in examining images of 'others', one has first to ask, who are the producers and consumers of these images, and only then to question who are the objects of representation. The key that unlocks these images is what whites have made of blacks, and why.

The phrase 'White on Black' refers to the whole spectrum of relations in which western interests were dominant—the trans-Atlantic slave trade, master-slave relations on plantations in the Americas, colonialism, the post-colonial era, and majority-minority relations in the western world. In each of these situations Europeans constructed images of Africa and blacks on the basis of selective perception, expedience, second-hand information, mingled with reconstructed biblical notions and medieval folklore, along with popular or 'scientific' ideas that were current at the time.

—Jan Nederveen Pieterse
White on Black: Images of Africans and Blacks in Western Popular Culture (1992)

I think, other than perhaps Native Americans, Blacks in the United States have had the biggest purchase on hope. How could we survive otherwise? We had to see another tomorrow, when everything—every-thing—in the environment told us that the situation was/is/and will forever be hopeless. Think of the Dred Scott case, decided by the Supreme Court in 1857. It ruled that Black folks, whether slave or free, could never become citizens. It also said that even their descendants, free or not, could never enjoy the rights ascribed in the Constitution. Boy, talk about a recipe for hopelessness! Black folks, for the most part, just kept on stepping! We are people partly composed of hope. In many ways, it is who we are.

—Mumia Abu-Jamal interviewed by Marc Lamont Hill
The Classroom and the Cell (2011)

Ten Things

IDEAS SENT TO PRESIDENT OBAMA IN 2009

1. Good Governance. Politicians and others in power need to stop lying to the citizens and stop treating us like brain dead children. The new President must be forceful against corruption in government, corporate America, and all aspects of the private and public sectors that affect our lives.

2. The rule of law must return first by upholding the constitution, repeal the Patriot Acts and stop illegal wire-tapping. This new administration must not govern by sound bites, talk radio, and Sunday morning visits to corporate "news" programs. Serious investigation of the last eight years is mandatory. Laws have been broken that have aided in breaking the nation economically and politically. To revise the spirit of the people, there must be accountability. A lot of people need to be in prison.

3. We need a children first superior education system. Free education for all citizens from preschool through Ph.D./professional school of skilled-based technical training (automobile, aircraft industry, construction, etc.). The new President could help create a nation of readers by recommending a book a week, thus helping to revitalize the nation's libraries. "Read to Lead" will hopefully help move the country away from the ignorant fear of intellectuals. To seek and possess knowledge is not elitism, it is wisdom.

4. Address the inequities of the criminal justice system. Over 2.5 million men and women are locked down in the nation's prisons. The overwhelming number are black and brown men who are poor and do not have proper legal representation. Recognize the role that state terrorism plays in the lives of poor people as local and state agencies' abuses of power go unnoticed and such actions encourage and enable the development of a prison industrial complex.

5. Help solve the inequities in the current economic system by:
    a. Stop rewarding banks and individuals who have brought this country and the world to the brink of disaster, and
    b. Dare to question the structural flaws of capitalism such as derivatives, credit default swaps, hedge funds, and lack of regulations in the banking industry. And move immediately state by state for infrastructure repair on schools, hospitals, sewer and water systems, bridges, and highways. And take seriously the call for a nation-wide light rail system; it is both technologically and environmentally green.
    c. *New York Times* columnist, Nicholas D. Kristof, calls for a "Secretary of Food" rather than agriculture. Part of his argument is that the country is subsidizing an unhealthy food system. Out of all the industrial nations, the United States has the worse obesity problem. By building a new single-payer health care system, the new President can stress preventive, wholistic health. He can also be the example of a President who exercises regularly and bases his primary diet on vegetables, grains, fruit, and juices that build the body rather than tear it down.

6. We need a peace and environmentalist or pro-environment President, not only in "words" but also in deeds. We must seriously move to reduce the military industrial complex and transfer those monies, knowledge and industrial base to new efforts in the creation of peace and green technology. Immediately move toward cessation of the current wars in Iraq, Afghanistan, and Israeli/ Palestine and use the monies saved for their reconstruction and reconstruction at home.

7. We need a "Secretary of Art and Humanities." We need to seriously bring artists and their work into the conversation of what America really is and can be. "Art is fundamental instruction and food for a people's soul as they translate the many languages and acts of becoming, often telling them in no uncertain terms that all humans are not pure or perfect. . . . Art allows and encourages love of self and others.... Art is elemental to intelligent intelligence, working democracy, freedom, equality and justice. Art, if used wisely and widely, early and often is an answer and a question."

8. Put Africa on the front burner in terms of foreign affairs and not just as a receiver nation for donations to fight AIDS, Malaria, bad governance, and a host of other problems. For the serious development of the 21st century, we must understand that geographically Africa is blessed with almost unlimited natural and human resource that other nations have begun to redefine in their foreign policy. For example, China and Japan are all over Africa making deals, buying natural resources, initiating student exchanges and helping to build infrastructure. We should do no less but do it in the right spirit of cooperation and sharing.

9. Change the climate of rewarding mediocrity and failure. Stop playing politics and cronyism with the lives of the citizens of the nation. A thorough review of the Justice Department, National Security Agency, Central Intelligence Agency and other agencies empowered to award contracts and make sensitive decisions about the nation's future need to be re-evaluated. The mechanism used to protect this country and its allies needs to be questioned. The overuse of the National Guard and reserve units has internally been very destructive. Question: Do we really need a fighting force aided by the no-bid contractors of Blackwater, Halliburton and others?

10. We need people in government with a conscience. Workers who will actively choose to do that which is good, just, fair and right for the great majority of citizens rather than the moneyed and elite few. The President must listen to others outside of his comfort zone or familial circle of extended family, friends, colleagues and advisors. He must never forget the majority of the United States population (as well as the world) consists of poor, working-poor, students, and middle-class of all cultures. Those persons, without serious money, "right" education, country club membership, or general assets or connections to power do think, work hard, vote, and experience the negative effects of bad decisions made by incompetent and connected insiders. This must change.

Excerpts from *Tikkun, see page 26*

Editorial excerpt from *Tikkun* by Rabbi Michael Lerner: Repenting for what Israel did to Gaza— Without Condoning the Wrongs Committed by Hamas

The outrage of the Palestinian people and the anger of the Hamas at Israel were certainly understandable. But Hamas's attempt to bomb civilian centers was also a huge violation of human rights, and its leaders, too, ought to face human rights trials through the International Criminal Court....

The damage to the Palestinian cause was immense. Netanyahu was suddenly faced with reinvigorated fascistic right, which criticized him for being too lenient with Gaza and threatened to bring down his government for its failure to conduct a more extensive war to kill every last member of Hamas (Racist) language against Palestinians and Muslims proliferated throughout Israeli society. Netanyahu was perceived by many Israelis as a centrist in comparison with more extreme political voices that emerged and sought to rid the land of Israel of its Palestinian population. The whole political spectrum in Israel, which was already tilted to the right, shifted even further rightward. The March 2015 elections confirmed that. In part due to the fear that Hamas's rocket attacks had triggered, Israelis gave Netanyahu a new mandate based on his promise to never allow a Palestinian state to emerge—which in turn strengthened the most military factions of Hamas that had always contended that the Palestinian Authority had been wasting its time and created illusory hopes among Palestinian by trying to find a peaceful solution to the Israeli occupation of the west bank and Gaza...

Shame on Hamas. Shame on Israel.

WE in the United States have a special responsibility. Our government has been providing military and political cover for Israel throughout the past several decades, and the Obama administration has gone out of its way to surpass previous administrations in supplying military equipment and expertise to the Israeli government. The American Israel Public Affairs Committee (AIPAC) and the Israeli right do not respond with gratitude in large part because they don't respect the easily-pushed-around Obama administration. So instead they ask for me—demanding that the United States become their proxy in declawing the Iranian government.

We at Tikkun are deeply saddened by this whole picture. And as we enter the High Holidays in the fall of 2015, we call for both sides to repent of their irresponsible behavior.

The full editorial is a statement of Fairness and must be read Vol. 30, No. 3, Summer 2015.

Editorial excerpt from *Tikkun* by Rabbi Michael Lerner: Except/War with Iran the disastrous aim of Israel and the Republicans

Israeli Prime Minister Benjamin Netanyahu and his supporters would love to see a series of military assaults on Iran. In particular, they are hoping for assaults that would decisively undermine Iran's ability to develop nuclear power, even for peaceful purposes. Netanyahu has felt this way for years, but after the disastrous war with Gaza in 2014, it was strategically clever for him to put the issue of Iran on the world's agenda in order to shift global attention away from the suffering of the Palestinian people.

Netanyahu's discussion of possible assaults by Israel or its sole ally, the United States, on Iran succeeded in steering Israeli voters away from discussions of Palestine in the runup to the March 2015 election...

Very few Israeli want their own soldiers to go to war with Iran. What they want most is for the United States to fight that war, which many Israelis believe is necessary in order to remove the threat to Israel's existence that Iran is thought to constitute.

Those Israelis who seek to encourage the United States to fight this war, as Benjamin Netanyahu did quite eloquently—though deceitfully—in his address to a joint session of the U.S. Congress on March 3, 2015, have a powerful ally in that quest, namely the Republican majorities in the U.S. Senate and House of Representatives. Most of these Republicans have never seen a war that they didn't yearn to get into, motivated in part by their funders in the military-industrial complex and in part by a lingering desire to reestablish the United States as the undisputed and sole major power of the world.

What makes war with Iran so particularly appealing to the militarists is that it hs the support of the many Democrats beholden to th American Israel Public Affairs Committee (AIPAC), as well as popular support from Christian Zionists, who are among the more vocal elements in the base of the Republican Party. Other proponents of an ill-advised war with Iran include the section of the American public who would love to watch the first African American president appear like a failure, thereby covertly validating the racism that has given the Republican Party its staying power, even among middle-income and poor people whose economic interests have been battered by Republican-instigated cuts to the already paltry safety pet.

The full editorial is insightful and clear and should be read for a better understanding the Israel, American and Iran disconnections. Vol. 30, No. 3, Summer 2015

United States Senate
WASHINGTON, DC 20510

March 9, 2015

An Open Letter to the Leaders of the Islamic Republic of Iran:

It has come to our attention while observing your nuclear negotiations with our government that you may not fully understand our constitutional system. Thus, we are writing to bring to your attention two features of our Constitution—the power to make binding international agreements and the different character of federal offices—which you should seriously consider as negotiations progress.

First, under our Constitution, while the president negotiates international agreements, Congress plays the significant role of ratifying them. In the case of a treaty, the Senate must ratify it by a two-thirds vote. A so-called congressional-executive agreement requires a majority vote in both the House and the Senate (which, because of procedural rules, effectively means a three-fifths vote in the Senate). Anything not approved by Congress is a mere executive agreement.

Second, the offices of our Constitution have different characteristics. For example, the president may serve only two 4-year terms, whereas senators may serve an unlimited number of 6-year terms. As applied today, for instance, President Obama will leave office in January 2017, while most of us will remain in office well beyond then—perhaps decades.

What these two constitutional provisions mean is that we will consider any agreement regarding your nuclear-weapons program that is not approved by the Congress as nothing more than an executive agreement between President Obama and Ayatollah Khamenei. The next president could revoke such an executive agreement with the stroke of a pen and future Congresses could modify the terms of the agreement at any time.

We hope this letter enriches your knowledge of our constitutional system and promotes mutual understanding and clarity as nuclear negotiations progress.

Sincerely,

The letter, spearheaded by Sen. Tom Cotton, was signed by 47 Republican senators. Seven GOP senators did not sign. Here's who signed:

SIGNATORIES:

Richard Shelby (Ala.)
Jeff Sessions (Ala.)
Dan Sullivan (Alaska)
John McCain (Ariz.)
John Boozman (Ark.)
Tom Cotton (Ark.)
Cory Garner (Colo.)
Marco Rubio (Fla.)
Johnny Isakson (Ga.)
David Perdue (Ga.)
Mike Crapo (Idaho)
Jim Risch (Idaho)
Mark Kirk (Ill.)
Chuck Grassley (Iowa)
Pat Roberts (Kansas)
Jerry Moran (Kansas)
Mitch McConnell (Ky.)
Rand Paul (ky.)
David Vitter (La.)
Bill Cassidy (La.)
Roger Wicker (Miss.)
Roy Blunt (Mo.)
Steve Daines (Mont.)
Deb Fischer (Neb.)
Ben Sasse (Neb.)
Dean Heller (Nev.)
Kelly Ayotte (N.H.)

Richard Burt
Thorn Tillis (N.C.)
John Hoeven (N.D.)
Rob Portman (Ohio)
Jim Inhofe (Okla.)
James Lankford (Okla.)
Pat Toomey (Pa.)
Lindsey Graham (S.C.)
Tim Scott (S.C.)
John Thune (S.D.)
Mike Rounds (S.D.)
John Cornyn (Texas)
Ted Cruz (Texas)
Orin Hatch (Utah)
Mike Lee (Utah)
Shelley Moore Capito (W.V.)
Ron Johnson (Wis.)
Mike Enzi (Wyo.)
John Barrasso (Wyo.)

DID NOT SIGN:

Lisa Murkowski (Alaska)
Jeff Flake (Ariz.)
Daniel Coats (Ind.)
Susan Collins (Maine)
Thad Cochran (Miss.)
Lamar Alexander (Tenn.)
Bob Corker (Tenn.)

The Constitution of the United States

We the People of the United States, in Order to form a more perfect Union, establish Justice, insure domestic Tranquility, provide for the common defence, promote the general Welfare, and secure the Blessings of Liberty to ourselves and our Posterity, do ordain and establish this Constitution for the United States of America.

ARTICLE. I.

THE LEGISLATIVE BRANCH

Section 1. All legislative Powers herein granted shall be vested in a Congress of the United States, which shall consist of a Senate and House of Representatives.

Section 2. The House of Representatives shall be composed of Members chosen every second Year by the People of the several States, and the Electors in each State shall have the Qualifications requisite for Electors of the most numerous Branch of the State Legislature.

No Person shall be a Representative who shall not have attained to the Age of twenty five Years, and been seven Years a Citizen of the United States, and who shall not, when elected, be an Inhabitant of that State in which he shall be chosen.

(Representatives and direct Taxes shall be apportioned among the several States which may be included within this Union, according to their respective Numbers, which shall be determined by adding to the whole Number of free Persons, including those bound to Service for a Term of Years, and excluding Indians not taxed, three fifths of all other Persons.)[1] The actual Enumeration shall be made within three Years after the first Meeting of the Congress of the United States, and within every subsequent Term of ten Years, in such Manner as they shall by Law direct. The Number of Representatives shall not exceed one for every thirty Thousand, but each State shall have at Least one Representative; and until such enumeration shall be made, the State of New Hampshire shall be entitled to chuse three, Massachusetts eight, Rhode Island and Providence Plantations one, Connecticut five, New York six, New Jersey four, Pennsylvania eight, Delaware one, Maryland six, Virginia ten, North Carolina five, South Carolina five and Georgia three.

---

[1] The sentence in parentheses was modified by the 14th Amendment, section 2.

The Constitution of the United States

When vacancies happen in the Representation from any State, the Executive Authority thereof shall issue Writs of Election to fill such Vacancies. The House of Representatives shall chuse their Speaker and other Officers; and shall have the sole Power of Impeachment.

Section 3. The Senate of the United States shall be composed of two Senators from each State, (chosen by the Legislature thereof,)[2] for six Years; and each Senator shall have one Vote.

Immediately after they shall be assembled in Consequence of the first Election, they shall be divided as equally as may be into three Classes. The Seats of the Senators of the first Class shall be vacated at the Expiration of the second Year, of the second Class at the Expiration of the fourth Year, and of the third Class at the Expiration of the sixth Year, so that one third may be chosen every second Year; (and if Vacancies happen by Resignation, or otherwise, during the Recess of the Legislature of any State, the Executive thereof may make temporary Appointments until the next Meeting of the Legislature, which shall then fill such Vacancies.)[3]

No person shall be a Senator who shall not have attained to the Age of thirty Years, and been nine Years a Citizen of the United States, and who shall not, when elected, be an Inhabitant of that State for which he shall be chosen.

The Vice President of the United States shall be President of the Senate, but shall have no Vote, unless they be equally divided.

The Senate shall chuse their other Officers, and also a President pro tempore, in the absence of the Vice President, or when he shall exercise the Office of President of the United States.

The Senate shall have the sole Power to try all Impeachments. When sitting for that Purpose, they shall be on Oath or Affirmation. When the President of the United States is tried, the Chief Justice shall preside: And no Person shall be convicted without the Concurrence of two thirds of the Members present.

Judgment in Cases of Impeachment shall not extend further than to removal from Office, and disqualification to hold and enjoy any Office of honor, Trust or Profit under the United States: but the Party convicted shall nevertheless be liable and subject to Indictment, Trial, Judgment and Punishment, according to Law.

Section 4. The Times, Places and Manner of holding Elections for Senators and Representatives, shall be prescribed in each State by the Legislature thereof; but the Congress may at any time by Law make or alter such

---

2 The words in parentheses superseded by 17th Amendment, section 1.
3 The words in parentheses were superseded by the 17th Amendment, section 2.

Regulations, except as to the Place of chusing Senators.

The Congress shall assemble at least once in every Year, and such Meeting shall (be on the first Monday in December,)[4] unless they shall by Law appoint a different Day.

Section 5. Each House shall be the Judge of the Elections, Returns and Qualifications of its own Members, and a Majority of each shall constitute a Quorum to do Business; but a smaller number may adjourn from day to day, and may be authorized to compel the Attendance of absent Members, in such Manner, and under such Penalties as each House may provide.

Each House may determine the Rules of its Proceedings, punish its Members for disorderly Behavior, and, with the Concurrence of two-thirds, expel a Member.

Each House shall keep a Journal of its Proceedings, and from time to time publish the same, excepting such Parts as may in their Judgment require Secrecy; and the Yeas and Nays of the Members of either House on any question shall, at the Desire of one fifth of those Present, be entered on the Journal.

Neither House, during the Session of Congress, shall, without the Consent of the other, adjourn for more than three days, nor to any other Place than that in which the two Houses shall be sitting.

Section 6. *Compensation.* (The Senators and Representatives shall receive a Compensation for their Services, to be ascertained by Law, and paid out of the Treasury of the United States.)[5] They shall in all Cases, except Treason, Felony and Breach of the Peace, be privileged from Arrest during their Attendance at the Session of their respective Houses, and in going to and returning from the same; and for any Speech or Debate in either House, they shall not be questioned in any other Place.

No Senator or Representative shall, during the Time for which he was elected, be appointed to any civil Office under the Authority of the United States which shall have been created, or the Emoluments whereof shall have been increased during such time; and no Person holding any Office under the United States, shall be a Member of either House during his Continuance in Office.

Section 7. *Revenue Bills, Legislative Process, Presidential Veto.* All bills for raising Revenue shall originate in the House of Representatives; but the Senate may propose or concur with Amendments as on other Bills.

---

4 These words in parentheses were superseded by the 20th Amendment, section 2.
5 These words in parentheses were modified by the 27th Amendment.

The Constitution of the United States

Every Bill which shall have passed the House of Representatives and the Senate, shall, before it become a Law, be presented to the President of the United States; If he approve he shall sign it, but if not he shall return it, with his Objections to that House in which it shall have originated, who shall enter the Objections at large on their Journal, and proceed to reconsider it. If after such Reconsideration two thirds of that House shall agree to pass the Bill, it shall be sent, together with the Objections, to the other House, by which it shall likewise be reconsidered, and if approved by two thirds of that House, it shall become a Law. But in all such Cases the Votes of both Houses shall be determined by Yeas and Nays, and the Names of the Persons voting for and against the Bill shall be entered on the Journal of each House respectively. If any Bill shall not be returned by the President within ten Days (Sundays excepted) after it shall have been presented to him, the Same shall be a Law, in like Manner as if he had signed it, unless the Congress by their Adjournment prevent its Return, in which Case it shall not be a Law.

Every Order, Resolution, or Vote to which the Concurrence of the Senate and House of Representatives may be necessary (except on a question of Adjournment) shall be presented to the President of the United States; and before the Same shall take Effect, shall be approved by him, or being disapproved by him, shall be repassed by two thirds of the Senate and House of Representatives, according to the Rules and Limitations prescribed in the Case of a Bill.

Section 8. *Powers of Congress.* The Congress shall have Power To lay and collect Taxes, Duties, Imposts and Excises, to pay the Debts and provide for the common Defence and general Welfare of the United States; but all Duties, Imposts and Excises shall be uniform throughout the United States;

To borrow money on the credit of the United States;

To regulate Commerce with foreign Nations, and among the several States, and with the Indian Tribes;

To establish an uniform Rule of Naturalization, and uniform Laws on the subject of Bankruptcies throughout the United States;

To coin Money, regulate the Value thereof, and of foreign Coin, and fix the Standard of Weights and Measures;

To provide for the Punishment of counterfeiting the Securities and current Coin of the United States;

To establish Post Offices and Post Roads;

To promote the Progress of Science and useful Arts, by securing for limited Times to Authors and Inventors the exclusive Right to their respective Writings and Discoveries;

To constitute Tribunals inferior to the supreme Court;

To define and punish Piracies and Felonies committed on the high Seas, and Offenses against the Law of Nations;

166

To declare War, grant Letters of Marque and Reprisal, and make Rules concerning Captures on Land and Water;

To raise and support Armies, but no Appropriation of Money to that Use shall be for a longer Term than two Years;

To provide and maintain a Navy;

To make Rules for the Government and Regulation of the land and naval Forces;

To provide for calling forth the Militia to execute the Laws of the Union, suppress Insurrections and repel Invasions;

To provide for organizing, arming, and disciplining the Militia, and for governing such Part of them as may be employed in the Service of the United States, reserving to the States respectively, the Appointment of the Officers, and the Authority of training the Militia according to the discipline prescribed by Congress;

To exercise exclusive Legislation in all Cases whatsoever, over such District (not exceeding ten Miles square) as may, by Cession of particular States, and the acceptance of Congress, become the Seat of the Government of the United States, and to exercise like Authority over all Places purchased by the Consent of the Legislature of the State in which the Same shall be, for the Erection of Forts, Magazines, Arsenals, dock-Yards, and other needful Buildings; And

To make all Laws which shall be necessary and proper for carrying into Execution the foregoing Powers, and all other Powers vested by this Constitution in the Government of the United States, or in any Department or Officer thereof.

Section 9. *Limits on Congress.* The Migration or Importation of such Persons as any of the States now existing shall think proper to admit, shall not be prohibited by the Congress prior to the Year one thousand eight hundred and eight, but a tax or duty may be imposed on such Importation, not exceeding ten dollars for each Person.

The privilege of the Writ of Habeas Corpus shall not be suspended, unless when in Cases of Rebellion or Invasion the public Safety may require it.

No Bill of Attainder or ex post facto Law shall be passed.

(No capitation, or other direct, Tax shall be laid, unless in Proportion to the Census or Enumeration herein before directed to be taken.)[6] No Tax or Duty shall be laid on Articles exported from any State.

No Preference shall be given by any Regulation of Commerce or Revenue to the Ports of one State over those of another: nor shall Vessels bound to, or from, one State, be obliged to enter, clear, or pay Duties in another.

---

[6] Section in parentheses clarified by the 16th Amendment.

No Money shall be drawn from the Treasury, but in Consequence of Appropriations made by Law; and a regular Statement and Account of the Receipts and Expenditures of all public Money shall be published from time to time.

No Title of Nobility shall be granted by the United States: And no Person holding any Office of Profit or Trust under them, shall, without the Consent of the Congress, accept of any present, Emolument, Office, or Title, of any kind whatever, from any King, Prince or foreign State.

Section 10. *Powers prohibited of States.* No State shall enter into any Treaty, Alliance, or Confederation; grant Letters of Marque and Reprisal; coin Money; emit Bills of Credit; make any Thing but gold and silver Coin a Tender in Payment of Debts; pass any Bill of Attainder, ex post facto Law, or Law impairing the Obligation of Contracts, or grant any Title of Nobility.

No State shall, without the Consent of the Congress, lay any Imposts or Duties on Imports or Exports, except what may be absolutely necessary for executing it's inspection Laws: and the net Produce of all Duties and Imposts, laid by any State on Imports or Exports, shall be for the Use of the Treasury of the United States; and all such Laws shall be subject to the Revision and Controul of the Congress.

No State shall, without the Consent of Congress, lay any duty of Tonnage, keep Troops, or Ships of War in time of Peace, enter into any Agreement or Compact with another State, or with a foreign Power, or engage in War, unless actually invaded, or in such imminent Danger as will not admit of delay.

ARTICLE. II.
THE EXECUTIVE BRANCH

Section 1. *The President.* The executive Power shall be vested in a President of the United States of America. He shall hold his Office during the Term of four Years, and, together with the Vice President chosen for the same Term, be elected, as follows:

Each State shall appoint, in such Manner as the Legislature thereof may direct, a Number of Electors, equal to the whole Number of Senators and Representatives to which the State may be entitled in the Congress: but no Senator or Representative, or Person holding an Office of Trust or Profit under the United States, shall be appointed an Elector.

(The Electors shall meet in their respective States, and vote by Ballot for two persons, of whom one at least shall not lie an Inhabitant of the same State with themselves. And they shall make a List of all the Persons voted for, and of the Number of Votes for each; which List they shall sign and certify, and transmit sealed to the Seat of the Government of the United States, directed to the President of the Senate. The President of the Senate shall, in the Presence of the Senate and House of Representatives, open all the Certificates, and the Votes shall then be counted. The Person having the greatest

Number of Votes shall be the President, if such Number be a Majority of the whole Number of Electors appointed; and if there be more than one who have such Majority, and have an equal Number of Votes, then the House of Representatives shall immediately chuse by Ballot one of them for President; and if no Person have a Majority, then from the five highest on the List the said House shall in like Manner chuse the President. But in chusing the President, the Votes shall be taken by States, the Representation from each State having one Vote; a quorum for this Purpose shall consist of a Member or Members from two-thirds of the States, and a Majority of all the States shall be necessary to a Choice. In every Case, after the Choice of the President, the Person having the greatest Number of Votes of the Electors shall be the Vice President. But if there should remain two or more who have equal Votes, the Senate shall chuse from them by Ballot the Vice President.)[7]

The Congress may determine the Time of chusing the Electors, and the Day on which they shall give their Votes; which Day shall be the same throughout the United States.

No person except a natural born Citizen, or a Citizen of the United States, at the time of the Adoption of this Constitution, shall be eligible to the Office of President; neither shall any Person be eligible to that Office who shall not have attained to the Age of thirty-five Years, and been fourteen Years a Resident within the United States.

(In Case of the Removal of the President from Office, or of his Death, Resignation, or Inability to discharge the Powers and Duties of the said Office, the same shall devolve on the Vice President, and the Congress may by Law provide for the Case of Removal, Death, Resignation or Inability, both of the President and Vice President, declaring what Officer shall then act as President, and such Officer shall act accordingly, until the Disability be removed, or a President shall be elected.)[8]

The President shall, at stated Times, receive for his Services, a Compensation, which shall neither be increased nor diminished during the Period for which he shall have been elected, and he shall not receive within that Period any other Emolument from the United States, or any of them. Before he enter on the Execution of his Office, he shall take the following Oath or Affirmation: "I do solemnly swear (or affirm) that I will faithfully execute the Office of President of the United States, and will to the best of my Ability, preserve, protect and defend the Constitution of the United States."

Section 2. *Civilian Power over Military, Cabinet, Pardon Power, Appointments.* The President shall be Commander in Chief of the Army and Navy of the United States, and of the Militia of the several States, when called into the actual Service of the United States; he may require the Opinion, in writing, of the principal Officer in each of the executive Departments, upon any subject relating to the Duties of their respective Offices, and he shall have Power to

---

7 This clause in parentheses was superseded by the 12th Amendment.
8 This clause in parentheses has been modified by the 20th and 25th Amendments.

Grant Reprieves and Pardons for Offenses against the United States, except in Cases of Impeachment.

He shall have Power, by and with the Advice and Consent of the Senate, to make Treaties, provided two thirds of the Senators present concur; and he shall nominate, and by and with the Advice and Consent of the Senate, shall appoint Ambassadors, other public Ministers and Consuls, Judges of the supreme Court, and all other Officers of the United States, whose Appointments are not herein otherwise provided for, and which shall be established by Law: but the Congress may by Law vest the Appointment of such inferior Officers, as they think proper, in the President alone, in the Courts of Law, or in the Heads of Departments. The President shall have Power to fill up all Vacancies that may happen during the Recess of the Senate, by granting Commissions which shall expire at the End of their next Session.

Section 3. *State of the Union, Convening Congress.* He shall from time to time give to the Congress Information of the State of the Union, and recommend to their Consideration such Measures as he shall judge necessary and expedient; he may, on extraordinary Occasions, convene both Houses, or either of them, and in Case of Disagreement between them, with Respect to the Time of Adjournment, he may adjourn them to such Time as he shall think proper; he shall receive Ambassadors and other public Ministers; he shall take Care that the Laws be faithfully executed, and shall Commission all the Officers of the United States.

Section 4. *Disqualification.* The President, Vice President and all civil Officers of the United States, shall be removed from Office on Impeachment for, and Conviction of, Treason, Bribery, or other high Crimes and Misdemeanors.

Article III.
The Judicial Branch

Section 1. *Judicial powers.* The judicial Power of the United States, shall be vested in one supreme Court, and in such inferior Courts as the Congress may from time to time ordain and establish. The Judges, both of the supreme and inferior Courts, shall hold their Offices during good Behavior, and shall, at stated Times, receive for their Services a Compensation which shall not be diminished during their Continuance in Office.

Section 2. *Trial by Jury, Original Jurisdiction, Jury Trials* (The judicial Power shall extend to all Cases, in Law and Equity, arising under this Constitution, the Laws of the United States, and Treaties made, or which shall be made, under their Authority; to all Cases affecting Ambassadors, other public Ministers and Consuls; to all Cases of admiralty and maritime Jurisdiction; to Controversies to which the United States shall be a Party; to Controversies between two or more States; between a State and Citizens of another State; between Citizens of different States; between Citizens of the same State claiming Lands under Grants of different States, and between a State, or the Citizens thereof, and foreign States, Citizens or Subjects.)[9]

In all Cases affecting Ambassadors, other public Ministers and Consuls, and those in which a State shall be Party, the supreme Court shall have original Jurisdiction. In all the other Cases before mentioned, the supreme Court shall have appellate Jurisdiction, both as to Law and Fact, with such Exceptions, and under such Regulations as the Congress shall make.

The Trial of all Crimes, except in Cases of Impeachment, shall be by Jury; and such Trial shall be held in the State where the said Crimes shall have been committed; but when not committed within any State, the Trial shall be at such Place or Places as the Congress may by Law have directed.

Section 3. *Treason.* Treason against the United States, shall consist only in levying War against them, or in adhering to their Enemies, giving them Aid and Comfort. No Person shall be convicted of Treason unless on the Testimony of two Witnesses to the same overt Act, or on Confession in open Court.

The Congress shall have power to declare the Punishment of Treason, but no Attainder of Treason shall work Corruption of Blood, or Forfeiture except during the Life of the Person attainted.

ARTICLE. IV.
THE STATES

Section 1. *Each State to Honor all others.* Full Faith and Credit shall be given in each State to the public Acts, Records, and judicial Proceedings of every other State. And the Congress may by general Laws prescribe the Manner in which such Acts, Records and Proceedings shall be proved, and the Effect thereof.

Section 2. State citizens, Extradition The Citizens of each State shall be entitled to all Privileges and Immunities of Citizens in the several States. A Person charged in any State with Treason, Felony, or other Crime, who shall flee from Justice, and be found in another State, shall on demand of the executive Authority of the State from which he fled, be delivered up, to be removed to the State having Jurisdiction of the Crime. (No Person held to Service or Labour in one State, under the Laws thereof, escaping into another, shall, in Consequence of any Law or Regulation therein, be discharged from such Service or Labour, But shall be delivered up on Claim

---

9 This section in parentheses is modified by the 11th Amendment.

of the Party to whom such Service or Labour may be due.)[10]

Section 3. *New States.* New States may be admitted by the Congress into this Union; but no new States shall be formed or erected within the Jurisdiction of any other State; nor any State be formed by the Junction of two or more States, or parts of States, without the Consent of the Legislatures of the States concerned as well as of the Congress. The Congress shall have Power to dispose of and make all needful Rules and Regulations respecting the Territory or other Property belonging to the United States; and nothing in this Constitution shall be so construed as to Prejudice any Claims of the United States, or of any particular State.

Section 4. The United States shall guarantee to every State in this Union a Republican Form of Government, and shall protect each of them against Invasion; and on Application of the Legislature, or of the Executive (when the Legislature cannot be convened) against domestic Violence.

ARTICLE. V.
AMENDMENT

The Congress, whenever two thirds of both Houses shall deem it necessary, shall propose Amendments to this Constitution, or, on the Application of the Legislatures of two thirds of the several States, shall call a Convention for proposing Amendments, which, in either Case, shall be valid to all Intents and Purposes, as part of this Constitution, when ratified by the Legislatures of three fourths of the several States, or by Conventions in three fourths thereof, as the one or the other Mode of Ratification may be proposed by the Congress; Provided that no Amendment which may be made prior to the Year One thousand eight hundred and eight shall in any Manner affect the first and fourth Clauses in the Ninth Section of the first Article; and that no State, without its Consent, shall be deprived of its equal Suffrage in the Senate.

ARTICLE. VI.
DEBTS, SUPREMACY, OATHS

All Debts contracted and Engagements entered into, before the Adoption of this Constitution, shall be as valid against the United States under this Constitution, as under the Confederation.

This Constitution, and the Laws of the United States which shall be made in Pursuance thereof; and all Treaties made, or which shall be made, under the Authority of the United States, shall be the supreme Law of the Land; and the

---

[10] This clause in parentheses is superseded by the 13th Amendment.

Judges in every State shall be bound thereby, any Thing in the Constitution or Laws of any State to the Contrary notwithstanding.

The Senators and Representatives before mentioned, and the Members of the several State Legislatures, and all executive and judicial Officers, both of the United States and of the several States, shall be bound by Oath or Affirmation, to support this Constitution; but no religious Test shall ever be required as a Qualification to any Office or public Trust under the United States.

ARTICLE. VII.

RATIFICATION

The Ratification of the Conventions of nine States, shall be sufficient for the Establishment of this Constitution between the States so ratifying the Same. Done in Convention by the Unanimous Consent of the States present the Seventeenth Day of September in the Year of our Lord one thousand seven hundred and Eighty seven and of the Independence of the United States of America the Twelfth. In Witness whereof We have hereunto subscribed our Names.

G. Washington - President and deputy from Virginia

New Hampshire - John Langdon, Nicholas Gilman

Massachusetts - Nathaniel Gorham, Rufus King

Connecticut - Wm Saml. Johnson, Roger Sherman

New York - Alexander Hamilton

New Jersey - Wil Livingston, David Brearley, Wm. Paterson, Jona. Dayton

Pennsylvania - B. Franklin, Thomas Mifflin, Robt. Morris, Geo. Clymer, Thos. FitzSimons, Jared Ingersoll, James Wilson, Gouv. Morris

Delaware - Geo. Read, Gunning Bedford jun, John Dickinson, Richard Bassett, Jaco. Broom

Maryland - James McHenry, Dan of St Thos. Jenifer, Danl Carroll

Virginia - John Blair, James Madison Jr.

North Carolina - Wm. Blount, Richd. Dobbs Spaight, Hu Williamson

South Carolina - J. Rutledge, Charles Cotesworth Pinckney, Charles Pinckney, Pierce Butler

Georgia - William Few, Abr Baldwin

Attest: William Jackson, Secretary The.

Amendments

The following are the Amendments to the Constitution. The first ten Amendments collectively are commonly known as the Bill of Rights.

The Bill of Rights

The Preamble To The Bill Of Rights

Congress of the United States begun and held at the City of New York, on Wednesday the fourth of March, one thousand seven hundred and eighty nine.

THE Conventions of a number of the States, having at the time of their adopting the Constitution, expressed a desire, in order to prevent misconstruction or abuse of its powers that further declaratory and restrictive clauses should be added: And as extending the ground of public confidence in the Government, will best ensure the beneficent ends of its institution.

RESOLVED by the Senate and House of Representatives of the United States of America, in Congress assembled, two thirds of both Houses concurring, that the following Articles be proposed to the Legislatures of the several States, as amendments to the Constitution of the United States, all, or any of which Articles, when ratified by three fourths of the said Legislatures, to be valid to all intents and purposes, as part of the said Constitution; viz.

ARTICLES in addition to, and Amendment of the Constitution of the United States of America, proposed by Congress, and ratified by the Legislatures of the several States, pursuant to the fifth Article of the original Constitution.

Amendment I.

Freedom of Religion, Press, Expression.

Congress shall make no law respecting an establishment of religion, or prohibiting the free exercise thereof; or abridging the freedom of speech, or of the press; or the right of the people peaceably to assemble, and to petition the Government for a redress of grievances.

Amendment II.

Right to Bear Arms.

A well regulated Militia, being necessary to the security of a free State, the right of the people to keep and bear Arms, shall not be infringed.

Amendments

Amendment III.
Quartering of Soldiers.

No Soldier shall, in time of peace be quartered in any house, without the consent of the Owner, nor in time of war, but in a manner to be prescribed by law.

Amendment IV.
Search and Seizure.

The right of the people to be secure in their persons, houses, papers, and effects, against unreasonable searches and seizures, shall not be violated, and no Warrants shall issue, but upon probable cause, supported by Oath or affirmation, and particularly describing the place to be searched, and the persons or things to be seized.

Amendment V.
Trial and Punishment, Compensation for Takings.

No person shall be held to answer for a capital, or otherwise infamous crime, unless on a presentment or indictment of a Grand Jury, except in cases arising in the land or naval forces, or in the Militia, when in actual service in time of War or public danger; nor shall any person be subject for the same offence to be twice put in jeopardy of life or limb; nor shall be compelled in any criminal case to be a witness against himself, nor be deprived of life, liberty, or property, without due process of law; nor shall private property be taken for public use, without just compensation.

Amendment VI.
Right to Speedy Trial, Confrontation of Witnesses.

In all criminal prosecutions, the accused shall enjoy the right to a speedy and public trial, by an impartial jury of the State and district wherein the crime shall have been committed, which district shall have been previously ascertained by law, and to be informed of the nature and cause of the accusation; to be confronted with the witnesses against him; to have compulsory process for obtaining witnesses in his favor, and to have the Assistance of Counsel for his defence.

Amendment VII.
Trial by Jury in Civil Cases.

In suits at common law, where the value in controversy shall exceed twenty dollars, the right of trial by jury shall be preserved, and no fact tried by a jury, shall be otherwise reexamined in any Court of the United States, than according to the rules of the common law.

AMENDMENT VIII.

Cruel and Unusual Punishment.

Excessive bail shall not be required, nor excessive fines imposed, nor cruel and unusual punishments inflicted.

AMENDMENT IX.

Construction of Constitution.

The enumeration in the Constitution, of certain rights, shall not be construed to deny or disparage others retained by the people.

AMENDMENT X.

Powers of the States and People.

The powers not delegated to the United States by the Constitution, nor prohibited by it to the States, are reserved to the States respectively, or to the people.

The Ninth and Tenth Amendments, taken together, mean that the federal government has only the authority granted to it, while the people are presumed to have any right or power not specifically forbidden to them. The Bill of Rights as a whole is dedicated to describing certain key rights of the people that the government is categorically forbidden to remove, abridge, or infringe. The Bill of Rights clearly places the people in charge of their own lives, and the government within strict limits - the very opposite of the situation we have allowed to develop today.

AMENDMENT 11 TO AMENDMENT 27

AMENDMENT XI.

Judicial Limits. Ratified 2/7/1795.

The Judicial power of the United States shall not be construed to extend to any suit in law or equity, commenced or prosecuted against one of the United States by Citizens of another State, or by Citizens or Subjects of any Foreign State.

AMENDMENT XII.

Choosing the President, Vice President. Ratified 6/15/1804.

The Electors shall meet in their respective states, and vote by ballot for President and Vice President, one of whom, at least, shall not be an inhabitant of the same state with themselves; they shall name in their ballots the person voted for as President, and in distinct ballots the person voted for as

Vice President, and they shall make distinct lists of all persons voted for as President, and of all persons voted for as Vice President and of the number of votes for each, which lists they shall sign and certify, and transmit sealed to the seat of the government of the United States, directed to the President of the Senate; The President of the Senate shall, in the presence of the Senate and House of Representatives, open all the certificates and the votes shall then be counted; The person having the greatest Number of votes for President, shall be the President, if such number be a majority of the whole number of Electors appointed; and if no person have such majority, then from the persons having the highest numbers not exceeding three on the list of those voted for as President, the House of Representatives shall choose immediately, by ballot, the President. But in choosing the President, the votes shall be taken by states, the representation from each state having one vote; a quorum for this purpose shall consist of a member or members from two-thirds of the states, and a majority of all the states shall be necessary to a choice. And if the House of Representatives shall not choose a President whenever the right of choice shall devolve upon them, before the fourth day of March next following, then the Vice President shall act as President, as in the case of the death or other constitutional disability of the President. The person having the greatest number of votes as Vice President, shall be the Vice President, if such number be a majority of the whole number of Electors appointed, and if no person have a majority, then from the two highest numbers on the list, the Senate shall choose the Vice President; a quorum for the purpose shall consist of two-thirds of the whole number of Senators, and a majority of the whole number shall be necessary to a choice. But no person constitutionally ineligible to the office of President shall be eligible to that of Vice President of the United States.

AMENDMENT XIII.

Slavery Abolished. Ratified 12/6/1865.

1. Neither slavery nor involuntary servitude, except as a punishment for crime whereof the party shall have been duly convicted, shall exist within the United States, or any place subject to their jurisdiction. 2. Congress shall have power to enforce this article by appropriate legislation.

AMENDMENT XIV.

Citizenship Rights. Ratified 7/9/1868.

1. All persons born or naturalized in the United States, and subject to the jurisdiction thereof, are citizens of the United States and of the State wherein they reside. No State shall make or enforce any law which shall abridge the privileges or immunities of citizens of the United States; nor shall any State

deprive any person of life, liberty, or property, without due process of law; nor deny to any person within its jurisdiction the equal protection of the laws.

2. Representatives shall be apportioned among the several States according to their respective numbers, counting the whole number of persons in each State, excluding Indians not taxed. But when the right to vote at any election for the choice of electors for President and Vice President of the United States, Representatives in Congress, the Executive and Judicial officers of a State, or the members of the Legislature thereof, is denied to any of the male inhabitants of such State, being twenty-one years of age, and citizens of the United States, or in any way abridged, except for participation in rebellion, or other crime, the basis of representation therein shall be reduced in the proportion which the number of such male citizens shall bear to the whole number of male citizens twenty-one years of age in such State.

3. No person shall be a Senator or Representative in Congress, or elector of President and Vice President, or hold any office, civil or military, under the United States, or under any State, who, having previously taken an oath, as a member of Congress, or as an officer of the United States, or as a member of any State legislature, or as an executive or judicial officer of any State, to support the Constitution of the United States, shall have engaged in insurrection or rebellion against the same, or given aid or comfort to the enemies thereof. But Congress may by a vote of two-thirds of each House, remove such disability.

4. The validity of the public debt of the United States, authorized by law, including debts incurred for payment of pensions and bounties for services in suppressing insurrection or rebellion, shall not be questioned. But neither the United States nor any State shall assume or pay any debt or obligation incurred in aid of insurrection or rebellion against the United States, or any claim for the loss or emancipation of any slave; but all such debts, obligations and claims shall be held illegal and void.

5. The Congress shall have power to enforce, by appropriate legislation, the provisions of this article.

Amendment XV.
Race No Bar to Vote. Ratified 2/3/1870.
1. The right of citizens of the United States to vote shall not be denied or abridged by the United States or by any State on account of race, color, or previous condition of servitude.

Amendments

2. The Congress shall have power to enforce this article by appropriate legislation.

AMENDMENT XVI.
Status of Income Tax Clarified. Ratified 2/3/1913.

The Congress shall have power to lay and collect taxes on incomes, from whatever source derived, without apportionment among the several States, and without regard to any census or enumeration.

AMENDMENT XVII.
Senators Elected by Popular Vote. Ratified 4/8/1913.

The Senate of the United States shall be composed of two Senators from each State, elected by the people thereof, for six years; and each Senator shall have one vote. The electors in each State shall have the qualifications requisite for electors of the most numerous branch of the State legislatures. When vacancies happen in the representation of any State in the Senate, the executive authority of such State shall issue writs of election to fill such vacancies: Provided, That the legislature of any State may empower the executive thereof to make temporary appointments until the people fill the vacancies by election as the legislature may direct. This amendment shall not be so construed as to affect the election or term of any Senator chosen before it becomes valid as part of the Constitution.

AMENDMENT XVIII.
Liquor Abolished. Ratified 1/16/1919. Repealed by Amendment 21, 12/5/1933.

1. After one year from the ratification of this article the manufacture, sale, or transportation of intoxicating liquors within, the importation thereof into, or the exportation thereof from the United States and all territory subject to the jurisdiction thereof for beverage purposes is hereby prohibited.

2. The Congress and the several States shall have concurrent power to enforce this article by appropriate legislation.

3. This article shall be inoperative unless it shall have been ratified as an amendment to the Constitution by the legislatures of the several States, as provided in the Constitution, within seven years from the date of the submission hereof to the States by the Congress.

Amendment XIX.

Women's Suffrage. Ratified 8/18/1920.

The right of citizens of the United States to vote shall not be denied or abridged by the United States or by any State on account of sex. Congress shall have power to enforce this article by appropriate legislation.

Amendment XX.

Presidential, Congressional Terms. Ratified 1/23/1933.

1. The terms of the President and Vice President shall end at noon on the 20th day of January, and the terms of Senators and Representatives at noon on the 3d day of January, of the years in which such terms would have ended if this article had not been ratified; and the terms of their successors shall then begin.

2. The Congress shall assemble at least once in every year, and such meeting shall begin at noon on the 3d day of January, unless they shall by law appoint a different day.

3. If, at the time fixed for the beginning of the term of the President, the President elect shall have died, the Vice President elect shall become President. If a President shall not have been chosen before the time fixed for the beginning of his term, or if the President elect shall have failed to qualify, then the Vice President elect shall act as President until a President shall have qualified; and the Congress may by law provide for the case wherein neither a President elect nor a Vice President elect shall have qualified, declaring who shall then act as President, or the manner in which one who is to act shall be selected, and such person shall act accordingly until a President or Vice President shall have qualified.

4. The Congress may by law provide for the case of the death of any of the persons from whom the House of Representatives may choose a President whenever the right of choice shall have devolved upon them, and for the case of the death of any of the persons from whom the Senate may choose a Vice President whenever the right of choice shall have devolved upon them.

5. Sections 1 and 2 shall take effect on the 15th day of October following the ratification of this article.

6. This article shall be inoperative unless it shall have been ratified as an amendment to the Constitution by the legislatures of three-fourths of the several States within seven years from the date of its submission.

Amendments

Amendment XXI.

Amendment 18 Repealed. Ratified 12/5/1933.

1. The eighteenth article of amendment to the Constitution of the United States is hereby repealed.

2. The transportation or importation into any State, Territory, or possession of the United States for delivery or use therein of intoxicating liquors, in violation of the laws thereof, is hereby prohibited.

3. The article shall be inoperative unless it shall have been ratified as an amendment to the Constitution by conventions in the several States, as provided in the Constitution, within seven years from the date of the submission hereof to the States by the Congress.

Amendment XXII.

Presidential Term Limits. Ratified 2/27/1951.

1. No person shall be elected to the office of the President more than twice, and no person who has held the office of President, or acted as President, for more than two years of a term to which some other person was elected President shall be elected to the office of the President more than once. But this Article shall not apply to any person holding the office of President, when this Article was proposed by the Congress, and shall not prevent any person who may be holding the office of President, or acting as President, during the term within which this Article becomes operative from holding the office of President or acting as President during the remainder of such term.

2. This article shall be inoperative unless it shall have been ratified as an amendment to the Constitution by the legislatures of three-fourths of the several States within seven years from the date of its submission to the States by the Congress.

Amendment XXIII.

Presidential Vote for District of Columbia. Ratified 3/29/1961.

1. The District constituting the seat of Government of the United States shall appoint in such manner as the Congress may direct: A number of electors of President and Vice President equal to the whole number of Senators and Representatives in Congress to which the District would be entitled if it were a State, but in no event more than the least populous State; they shall be in addition to those appointed by the States, but they shall be considered, for the purposes of the election of President and Vice President, to be electors

appointed by a State; and they shall meet in the District and perform such duties as provided by the twelfth article of amendment.

2. The Congress shall have power to enforce this article by appropriate legislation.

AMENDMENT XXIV.
Poll Tax Barred. Ratified 1/23/1964.

1. The right of citizens of the United States to vote in any primary or other election for President or Vice President, for electors for President or Vice President, or for Senator or Representative in Congress, shall not be denied or abridged by the United States or any State by reason of failure to pay any poll tax or other tax.

2. The Congress shall have power to enforce this article by appropriate legislation.

AMENDMENT XXV.
Presidential Disability and Succession. Ratified 2/10/1967.

1. In case of the removal of the President from office or of his death or resignation, the Vice President shall become President.

2. Whenever there is a vacancy in the office of the Vice President, the President shall nominate a Vice President who shall take office upon confirmation by a majority vote of both Houses of Congress.

3. Whenever the President transmits to the President pro tempore of the Senate and the Speaker of the House of Representatives his written declaration that he is unable to discharge the powers and duties of his office, and until he transmits to them a written declaration to the contrary, such powers and duties shall be discharged by the Vice President as Acting President.

4. Whenever the Vice President and a majority of either the principal officers of the executive departments or of such other body as Congress may by law provide, transmit to the President pro tempore of the Senate and the Speaker of the House of Representatives their written declaration that the President is unable to discharge the powers and duties of his office, the Vice President shall immediately assume the powers and duties of the office as Acting President. Thereafter, when the President transmits to the President pro tempore of the Senate and the Speaker of the House of Representatives his written declaration that no inability exists, he shall resume the powers and duties of his office unless the Vice President and a majority of either the principal

officers of the executive department or of such other body as Congress may by law provide, transmit within four days to the President pro tempore of the Senate and the Speaker of the House of Representatives their written declaration that the President is unable to discharge the powers and duties of his office. Thereupon Congress shall decide the issue, assembling within forty eight hours for that purpose if not in session. If the Congress, within twenty one days after receipt of the latter written declaration, or, if Congress is not in session, within twenty one days after Congress is required to assemble, determines by two thirds vote of both Houses that the President is unable to discharge the powers and duties of his office, the Vice President shall continue to discharge the same as Acting President; otherwise, the President shall resume the powers and duties of his office.

AMENDMENT XXVI.
Ratified July 1, 1971.

Note: Amendment 14, section 2, of the Constitution was modified by section 1 of the 26th amendment.

Section 1. The right of citizens of the United States, who are eighteen years of age or older, to vote shall not be denied or abridged by the United States or by any State on account of age.

Section 2. The Congress shall have power to enforce this article by appropriate legislation.

AMENDMENT XXVII.
Originally proposed Sept. 25, 1789. Ratified May 7, 1992.

No law, varying the compensation for the services of the Senators and Representatives, shall take effect, until an election of Representatives shall have intervened.

United Nations
Universal Declaration of Human Rights

Preamble

Whereas recognition of the inherent dignity and of the equal and inalienable rights of all members of the human family is the foundation of freedom, justice and peace in the world,

Whereas disregard and contempt for human rights have resulted in barbarous acts which have outraged the conscience of mankind, and the advent of a world in which human beings shall enjoy freedom of speech and belief and freedom from fear and want has been proclaimed as the highest aspiration of the common people,

Whereas it is essential, if man is not to be compelled to have recourse, as a last resort, to rebellion against tyranny and oppression that human rights should be protected by the rule of law,

Whereas it is essential to promote the development of friendly relations between nations,

Whereas the peoples of the United Nations have in the Charter reaffirmed their faith in fundamental human rights, in the dignity and worth of the human person and in the equal rights of men and women and have determined to promote social progress and better standards of life in larger freedom,

Whereas Member States have pledged themselves to achieve, in cooperation with the United Nations, the promotion of universal respect for and observance of human rights and fundamental freedoms,

Whereas a common understanding of these rights and freedoms is of the greatest importance for the full realization of this pledge,

Now, therefore, The General Assembly, Proclaims this Universal Declaration of Human Rights as a common standard of achievement for all peoples and all nations, to the end that every individual and every organ of society, keeping this Declaration constantly in mind, shall strive by teaching and education to promote respect for these rights and freedoms and by progressive measures, national and international, to secure their universal and effective recognition and observance, both among the peoples of Member States themselves and among the peoples of territories under their jurisdiction.

Universal Declaration of Human Rights

ARTICLE I

All human beings are born free and equal in dignity and rights. They are endowed with reason and conscience and should act towards one another in a spirit of brotherhood.

ARTICLE 2

Everyone is entitled to all the rights and freedoms set forth in this Declaration, without distinction of any kind, such as race, colour, sex, language, religion, political or other opinion, national or social origin, property, birth or other status. Furthermore, no distinction shall be made on the basis of the political, jurisdictional or international status of the country or territory to which a person belongs, whether it be independent, trust, non-self-governing or under any other limitation of sovereignty.

ARTICLE 3

Everyone has the right to life, liberty and security of person.

ARTICLE 4

No one shall be held in slavery or servitude; slavery and the slave trade shall be prohibited in all their forms.

ARTICLE 5

No one shall be subjected to torture or to cruel, inhuman or degrading treatment or punishment.

ARTICLE 6

Everyone has the right to recognition everywhere as a person before the law.

ARTICLE 7

All are equal before the law and are entitled without any discrimination to equal protection of the law. All are entitled to equal protection against any discrimination in violation of this Declaration and against any incitement to such discrimination.

ARTICLE 8

Everyone has the right to an effective remedy by the competent national tribunals for acts violating the fundamental rights granted him by the constitution or by law.

ARTICLE 9

No one shall be subjected to arbitrary arrest, detention or exile.

ARTICLE 10

Everyone is entitled in full equality to a fair and public hearing by an independent and impartial tribunal, in the determination of his rights and obligations and of any criminal charge against him.

ARTICLE 11

1. Everyone charged with a penal offence has the right to be presumed innocent until proved guilty according to law in a public trial at which he has had all the guarantees necessary for his defense.

2. No one shall be held guilty of any penal offence on account of any act or omission which did not constitute a penal offence, under national or international law, at the time when it was committed. Nor shall a heavier penalty be imposed than the one that was applicable at the time the penal offence was committed.

ARTICLE 12

No one shall be subjected to arbitrary interference with his privacy, family, home or correspondence, nor to attacks upon his honour and reputation. Everyone has the right to the protection of the law against such interference or attacks.

ARTICLE 13

1. Everyone has the right to freedom of movement and residence within the borders of each State.

2. Everyone has the right to leave any country, including his own, and to return to his country.

ARTICLE 14

1. Everyone has the right to seek and to enjoy in other countries asylum from persecution.

2. This right may not be invoked in the case of prosecutions genuinely arising from non-political crimes or from acts contrary to the purposes and principles of the United Nations.

Universal Declaration of Human Rights

ARTICLE 15

1. Everyone has the right to a nationality.
2. No one shall be arbitrarily deprived of his nationality nor denied the right to change his nationality.

ARTICLE 16

1. Men and women of full age, without any limitation due to race, nationality or religion, have the right to marry and to found a family. They are entitled to equal rights as to marriage, during marriage and at its dissolution.

2. Marriage shall be entered into only with the free and full consent of the intending spouses.

3. The family is the natural and fundamental group unit of society and is entitled to protection by society and the State.

ARTICLE 17

1. Everyone has the right to own property alone as well as in association with others.
2. No one shall be arbitrarily deprived of his property.

ARTICLE 18

Everyone has the right to freedom of thought, conscience and religion; this right includes freedom to change his religion or belief, and freedom, either alone or in community with others and in public or private, to manifest his religion or belief in teaching, practice, worship and observance.

ARTICLE 19

Everyone has the right to freedom of opinion and expression; this right includes freedom to hold opinions without interference and to seek, receive and impart information and ideas through any media and regardless of frontiers.

ARTICLE 20

1. Everyone has the right to freedom of peaceful assembly and association.
2. No one may be compelled to belong to an association.

ARTICLE 21

1. Everyone has the right to take part in the government of his country, directly or through freely chosen representatives.

2. Everyone has the right to equal access to public service in his country.

3. The will of the people shall be the basis of the authority of government; this will shall be expressed in periodic and genuine elections which shall be by universal and equal suffrage and shall be held by secret vote or by equivalent free voting procedures.

ARTICLE 22

Everyone, as a member of society, has the right to social security and is entitled to realization, through national effort and international co-operation and in accordance with the organization and resources of each State, of the economic, social and cultural rights indispensable for his dignity and the free development of his personality.

ARTICLE 23

1. Everyone has the right to work, to free choice of employment, to just and favourable conditions of work and to protection against unemployment.

2. Everyone, without any discrimination, has the right to equal pay for equal work.

3. Everyone who works has the right to just and favourable remuneration ensuring for himself and his family an existence worthy of human dignity, and supplemented, if necessary, by other means of social protection.

4. Everyone has the right to form and to join trade unions for the protection of his interests.

ARTICLE 24

Everyone has the right to rest and leisure, including reasonable limitation of working hours and periodic holidays with pay.

ARTICLE 25

1. Everyone has the right to a standard of living adequate for the health and well-being of himself and of his family, including food, clothing, housing and medical care and necessary social services, and the right to security in the event of unemployment, sickness, disability, widowhood, old age or other lack of livelihood in circumstances beyond his control.

2. Motherhood and childhood are entitled to special care and assistance. All children, whether born in or out of wedlock, shall enjoy the same social protection.

ARTICLE 26

1. Everyone has the right to education. Education shall be free, at least in the elementary and fundamental stages. Elementary education shall be compulsory. Technical and professional education shall be made generally available and higher education shall be equally accessible to all on the basis of merit.

2. Education shall be directed to the full development of the human personality and to the strengthening of respect for human rights and fundamental freedoms. It shall promote understanding, tolerance and friendship among all nations, racial or religious groups, and shall further the activities of the United Nations for the maintenance of peace.

3. Parents have a prior right to choose the kind of education that shall be given to their children.

ARTICLE 27

1. Everyone has the right freely to participate in the cultural life of the community, to enjoy the arts and to share in scientific advancement and its benefits.

2. Everyone has the right to the protection of the moral and material interests resulting from any scientific, literary or artistic production of which he is the author.

ARTICLE 28

Everyone is entitled to a social and international order in which the rights and freedoms set forth in this Declaration can be fully realized.

ARTICLE 29

1. Everyone has duties to the community in which alone the free and full development of his personality is possible.

2. In the exercise of his rights and freedoms, everyone shall be subject only to such limitations as are determined by law solely for the purpose of securing due recognition and respect for the rights and freedoms of others and of meeting the just requirements of morality, public order and the general welfare in a democratic society.

3. These rights and freedoms may in no case be exercised contrary to the purposes and principles of the United Nations.

ARTICLE 30

Nothing in this Declaration may be interpreted as implying for any State, group or person any right to engage in any activity or to perform any act aimed at the destruction of any of the rights and freedoms set forth herein.

Suggested Organizations to Support

It is important that we support and encourage organizations that educate, mentor, enrich, nurture and protect young people in our communities. These are a few of the local and national organizations that I support without question.

1. The National CARES Mentoring Movement
   Susan L. Taylor, Founder and CEO
   www.caresmentoring.org

2. Black Star Project
   Phillip Jackson, Executive Director
   www.blackstarproject.org

3. Betty Shabazz International Charter Schools
   Dr. Carol Lee, Co-founder and Chair of the Board
   www.bsics.org

4. Detroit Public Library
   Jo Anne G. Mondowney, Executive Director
   www.detroitpubliclibrary.org

5. Third World Press Foundation
   Dr. Haki R. Madhubuti, Founder
   www.thirdworldpressbooks.com

6. Native American Rights Fund
   www.narf.org/

7. The Institute of the Black World Twenty-First Century (IBW)
   Dr. Ron Daniels, Executive Director
   www.ibw21.org

8. Carter G. Woodson Regional Library
   Chicago Public Library
   woodsonregional@chipublib.org

9. Continue this list by adding your own organizations

ALSO BY HAKI R. MADHUBUTI

Non-Fiction
Freedom to Self-Destruct: Easier to Believe than Think—New and Selected
   Essays (forthcoming)
YellowBlack: The First Twenty-One Years of a Poet's Life, A Memoir
Tough Notes: A Healing Call for Creating Exceptional Black Men
Claiming Earth: Race, Rage, Rape, Redemption: Blacks Seeking a Culture of Enlightened
   Empowerment
Dynamite Voices: Black Poets of the 1960s
Black Men: Obsolete, Single, Dangerous? The Afrikan American Family in Transition
From Plan to Planet: Life Studies; The Need for Afrikan Minds and Institutions
Enemies: The Clash of Races
A Capsule Course in Black Poetry Writing (co-author)
African Centered Education (co-author)
Kwanzaa: A Progressive and Uplifting African American Holiday

Poetry
Taught By Women (Forthcoming)
Honoring Genius, Gwendolyn Brooks: The Narrative of Craft, Art, Kindness and Justice, Poems
Liberation Narratives: New and Collected Poems 1966-2009
Run Toward Fear: New Poems and A Poet's Handbook
HeartLove: Wedding and Love Poems
Ground Work: New and Selected Poems of Don L. Lee/Haki R. Madhubuti from 1966-1996
Killing Memory, Seeking Ancestors
Earthquakes and Sunrise Missions
Book of Life
Directionscore: New and Selected Poems
We Walk the Way of the New World
Don't Cry, Scream
Black Pride
Think Black

Edited Works
By Any Means Necessary, Malcolm X: Real, Not Reinvented (co-editor)
Releasing the Spirit: A Collection of Literary Works from Gallery 37 (co-editor)
Describe the Moment: A Collection of Literary Works from Gallery 37 (co-editor)
Million Man March/Day of Absence: A Commemorative Anthology (co-editor)
Confusion by Any Other Name: Essays Exploring the Negative Impact of
  The Black Man's Guide to Understanding the Black Woman (editor)
Why L.A. Happened: Implications of the '92 Los Angeles Rebellion (editor)
Say that the River Turns: The Impact of Gwendolyn Brooks (editor)
To Gwen, With Love (co-editor)

Recordings: Poetry and Music
Rise Vision Comin' (with Nation: Afrikan Liberation Arts Ensemble)
Medasi (with Nation: Afrikan Liberation Arts Ensemble)
Rappin' and Readin'

About the Author

A leading poet and one of the architects of the Black Arts Movement, Haki R. Madhubuti—publisher, editor, educator and activist—has been a pivotal figure in the development of a strong Black literary tradition. He has published more than 31 books (some under his former name, Don L. Lee) and is one of the world's best-selling authors of poetry and non-fiction. His *Black Men: Obsolete, Single, Dangerous? The African American Family in Transition* (1990) has sold more than 1 million copies. His publications include *Liberation Narratives: New and Collected Poems 1966-2009* (2009); *Honoring Genius: Gwendolyn Brooks: The Narrative of Craft, Art, Kindness and Justice* (2011) and *By Any Means Necessary, Malcolm X: Real, Not Reinvented* (co-editor, 2012). His poetry and essays were published in more than 85 anthologies from 1997 to 2015. Two book-length critical studies on Madhubuti's literary works are *Malcolm X and the Poetics of Haki Madhubuti* by Regina Jennings (2006) and *Art of Work: The Art and Life of Haki R. Madhubuti* by Lita Hooper (2007).

Professor Madhubuti founded Third World Press in 1967. He is a founder of the Institute of Positive Education/New Concept School (1969), and a co-founder of Betty Shabazz International Charter School (1998), Barbara A. Sizemore Middle School (2005), and DuSable Leadership Academy (2005). Professor Madhubuti is an award-winning poet and recipient of the National Endowment for the Arts and National Endowment for the Humanities fellowships, the American Book Award, an Illinois Arts Council Award, the Studs Terkel Humanities Service Award and others. In 2014, Dr. Madhubuti received the Barnes & Noble Writers for Writers Award presented by *Poets & Writers* Magazine. In 2015, Madhubuti was the first poet to receive a Life Time Achievement Award at the Juneteenth Book Festival Symposium at the Library of Congress; and he was honored by the Congressional Black Caucus Foundation with a Lifetime Achievement Award for Leadership in the Fine Arts and he received the Fuller Award for Lifetime Achievement from the Chicago Literary Hall of Fame.

He is the former University Distinguished Professor and a professor of English at Chicago State University where he founded and was director-emeritus of the Gwendolyn Brooks Center and director of the Master of Fine Arts in Creative Writing Program. Professor Madhubuti served as the Ida B. Wells-Barnett University Professor at DePaul University for 2010-11.

Contact: twpress3@aol.com | 773-651-0700

CPSIA information can be obtained
at www.ICGtesting.com
Printed in the USA
BVOW07s0235010516

446081BV00001B/1/P